PRAISE FOR **PORTRAITS** FROM **PARIS**

"Gavin Cologne-Brookes has lived a remarkable life and is a gifted storyteller. The writing thrums with energy and color and humor.... The whole insightful performance is embedded to a quite extraordinary degree in artistic and literary lore. Stunning."

—**JONATHAN CARR**, author of *Make Me a City*

"The strands are woven together beautifully. The brutality of school opens the reader's heart (and eyes) to the brutality that lies behind so much of the art that Cologne-Brookes observes. The grimness of this very clear vision works with the elegant prose and his obvious delight in his current life to make a compelling statement of transcendence and *joie de vivre*. A powerful memoir that dramatizes a dynamic interplay between art, temporality, and the self."

—**MIMI THEBO**, author of *Dreaming the Bear*

"A beautifully written painter's portrait of surviving boarding school and finding validation in art. This book is a touching and evocative journey that takes in some of the world's great artworks, described with an artist's palette."

—**ROBERT VERKAIK**, author of *Posh Boys* and *The Traitor of Colditz*

PORTRAITS FROM PARIS

PORTRAITS FROM PARIS
SCHOOL & TRAVEL REMEMBERED FROM THE CITY OF LIGHT

GAVIN COLOGNE-BROOKES

LOUISIANA STATE UNIVERSITY PRESS
BATON ROUGE

Published by Louisiana State University Press
lsupress.org

Copyright © 2025 by Gavin Cologne-Brookes
All rights reserved. Except in the case of brief quotations used in articles or reviews,
no part of this publication may be reproduced or transmitted in any format or by any means
without written permission of Louisiana State University Press.

LSU Press Paperback Original

DESIGNER: Michelle A. Neustrom
TYPEFACES: Calluna, text; Jachoust Sans, display

COVER ILLUSTRATION: *Smile*, 2020, by Gavin Cologne-Brookes.

Cataloging-in-Publication Data are available at the Library of Congress.

ISBN 978-0-8071-8395-3 (paperback) | ISBN 978-0-8071-8480-6 (epub) |
ISBN 978-0-8071-8481-3 (pdf)

for Nicki, Xenatasha, and Anastasia

What is important for a painter is not a thing's reality but its shape, and what is important for a novelist is not the course of events but their ordering, and what is important for a memoirist is not the factual accuracy of the account but its symmetry.

—ORHAN PAMUK, *Istanbul: Memories and the City*

If our view of memory is correct, in higher organisms every act of perception is, to some degree, an act of creation, and every act of memory is, to some degree, an act of imagination.

—GERALD EDELMAN AND GIULIO TONONI, *A Universe of Consciousness: How Matter Becomes Imagination*

The art of losing isn't hard to master.

—ELIZABETH BISHOP, "One Art"

CONTENTS

Acknowledgments xi

Present in Past: Severance 1

CHILD & YOUTH

1. Departure 9
2. Paris 17
3. Taxidermy 21
4. Blitzkrieg 25
5. Omaha 33
6. Necessity 40
7. Breakage 43
8. Vancouver 46
9. Garçon 53
10. Budgerigar 62
11. Moscow 67
12. Stripe 72
13. Latin 82
14. Rome 91
15. Ports 96
16. Comfort 100
17. Istanbul 108
18. Leaving 112
19. Expectations 116
20. Lisbon 120

YOUTH & ADULT

1. Arrival 129
2. Montevideo 133
3. Corps 139
4. Community 144
5. San Francisco 150
6. Fosse 157
7. Chapel 161
8. Nairobi 168
9. Zilch 175
10. Crypt 179
11. Kyiv 183
12. Recluse 191
13. Love 197
14. Kraków 203
15. Canvas 209
16. Mural 218
17. Kolkata 222
18. Exhibition 228
19. Freedom 231
20. Rio 236

Past in Present: Reunion 241

ACKNOWLEDGMENTS

This is a work of creative nonfiction based on remembered events and encounters shaped to the needs of narrative. It involves imaginative reconstructions to bring to life unreliable recollections. Many events and incidents are either rendered in a fictitious manner or adapted for dramatic purposes to illustrate emotional truths. To indicate the fictional nature of much memory, and to protect privacy, where necessary I have changed the names, attributes, and circumstances of individuals.

But I would like to acknowledge all the people I've known over the years who may in one way or another have participated in, populated, stimulated, or facilitated these memories, as well as those who have aided the creation of the book, shaped my painting career, or been part of my time in Paris.

In general, they include Nik Ansell, Belinda Cash, Cameron Cologne-Pool, Siân Melangell Dafydd, Richard Francis, Tim Liardet, Rebecca McGuire-Snieckus, Mark Olney, Doug Owens, Richard Parfitt, Rowena and Elspeth Rae, Andrew and Chris Sampson, Robert Shakespeare, Luke Smith, Mimi Thebo, and Barry Walsh. In specific terms, I thank the staff of LSU Press for their work on this book, with special thank-yous to James W. Long, Ashley Gilly, Michelle Neustrom, Sunny Rosen, and James Wilson, along with freelance editor Susan Murray. Friends, colleagues, or acquaintances who have facilitated travel experiences include Lynda Bevan, Maggie and David Christensen, Margaret Chungali, Claudio "Toti" Lino da Costa; Leandro Delgado, Dan Disch and his parents and siblings, Paul Hyland, Angulu Kennedy, Danny Kyalo, Hilde and Marco Lissoni, Matt Martin, Bogdana Nosova, Luisa Peirano, Vira Ponomaryova, Juan Ravecca, Susan Shillinglaw, Daniel Supervielle, and Marina Vanderput. Friends, acquaintances, and professionals who have facilitated our time in France include Amine Bahnini, John Baxter, Frédéric Benhaïm, Kahina Betroune, Henri and Delphine de Drouas, Christina Fiorentini, Tanya Giraud (the only Alaskan I know in Provence), Steve and Tessa Green, Fiona Hamilton, Andrew Hately, Elizabeth Heudebourg, David Parlier, Gérald Preher, Muriel and Simon Reeves, Fotis Vaitsopoulos, and Thierry Watrin, along with Jerome and Hugo of Comptoir des Deux Frères, and Jen, Simon, Rosie, and Ottilie Biddel, who looked after our cat, Socrates. In terms of my artistic interests, I'd like to acknowledge Rantiba Bendali and other staff of the Louvre; Georgina Dhillon and Rinald Mamashev of the Zari Gallery, London; Spencer Ewen and his late parents, Richard and Andi; Ron George and John Strachan of Bath Spa University; my one-time art master, the late Tom Griffiths; Nadège Horner and Philippe Mariot of the Musée d'Orsay, along with Pierre Jourjon for information related to Paris cemeteries; Angus MacLennan of the White Horse Gallery, Marlborough, and Adam Smith, Hannah Greiving, and Katy Long of the Rothermere American Institute, University of Oxford.

Aspects of the "Rome" chapter were published in the *Sewanee Review* as "Rome to Ravello with *Set This House on Fire*." A version of the "Kraków" chapter appeared in *Thoughts of Love,* edited by Gary and Fiona Peters, as "A Stroll through Hell in Search of Love: Responses to a Century of Polish Suffering." Sections of "Past in Present: Reunion" appeared as "Try to Make It Real: A Bruce on Broadway Tale," in *Interdisciplinary Literary Studies.*

My late parents, Bobbi and Philip, and my siblings, Bruce and Amelia, would be right not to recognize themselves in this account, since narratives are often more about shape than strict adherence to fact. Perhaps my wife, Nicki, and our daughters, Xenatasha and Anastasia, will not recognize themselves or these family members either. This is not a memoir about them but about my experiences of school, travel, Paris, and painting. Nevertheless, it is dedicated to them with love.

PORTRAITS FROM PARIS

PRESENT IN PAST

SEVERANCE

Fourmillante cité, cité pleine de rêves, / Où le spectre en plein jour raccroche le passant!
Swarming city, city of dreams / Where ghosts in daylight accost the passerby!
—CHARLES BAUDELAIRE, "LES SEPT VIEILLARDS" / "THE SEVEN OLD MEN"

I learned this as a child. Never look up to someone. Never look down on them. Always look at them. What I did as a child I do all the more at present. I've taken severance and become an emeritus professor. My wife, Nicki, teaches mathematics here in Paris, while I explore the city. A Carte Louvre Professionnel provides access to the Louvre and Musée Delacroix and helps me feel I belong somewhere. A Carte Blanche gets me into the Musée d'Orsay and Orangerie. I wander at will through free venues like the Petit Palais and La Vie Romantique, and in time will visit everywhere from the Picasso to the Pompidou, the Rodin to the Cognacq-Jay. I go where my mood suits. This includes cafés in every arrondissement; the cemeteries of Père-Lachaise, Montmartre, and Montparnasse; the Palais-Royal, Luxembourg and Tuileries Gardens; parks from Buttes-Chaumont to Montsouris, and all over the transport system that interlinks a city materializing for me like a painting.

It's time to take stock. I'm doing this not just by discovering Paris but also through oil painting and constructing a memoir of childhood entrapment and adult freedom. Painting and writing are not dissimilar activities. As products of selves over time, both involve multiple markings—flecks or words—manipulated until you produce something far superior to your everyday intelligence. The difference is mainly for the recipient. Paintings can be quickly internalized. Books must be read. But in either case my current interests have to do with my boarding experience, my present life abroad, and travel in between. For the two clear gains from those schooldays were my discovery of painting, and my desire to be elsewhere.

I take it as given that past and present creatively interpret one another. We shape memories into narrative. Meanwhile memories affect our assessment of the present. Recollections of childhood differ from adult memories. Try as we might to look directly, the closer we peer, the more obvious is the need to invent. Nietzsche famously writes that we make each other up and forget we've done so. But we also make ourselves up, fabricating blank sections of our distant past to create bridges between free-floating memories. In maturity we have more capacity to evaluate what confronts us. Our exaggerated, novelistic childhood recollections can therefore give way, when it comes to adult experiences, to something nearer documentary journalism. But the tendency to fabricate, learned early as a survival imperative, may never entirely dissolve.

"What does please me," wrote Delacroix in his twenties, "is that I am gaining in reason and good sense without losing the faculty of being excited by beauty." He valued childlike awe as much as the more rational observations of adulthood. Past and present dispositions must exist together if memory is to be coherent, just as an interaction of elements is essential to painting. "Cohesion," he wrote, involves the art of binding "different parts of the picture by means of effect, color, line, reflections." There's a Charles Blanc story of how, early in Delacroix's career, using up all his yellows but failing to lighten the golden cloaks in *The Execution of the Doge Marino Faliero,* he hailed a cab to examine the work of Rubens in the Louvre. But as he did so, sudden sunshine turned the shadowy gravel violet. The yellow cab at once looked brighter and blacks more mauve. Realizing that our perception of a color depends upon what it's set against, he headed back to his studio and resolved the problem.

As in painting so in memoir, dualities aid coherence. Reimagining my childhood from maturity, I'll set one element against another: impressionistic against detailed, unreliable against reliable, invented against factual. Equally, in studying portraits and people, including people viewing portraits, I find myself combining the actual and the artistic. Perhaps my physical eyesight is relevant here. I'm not like the one-eyed flautist of the mysterious 1566 portrait attributed to Marc Duval that I often pass in Room 823 of the Louvre's Richelieu wing. But, for reasons I'll touch on later, while my right eye sees fairly clearly, a corneal scar in front of the pupil means that my left eye sees the world through a fuzzy gauze. Likewise, I see the present moment sharply. The more distant the memory, the murkier the vision.

Whatever museum or gallery I'm in, I therefore divide attention between yesterday's creations and today's human traffic. I'm not just pondering the solidified past but also the fleeting present. In contrast to the proverbial portrait that seems to watch you, people rarely look back at me. Focused on the work displayed, it's remarkable how few realize they themselves are being viewed. They're very self-aware, taking selfies in front of this or that Monet or Morisot, but are generally either absorbed with an artwork or with photographing one. In such places I can watch them like almost nowhere else.

The Louvre is, of course, an intoxication of treasures so, while I don't personally take selfies, walking through the wings—Richelieu, Sully, and Denon—I do take photos. Let's say I'm in Rooms 950–52 of Sully's upper level. This may be to reacquaint myself with Corot's *La Dame en bleu*, or Géricault's second sketch for *The Raft of the Medusa* (the first being in nearby 941). But it may also involve observing what others pause at or pass by. I follow what Robert Doisineau, famous for his photograph of lovers kissing, *Le Baisir de l'Hôtel de Ville*, called "the religion of looking." Such engagement with people in or beyond the paintings means that even in apparent solitude I have stimulation enough. As Vincent van Gogh writes, a painting "is a personality." I therefore leave galleries feeling I've had intense conversations, though I've hardly spoken all day.

My change in circumstances may account for the current vividness of my dreams, or maybe, in seeking to make sense of life, I'm experiencing a low-level need to resolve something. For the first time since I arrived at boarding school aged eight, followed by a teenage relapse, they're accompanied by grinding teeth. On recent nights I've joined Colette for coffee with a one-legged Sarah Bernhardt in her silk-lined coffin; supplied General de Gaulle with indigestion tablets; been manhandled from Opéra Garnier by Charles Aznavour and Juliette Gréco; taken the captain's armband from Kylian Mbappé at the Stade de France, and had a recurrence of a terrible dream I first experienced in the early weeks at school.

As a student of portraiture, I don't entirely distinguish between visitors and portraits. Look long enough at Rembrandt and everyone acquires the brown line of a Rembrandt mouth. Drawn to the multiplicity of framed individuals preserved for posterity, I'm struck by the illusion that they really do observe us ephemeral beings. Often a demeanor reminds me of someone. Like Marcel Proust, I trace not just the "general characteristics" of people I've known but also their "individual features." Georges de La Tour's *Madeleine à la veilleuse* could be a girl I met aged fifteen in the Dordogne. Frans Pourbus I's portrait of sixteenth-century Dutch jurisconsult, Viglius van Aytta, looks remarkably like a teacher we knew as the Major. Ingres's Louis-François Bertin resembles the man who tried to teach us Latin. But even if I don't recognize the portraits from life, they still take on attributes beyond mere paint.

The reading experience, too, can seep into life itself and vice versa. If after a day in galleries every bus, RER, or métro ride is a gathering of portraits, so characters created by Flaubert, Maupassant, Balzac, Zola, and others populate my Paris. Head against the window, Emma Bovary daydreams on the overground section of Line 2 from Pigalle to Père-Lachaise. Georges Leroy, whose adventures in *Bel-Ami* intrigued me in youth, frequents Clichy cafés, the pinprick pupils of his cold blue eyes sizing up prey. Père Goriot rants about his daughters on the top deck of the RER C train from Notre-Dame to Versailles. Gervaise sits at a checkout in a Monoprix in Les Sablons. Museums and books are time machines and magic boxes, and this suits me well: the past being very present, the present swiftly past, and the imagined and actual not always extricable.

Such preoccupations may have a psychological explanation. Severed from the joyful burden of employment, I'm aware of Stendhal's observation that "without work the ship of life has no ballast" and Delacroix's that work affords "a genuine sense of well-being." Perhaps most apt of all is Balzac's sentiment in *Cousin Bette*. "Constant labor is the law of art as well as the law of life," he writes, "for art is the creative activity of the mind."

My place of study is therefore the Louvre, with satellite campuses such as the Orsay. My work involves learning to paint better, and seeking answers to two questions. The first is what effect my boarding school childhood has had on my subsequent life. The second is how this relates to my tendency, via haphazard travel, to become l'étranger. This meditation on entrapment and escape is also a drama of engagement with the parochial worlds of my childhood, with my own and others' imaginations, and with cultures I've visited. Using the Vélib' system of bikes and e-bikes, I fly around Paris unknown, invisible, living partly in the present and partly in the past, partly here and partly somewhere else.

This brings me to the recurring dream. A drama of arrival and departure, it involves my parents and I drifting through the night on a small boat with a candle in place of a steam funnel. We bump into a sandy beach. I understand I'm to jump ashore. But when I turn round, they've stayed aboard. The boat is already drifting back into the darkness. My parents gaze from either side of the candle at their marooned son. Soon they're so far away as to be featureless. I cup my hands: What if the candle fails? Perhaps they reply but I hear nothing. Swallowed by the night, my parents and the candle boat recede to resemble a floating star. With nothing to look at but immensity, I close my eyes. Depending upon my mood, I open them to find myself either an adult in my current life in Paris, or a child in a dormitory.

Away to School, 2003, by Gavin Cologne-Brookes.

CHILD & YOUTH

The snail, of course, has to be taken out of his shell to be prepared for cooking. The shell he is forced back into may not be his own.

—A. J. LIEBLING, *Between Meals: An Appetite for Paris*

1 DEPARTURE

One day, long ago and far away, a boy is sent to boarding school. He has no idea that he won't see home for several weeks, and will never again live there permanently. Home is a house in the countryside, on the border of Surrey and Sussex, opposite a green field that rises to a solitary oak on the horizon. The house has a square tower rising from the roof like a humanoid head and shoulders. The tower roof resembles a tiled sunhat that shades its one long window, giving it as much personality as any actual being the boy has known.

The nearest shops are in the village of Ockley three miles north, with Horsham five miles south. For the next decade the boy spends school breaks and occasional Sundays at home, whether in the tower, in his bedroom, or in the walled garden with its old, evermore-leaning apple tree. For five years he'll attend a "preparatory" school, Thornditch, on the edge of a Sussex town. For the next four years he'll be at a "public" school, Grimpton College, on a hill dominated by a so-called chapel that's far bigger than any normal church, but without a steeple—a kind of concrete cornflake box with stained glass windows and an apex lid. Each school is up a driveway that separates it from the ordinary world. Each offers a distant view of wide waters. Thornditch looks out at a reservoir sprinkled with sailboats, Grimpton at the South Downs and the sea. These are mainly male institutions dotted with females, as the wide swathes of the Maasai Mara are dotted with clumps of greenery.

Until the moment of arrival at Thornditch the boy has been content enough in his world. Only two major changes have occurred. A sister has appeared and an older brother has gone missing for weeks at a time. But soon after the boy's eighth birthday things take a downward turn. The mother drives him to Kick & Birch Ltd. to be fitted into uncomfortable clothes. On a blossom-spattered Sunday evening in April 1969, the father snaps a photo with his Polaroid Instamatic. Out slides a blank shiny card. Boy, mother, and brother materialize like ghosts: the mother in the middle, the brother, aged nine, shoulder height to the mother, and the boy himself, freckled, frowning. The boys wear the Sunday uniform of black lace-ups, woolen pink-trimmed socks held up by garters, gray flannel shirt, suit shorts and jacket, pink tie with flat bottom as if snipped off, and pink school cap. The brother stands at attention, head straight, expression inscrutable. A year already at the school, he's outgrown his uniform. In contrast, the boy's hands are in his jacket pockets, despite the mother's hand in the crook of his arm, his thin legs—Knobbly Knees being another family nickname—in the position he'll come to know of as "at ease."

Years later, the boy uses the photograph to create a painting. It's so small that the slightest touch makes a difference, especially around the eyes. The mother's harsh expression, for instance, might be to do with too heavy a shaping of her eyebrows. In the fashion of the sixties, she wears a jacket and miniskirt. They appear orange in the painting, though in the photo they're closer to what Winsor & Newton call Scarlet Lake. But the faded ties and caps are true enough. The uniforms being secondhand, it's not just the brothers in them but the ghosts of previous owners. For all the boy knows, his tie and cap may once have belonged to a child later obliterated on the Somme or burned alive in a Spitfire before being doused in the waves off the coast of Kent.

"Okay," the father says, "into the car."

The brothers climb into the yellow Cortina. Trunks and tuck boxes jut from the back of the car. The sister isn't there. Perhaps the parents have arranged a babysitter.

"Can I say goodbye to Tina?" says the boy.

"Being a cat she won't know you're gone," says the father. "You'll see her soon."

The boy sits behind the father so he can see the mother's profile. The father pulls out of the driveway and speeds down country lanes toward Thornditch.

Never before has the boy felt such discomfort. The jacket presses the scratchy shirt into his shoulders. The collar and tie chafe his neck. The shorts rub the top of his legs. The garters pinch his shins. The socks scratch his calves. The brand-new lace-ups press the bone in line with his big toe.

"Mummy," he says, "the uniform itches."

"Don't be a sissy. And it's Mother and Father now you're a big boy."

She takes her compact case from her handbag, clicks it open, dabs her nose with the powdery disk. She snaps it shut, puts it back in her bag, and pulls down the sunshade to look in the mirror. She backcombs her hair with a fut-fut sound, lifting the front and combing part of it down, then opens pale lipstick and makes her mouth an O.

"Mummy? Why are we going to school on a Sunday?"

"Mother. You're going to board."

"What's board?"

"Stay overnight."

"Until tomorrow?"

"For three weeks."

"Then I come home?"

"For an exeat," says the brother.

"I don't want an exeat," says the boy.

"You will," says the brother.

"An exeat," the father explains, "is like parole. You get out for good behavior."

"Then you go back," says the brother, "and start all over again."

The mother has finished reapplying her lipstick. She slides her lips, smiles into the mirror, and brushes the corner of her mouth with her little finger. She rolls back the lipstick, replaces the lid, and flips the mirror.

"Who will look after us?"

"The matrons," says the father.

The boy doesn't like to twist his neck because his collar chafes, but does so enough to see the brother looking out of his window. The boy turns to his own window. He entertains himself with a silent interview. He's a spaceman heading for the rocket at Cape Canaveral.

What do you most look forward to about the launch, Commander?

I most look forward to the juddering power of the engines beneath me.

What do you least like about space travel, Commander?

I least like the itchy spacesuit.

What is the purpose of your journey, Commander?

A mission to the moon to destroy matrons for the benefit of all mankind.

What are matrons, Commander?

Machines designed by aliens to destroy all known life in the galaxy.

Why not destroy the aliens, Commander?

The matrons have killed all the aliens with exeats.

At this point the boy's Head Cinema distracts him, superimposing a cowboy on a black stallion keeping pace with the car, galloping through fields, leaping fences, walls, even buildings. He wears a black hat and a red shirt with a black waistcoat. Close behind on a white horse another cowboy fires a pistol. He wears a white hat, blue shirt, and yellow waistcoat pinned with a star. The fugitive falls off his horse and plunges into a lake.

Dusk approaches. The sky melts from blue to the orange-red of the mother's skirt-suit. She's dressed to match a sunset. The landscape skims up close and floats in the distance. The sun stumbles across ploughed fields, peeps down streets, pops from behind houses, winks through hedgerows, then detonates in a copse, splintering the silhouetted branches in a final fire. The sky dissolves to yellow over dark hills, then violet, then blue, and finally, between the neon strokes of street lighting, to black. At traffic lights, specks of rain hit the windows and redness shines in every droplet. The lights turn to amber and green. The droplets change, too. The father switches on the wipers. The car speeds into the darkness. He turns on the radio. For a while there's tinkly music, then the weather forecast.

There are warnings of gales in Finisterre, Sole, Fastnet, and Shannon, the crisp radio voice announces. *The general synopsis at one nine double-o: low Shannon, nine hundred and eighty, expected Lundy nine hundred and ninety-one by one double-o tomorrow.* The boy twists his neck in his collar. His Head Cinema shows a pipe smoker in a captain's hat and knitted polo neck turning dials in a tackle-strewn cabin tossed in a stormy sea. *Southeasterly three or four, occasionally five. Showers. Good. Fisher, German Bite south backing southeast, four or five, occasionally six, showers. Good.*

It's unclear what's good about bad weather. Maybe the crisp-voiced man likes storms. Soon he sails off the airwaves, replaced again by tinkly music.

The boy leans forward out of the darkness. "Will I see you again on a Sunday?"

"Yes." The mother puts on the overhead light and pulls down her mirror. She pouts, reapplying lipstick. The angle of the light hollows her eye sockets. "Three Sundays' time."

The boy slumps back. Fut-fut. They reach a town. He feels a familiar ooze in his nostril. "Nosebleed," he reports. This regular occurrence requires no explanation.

"Tissue," says the mother, reaching back, a copilot assisting a navigator. "Head back. Squeeze nose. Don't swallow. Don't spit."

The boy's uniform imprisons his skin. He thinks the collar is bruising his neck. The mother says it's a rash. A bruise is when you bleed within. A rash is when you scrape your skin. In either case, he thinks, borrowing one of the mother's phrases, it really is the end.

The car turns up a dark driveway flanked with pale rhododendrons and reaches a gravel circle beneath the silhouette of a turreted building with windows lit up yellow. Cars park either side of a huge doorway and around the outer rim of the circle. Parents and boys carry the boys' belongings across the windswept gravel and through the doorway.

The boy waits in the car for the nosebleed to stop. The parents and brother take the brother's trunk and tuck box through the doorway. The boy won't see the brother for some time. When they return, the parents fetch the boy's trunk and he follows them with his tuck box into an oak-paneled hallway. A white-coated lady named Matron McRipp leads them past portraits of stern men, a set of African gongs, and a tiger skin with a snarling head. Opposite the foot of a wide staircase is a list of boys' names under dormitories with strange names like Drake, Gordon, Kitchener, Marlborough, and Nelson. The door the boy is ushered through is labeled Wellington.

The long room is like a hospital ward with a parquet floor, white pillars, a floor-to-ceiling bow window with blinds pulled down, and two long rows of beds with bars at the head like prisons in cowboy films. A single bar at the foot of each shows boys' surnames alphabetically down the line. The boy's is second on the left, after Aitkin II and Bunting and before Cribley, who has scabby hands and says he was "adopted" and has now been "abducted." The only new boys this term, they happen to suit the alphabetical arrangement.

The boy copies others and pushes his tuck box under the bed. He's concerned that the fruit in there might rot. The parents place the trunk at the end. The mother wets her fingers and rubs his fringe to one side.

"When can I come home?"

"Soon."

"When's soon?"

"On the Sunday Out."

"The exit?"

"The exeat. Be a big boy and have a lovely time!"

"I have fruit in my tuck box," says the boy. "I don't know where to put it."

"Don't be childish, darling. There'll be a fruit cupboard. Ask the matron."

They leave. Some of the boys have red eyes.

"Bunting is blubbering," says Cribley.

Aitkin II, a dark-haired, wide-faced boy, sits on his bed and repetitively raises and lowers his head, hands fluttering beside him, like a baby bird awaiting food.

Bunting has an odd expression. Straw hair partly covering one eye, he's crying from the uncovered eye but not the half-covered one. The boy later learns that Bunting has a glass right eye. His father asked him to watch from behind a fence to say when the drill came through but when it did it drilled through Bunting's eye so he wears a pretend one.

The dormitory captain is a thirteen-year-old "officer." Officers have black diagonal stripes on their ties.

"I am Dobson, dormitory captain," he shouts, though no one's talking. "Dormitory Dobson. Obey or suffer! Now, undress! Fold clothes on chair! Place socks and garters in shoes! Place shoes under chair! Don pajamas and dressing gown! Stand to attention!"

Every boy does as he's told.

"Face door! Single file, this row first, quick march! Into corridor! Up Grand Staircase! Into bathroom! Wash face! Brush teeth! Comb hair!"

The boys troop up the oak staircase. Above the bend is a portrait of a woman in a green dress. On the other wall a stained glass window depicts the school coat of arms: a sword crossed with a cricket bat. Each boy stands before a basin with his flannel, toothpaste, toothbrush, and comb. The boy doesn't speak to anyone else. He looks at his eight-year-old self in the mirror. The officer repeats the orders in reverse. The boys march back downstairs, turning at the painting of the lady in green by the stained glass window, and get into bed. All this is done to no other sound than the slap of slippers on the staircase.

The boy lies in the tucked sheets. His feet stick up beneath the blanket. Year by year they get farther away. The high ceiling is patterned like a christening cake. The lights flick off suddenly, leaving an image in his head of the white curves and cornices.

"Silence!" A bed creaks. Something snaps. "That's my belt," shouts Dobson, "my whip!" He snaps it again. "Order will be maintained. My whip demands total silence. No sniveling, no blubbering. If I hear so much as a rustle I'll flash my torch at you and you'll get out of bed and stand in the middle of the dormitory with a pillow on each arm. Drop a pillow and you'll see Glinty in the morning to be whacked." Dobson's shoes crackle on the parquet floor like tearing flesh. "As all of you except the new boys will know, when the morning bell rings, get up. Dress. Stand by bed. Await instructions."

Glinty, the boy will learn, is the bespectacled Headmaster, Mr. Gladmere.

Dobson flashes his torch around the dormitory then flicks it off. The boy's eyes adjust to the darkness. The huge windows are pale behind the blinds. Boys are sniffling. Maybe he'd better say his prayers. God Bless Mummy, God Bless Daddy is the start, but he can't recall the rest. Even that may now have to be God Bless Mother, God Bless Father. He doesn't want to be here but at least he can go anywhere in his head. As Commander, he directs his rocket up out of Earth's orbit toward Planet Silence in the Outer Hebrides Galaxy where he shoots matrons with exeats. Matrons pulverized, he sets his dials for home. As the blue Earth fills his vision, he ejects and drifts down in a memory that's halfway toward a dream.

He's in his room in the moonlight. A corner box holds the tangled figures of his inch-high Timpo Cowboys and Indians. Grandma Cologne says those with black hats are outlaws, those with white hats are good men. The rest are ordinary Cowboys. The bookshelves contain *Asterix* and *Tintin* books, full of adventures to far-off lands; *Chocky,* about a boy named Matthew with an alien in his head who helps him win swimming races; *Tom's Midnight Garden,* about a boy who creeps downstairs at midnight to see why a clock has struck thirteen and finds himself in Victorian times, and *Marianne Dreams,* about a girl who draws a house then dreams of it.

At home there's a wall clock. Hearing it chime, he creeps from his bedroom along the landing, down to the hallway to the garden door. Across the terrace, moonlight lacquers the well and rusty swing. He climbs the shallow steps through the archway to the big lawn. An owl hoots in the pines. He wanders past the vegetable patch to the potting shed, then across to the summerhouse, and round again to the courtyard and roadside gate. Someone's calling from far away: Everything is ruined, ruined! Then he's in the classroom of the village school, leaning back on his chair and telling a girl, Carolyn, whom he admires as the best at drawing in the class, that everything is ruined. Carolyn asks why. Because I'm leaving, says the boy. I'm going to boarding school. Carolyn asks what that is.

The boy opens his eyes. There's no moonlight. He can just make out the christening cake ceiling of the dormitory and the blinds on the floor-to-ceiling windows.

I really don't know, he thinks, but I'm beginning to find out.

2 PARIS

Room 719 on the upper level of Denon is a cul-de-sac at the end of the Spanish collection. A lesser-known entrance to the Louvre, the Porte des Lions, provides a shortcut to this space by way of the stairway up from the Arts of Africa, Asia, Oceania and the Americas. On the right are three individual seats in their own alcoves, each with a window onto the endless busyness of ant-sized people traversing the Tuileries's sandy paths against a backdrop of the Rue de Rivoli. The first of these is my self-designated office from which I gaze at Paris and into my past. The handful of paintings here keep me focused. Luis Meléndez's self-portrait is next to trompe l'oeil still lifes by Bernardo Germán de Llórente and Goya's *Still Life with a Sheep's Head.* Farther along, I'm watched by his portrait of Mariana Waldstein, intimate of Napoléon's brother Lucien. On the end wall is one of Ferdinand Guillemardet, ambassador to Spain. Two more Goya portraits, one of Don Evaristo Pérez de Castro, the other titled *Woman with a Fan,* complete our select company.

Prior to moving into an apartment on Rue Chauveau in Neuilly, home is a self-catering suite in the Adagio Aparthotel at the Seine end of Rue du Théâtre. The restaurant opposite the entrance appears as a murder setting at the start of series seven of the television drama *Engrenages*—known in English as *Spiral.* But really the area is perfectly safe. Our large windows look out at half of Tour Eiffel. The other half is obscured by the Cheminée du Front de Seine, a steam ventilator tower that resembles an Apollo rocket on its launchpad.

On the 72 bus here this morning I witnessed a curious incident. Finishing an apple, a smartly dressed woman placed the core in her handbag. Exchanging a smile with an old man eating an apple of his own, she then retreated inward and began to move her lipsticky lips as if still munching. Her contemplative expression revived the memory of my mother's death from cancer some years ago, her world shrinking from the wildly social to the domestic indoors to the single room and finally the bed. It was as if, in Zola's phrase from *The Masterpiece*, she "could see the invisible and hear the silence calling." Something else caught my attention. When I looked again both passengers had gone. I left the bus and crossed Quai François Mitterrand at Pont des Artes for the Louvre.

I'm not writing this memoir in Paris entirely by chance. I've long expected to live here. Many years ago a Grimpton art master, Mr. Popjoy (of whom more later), gave me a fifties map of Paris. Dating from his time as a student at École des Beaux-Arts, it's taped across torn sections ("just as one dresses a wound," writes Patrick Modiano of map-mending in his novella *In the Café of Lost Youth*). But it's on the hotel wall and will be on the wall in the Neuilly apartment.

France is also the land of my Huguenot ancestors, and Paris the traumatic epicenter of their fate. There's a family story of a long-lost oar handle with names and dates recording an illustrious lineage. Evidently it stated that my forebear was the Huguenot leader Admiral Gaspard II de Coligny, assassinated at the start of the Saint Bartholomew's Day Massacre in 1572. Uncle Gaspard's statue stands behind railings on Rivoli by the Oratoire du Louvre a few hundred yards from where I'm sitting. Marc Duval, painter of the one-eyed flautist, spelled their name Colignej on his 1550 sketch of the brothers. The oldest, Odet, seems to have adjusted his name to Coligne on coming to England with his wife, Ysabel de Hauteville. Poisoned on the orders of the French authorities (claimed Ysabel) shortly after the suspicious death of the younger brother François, and not long before the Admiral's assassination, Coligne is buried in Canterbury Cathedral. The story goes that they had a son named Zacharie. To camouflage his Huguenot connections, Ysabel tweaked Coligne by one letter to Cologne, thereby redirecting his identity toward that city, and a name that, while less obviously linked with the Huguenot movement, was still associated with migration. For Colognes were certainly escapists. This is evident from the fact that, while there aren't many people with that name in Europe, there are several in the American South, notably Louisiana.

"As a boy, the first Cologne in England," Grandma Cologne told me, "fled for his life in a rowboat after his father's death in the French Wars of Religion."

This suggests that, after Odet's death, Ysabel sent Zacharie up the Thames to seek his fortune in London, aware of but unburdened by the names Coligny or Coligne. Records show that several of my Cologne ancestors were carvers of fine cabinets. Zacharie seems to have carved his lineage on the handle of one of the oars. The skill would have passed down through various Colognes even if the handle itself was lost.

Odet, Gaspard, and François were sons of a hero of the Italian Wars, Gaspard I de Coligny, and a Première Dame d'Honneur to Eleanor of Austria, Louise de Montmorency. Louise was a daughter of Anne Pot and William of Montmorency. Louise's brother, Anne, witnessed the Field of the Cloth of Gold and died of wounds after leading the Royal army to victory at Saint-Denis. Feeling one should keep in touch with relatives, I occasionally greet his gisant in Richelieu. I also visit Room 946 of Sully, where two nineteenth-century paintings depict scenes from the Saint Bartholomew's Day Massacre. Alexandre-Évariste Fragonard, son of celebrated Rococo painter Jean-Honoré, depicts a soldier leaning across a woman in a marital bed to crush her husband's skull with a musket. Robert-Fleury seems to show the start of Uncle Gaspard's gruesome expiration. Beside an open window a bearded man lies at the mercy of a red-headed soldier about to pierce him with a pike.

Perhaps at the behest of Catherine de' Medici, on 22 August 1572, near Église Saint-Germain-l'Auxerrois, east of the Louvre—only a few yards from my favorite Paris cocktail bar, Le Fumoir, on what is now Rue de l'Amiral Coligny—one Seigneur de Maurevert shot a finger from Gaspard's right hand and shattered his left elbow. Two nights later a group stabbed him in his lodgings and defenestrated him to the feet of the Duke of Guise, where another Guise associate beheaded him.

I was recently in Deyrolle, on Rue du Bac, pondering the taxidermy shop's array of specimens, from camels to ravens to tarantulas. Fortunately, humans are not popular subjects for this art form, certainly not murdered ones. Statues, on the other hand, don't always shy away from the gruesome. Saint Denis stands holding his severed head beside the Miraculous fountain of Montmartre (or Martyr Mountain). Likewise in the Louvre Saint Valerie, another céphalophore, carries her head, supposedly toward the altar in Limoges; the gisant of Jeanne de Bourbon Vendôme depicts an emaciated corpse with stone maggots crawling from her intestines, and Girolamo Della Robbia portrays Gaspard's probable nemesis Catherine de' Medici, as per her instructions, as a corpse-on-a-slab. In contrast, Montmorency's gisant, adjacent to Robbia's Medici, has him suited and booted in full armor, his and his wife's hands in prayer and, across from the Louvre, Gaspard's statue on Rivoli depicts him intact.

There is, however, currently an exhibition in the church courtyard of Gaspard's assassination and its aftermath. Cartoons show his dismembered corpse being dragged through the streets and thrown in the Seine. What they don't show is that the mob cut off his extremities, and his remains were left to rot on the gibbet of Montfaucon. (The body of a dead enemy never smells bad, the visiting Charles IX told his gagging courtiers.) If one wants further embellishment, there's Joseph Hornung's painting, in London's Victoria and Albert Museum, of Medici contemplatively stroking the hair on the admiral's amputated head. But, whatever the truth of Uncle Gaspard's murder and the massacre that followed, I'm drawn both to Paris and into a personal past, and this lineage, however tenuously, connects them. On that personal level, I need to record, or more likely re-create, a past in pursuit of identity, or completion, or reconciliation between the two beings that I am: child and adult.

3 TAXIDERMY

After Lights Out some weeks into term, the boy has a whispered conversation with Aitkin about the masters: the bewhiskered Mr. Croulebarbe (History); the sinewy Horatio Greatorex (Sport); the droopy-faced Major Nott (Geography); the narrow-eyed Mr. Pavilion (Mathematics); the terrifying Mr. Flat (Music), Captain Bullet (Gymnastics and Religion)—a tall, ashen man whose neck and head are of equal diameters—and Colonel Puterbaugh (Physics and Shooting) with his empire-pink face, barrel chest, and mustache the size of a postage stamp. But Aitkin falls asleep and Dormitory Dobson catches the boy whispering his opinions to himself. He tells him that he'll be taken at dawn to Glinty's study to be "threshed." It feels like his last night on Earth. He expects to be scythed to ribbons or beheaded like an ear of corn. He wakes in a sweat, then dreams he's being led to Glinty's study. Soon enough Dobson shakes him at dawn.

"Don gown and slippers. Follow me." Watched by dozens of eyes, Dobson marches him past the headmasters' portraits and tiger skin to Glinty's study. "Wait here."

Above a bench on the oak-paneled wall opposite the study hangs a portrait of Glinty's father. The balding, white-haired, one-time headmaster stares at the boy down his veiny nose. The boy climbs up on the bench and traces the paint with a finger. The skin looks real. Actual liquid seems to sit in the corner of the eyes. The boy traces the forehead, reaches a bubbly texture at the bridge of the nose, and presses, denting the nose. He jumps down with a thump. The study door opens and Glinty appears, wearing tortoiseshell spectacles and a black gown over a pin-striped suit. He has the same veiny nose as the portrait.

"Enter."

The study smells Victorian. Sunlight streams from a window onto a leather-topped desk. Behind it is a painting of elephants charging through grass under stormy skies.

"Abide." Glinty disappears through a side door.

The red-patterned carpet looks oriental. In the shadows to the right of the window is a glass case full of birds, and another against the opposite wall. The boy peers back and forth between the labels and the birds, some perched on branches, including a wren, a blackbird, and a sparrowhawk. A house martin and a swallow, their wings stretched as if in flight, are double-clamped to the bark. There are several woodpeckers. Greater Spotted Woodpecker, reads one label, by a big red, black, and white bird, beak against a bit of tree trunk. Lesser Spotted Woodpecker, reads another. This is a smaller version of the same bird, but neither is exactly spotted so maybe it's just Less Often Seen. The Lesser Spotted Woodpecker clings to a twig and stares at the boy. There's also a Green Woodpecker, barely green at all now, and a Pied Woodpecker label without a bird. Maybe Pied means Missing.

A case by the door contains a large bird, labeled Lady Amherst's Pheasant, standing in dry grass. The boy assumes Lady Amherst left the pheasant to the school in her will, or maybe a gamekeeper shot it accidentally, upsetting Lady Amherst so much that she had it stuffed. High up along the wall, opposite bookshelves, rows of dusty little birds, encased and unblinking, eye him from the gloom.

Glinty reappears holding a long, pale stick. He switches on a lamp and places the stick on the desk. "Have you anything to say?"

"How old are the birds?"

Glinty peers at the birds as if he hasn't noticed them before. "Ooh, I should think a hundred years or more. They'd have been treated by a taxidermist and encased as if in flight—or song."

"What do you mean?"

"Sir. What do you mean, sir?"

"What do you mean, sir?"

"The birds are stuffed."

"They look hungry."

"Stuffed with sawdust and wool."

The boy looks again at the dusty birds. "Who killed them?"

Glinty takes the folded handkerchief from his breast pocket and blows his veiny nose until it's red. "When I asked you if you had anything to say, I didn't intend you to embark upon a conversation about taxidermy." He folds the handkerchief and puts it back in his pocket. "Have you evidence to mitigate your misdemeanor?"

"There's a painting of elephants behind you."

"That's a print," says Glinty. "Those are *Keenyan* elephants in the Maasai Mara, the *Keenyan* wilderness." The boy has no idea what he's talking about. Perhaps Kenyan is a make of elephant. "*Keenya* was once upon a time part of the Empire. We ruled half the world."

"Where's my brother?"

"Brother? No doubt behaving appropriately somewhere. Is that all you have to say?"

"I don't like kippers."

"That's a red herring."

This confuses the boy further.

"You talked after Lights Out." The carpet has lots of different reds. The boy studies the patterns in search of herrings. "I must therefore eat you."

"Eat me?"

"Beat. I intend to *thresh* you."

"Has the grass in the painting been threshed, sir?"

"Remove gown. Drop pajamas. Bend over chair." There's a chair to the left with a green cushion. The boy pulls his pajamas down and holds the chair handles.

Whack!

Burning. Stinging.

Whack!

Two. The boy counts. He does this when gassed by the dentist, Mr. Dixon, who is always looking to gas you and take out your teeth.

Whack!

Three. Some adults like to damage you. That's why you need to be brave. You must hide within yourself. They batter the door and tap the window but you pretend no one's there.

Whack!

Four. The boy grips the chair. The wall is mildewed. The door is shut. Is this what you came to the moon for, Commander?

Whack!

Five. A pause. Maybe it's over. The matrons have caught him and taken him to Emperor Minus Zed.

Whack!

Six.

"Raise pajamas. Don gown. Return to dormitory."

As he leaves, his bottom set to sting all morning, the boy glances up at the portrait of Glinty's father. Due to the dent at the bridge of his veiny nose, the man's expression now has the hint of a sneer.

4 BLITZKRIEG

Like lots of things, Sundays Out, or exeats, start as thrilling then disappoint. Once home and in civilian clothes, the boy plays with his Cowboys and Indians. The fifty Indians charge—moved one by one—from under the sofa. The hundred-plus Cowboys and Cavalry circle their wagons. The parents and grandparents gather round the log fire. Granny and Grandpa and the parents have gin and tonic. Grandma Cologne has neat gin. At lunch, the brother and sister talk in hushed tones, each hoping for the best potatoes. The adults drink wine. By pudding, the father is talking of British superiority, which is why, led by England, they won wars and had an Empire. After educating the foreigners, they gave them back their countries and now help them not to make a mess of things. The brother wants to be an officer, first at school then in the army. After lunch, the adults fall asleep in the sitting room until the grandparents leave. After supper, the boy puts on his nettle suit. On the drive back the father listens to Charlie Chester's tunes for elderly people. "With a box full of records and a bag full of post, it's Radio Soapbox and Charlie your host!" In chapel the school sings "Abide with Me"—*Fast falls the eventide. Hold now thy cross before my failing eyes*—then exits beneath a print of what the boy will later learn is Salvador Dalí's *Christ of Saint John of the Cross*.

Film Night, too, promises more than it gives. The boys are sent to bed at their allotted time, even when the film hasn't finished. Only the nine o'clock dormitories see to the end. A projector and screen are set up in the library which has prints on the oak-paneled walls by a painter called Rembrandt. One is of an old man who observes you with gentle eyes. Another is of a lady holding up her nightshirt to wade in water. The library buzzes with anticipation. The lights go out and the projector whirls, starting with specks and flashes before a picture materializes with writing saying what the film is.

The boys watch the start of *The Admirable Crichton, The Flight of the Phoenix, Lord of the Flies,* and other films about strange islands and castaways. There are also films like *Zulu,* where British soldiers fight off hordes of Zulus who then—an older boy later explains—announce respect for British bravery by doing a dance. Sometimes there are World War II films. *Night of the Generals* is so dark that all you see are the red stripes down the generals' trousers. But at least it's in color, unlike *The Dambusters,* although the theme tune does make you want to fly off and bust a dam. Also, he likes the spookiness of black-and-white sunlight in films like *Reach for the Sky,* about a pilot called Bader who flies legless. *The First of the Few* is about a man named Mitchell who invents the Spitfire but has cancer. Of the color films, while *The Cockleshell Heroes* has a jolly theme tune, the best is *Spartacus,* about a slave with a cleft chin, and armor on one shoulder, about whom every other slave says, "I'm Spartacus." It's still exciting, even though the boy never gets to see Mitchell succeed in making a Spitfire or the Dambusters bust successfully, or what happens to the generals or Spartacus, or whether the castaways get home.

Often the film breaks down, goes too fast or slow or loses sound. The reel cuts remind you they're made-up stories or actors pretending to do historical events. Sometimes there's a break for High Tea, which on Film Night is a rubbery fried egg and brown chips that ping from your plate. The state of the egg and chips is because the reel has gone on longer than Maria and Miguel expect. Maria is small and round and wears a dark-blue outfit. Miguel's bow legs are clad in black trousers beneath his white jacket and black tie. They are the Portuguese "domestics" in charge of the dining hall.

If the British face dangers, they triumph. Britain has the best history. The boys are lucky to be born in the most victorious country with the bravest, most civilized people as opposed to being foreign. They're also lucky to be selected as the next British leaders. It's especially great to be English because they won the World Cup as well as all the wars, nobly supported by others who, while also British, are Scottish or Welsh or Irish, as well as people like Australians and Canadians. But if you're English and at a boys' preparatory school you just learn Latin and History and read H. E. Marshall's *Our Island Story* and become dashing gentlemen with David Niven mustaches.

The boy is half English from the father except for a bit of French, which he knows from his name and from the legend of the oar handle that has the

French family history about an Admiral who had his head cut off, and a quarter Scottish and a quarter Welsh from the mother. He rather wishes he was something different, like Namibian, or Tibetan, but you don't get a choice in these things.

History means the Empire and World Wars I and II. On Remembrance Sundays the boys are told to be proud of their predecessors, or Old Boys, who died nobly. There's a photograph of an Old Boy by the steps to the altar. He died aged twenty in 1944. One frosty Remembrance Sunday a wreath hangs on the altar and red poppies are glued to little crosses sprouting from a box on the step. The boys wear paper poppies on plastic green stems. Glinty reads the names of every Old Boy who died in a war since the school was founded. This gives the boy time to plan the afternoon battle in the trenches the Old Boys themselves probably dug in the School Woods before they died in real battles. One day the boy will himself be an Old Boy, though they're hard to imagine. He pictures ordinary boys with boys' faces but bigger and older. They seem monstrous and better off dead.

As usual, lunch is horrible. The boys eat at benches with a master at one end of the table. Breakfast is the worst meal, consisting of gray tea and porridge with dark lumps. But all school food is grim. The biggest horror, surpassing even porridge, liver, and rhubarb, is compulsory custard passed round in a jug. No one wants the dried skin to drop into their bowl. As a constant chatterer during Silence Time the boy usually ends up eating at the Pigs' Table in the middle of the dining hall. This means standing facing the School Shield beneath the print of a man leaning on a stick and gazing across a mountainous vista.

After lunch they lie on their beds for an hour before Free Time then put on gumboots and khaki shorts and jackets to race to the trenches. They divide into a German and a British army. Today the boy is German. The Germans meet the British in No-Man's-Land and agree to fight the Somme. The boy assumes it was named the Somme because it was somber, but it was still a great battle of the Great War. Lots of soldiers were killed, including Old Boys. No-Man's-Land is only yards across. You fling clumps of earth at each other. They explode on impact. Dust drifts across the trenches like gas. A horse-faced boy called Dollaton IV, youngest of four, who for the battle is known as Baron von Dollaton, keeps charging over the top. He's very tall and enjoys dying. He's good at sprawling just as he reaches the British trench. The boy himself only dies once because it's a bit muddy. He prefers being a clump-flinging machine gunner. By the time the bell goes, it's dusk and they use torches as flares and machine gun sprays. After Low Tea of marmite sandwiches, they shower, put on itchy Sunday suits, sit on lockers in the main hall, then parade into Evensong.

Evensong feels longer than Eternity. The boy's legs are sore between the shorts and gartered socks. Matron McRipp says his legs are "chapped." "Chapped" must be to do with being a "chap," and maybe only chaps get their legs chapped. Chapped legs are from being outside in the cold then coming into the warm. You can also get chilblains. The boy thinks he might change his name to Chilblain.

"Let us sing 'Abide with me,' Hymn Two Hundred and Sixty-Two," says Glinty.

Not unexpected, this is still disappointing. The boy's favorite hymn is "For Those in Peril on the Sea." It's exciting, easy to picture, and he likes the word Peril.

Eventually it's time to parade into High Tea followed by bed. The boy lies in the dark and thinks how odd it is that this day, like all days, seems long but is one of many. Soon today will be history. He imagines being as old as eleven, or a teenager, or as old as an Old Boy, or actually dead. Dying is like a black cloth wrapped round your neck so tight that you wither. He wonders if he's lived before and maybe been a Knight of the Round Table, or one of Robin Hood's Merry Men, carousing with vittles and ale. He thinks about how they missed Bonfire Night and only saw fireworks in the distance where ordinary people were having fun. His Head Cinema shows him at home with the family, pulling on hats and scarves and gloves and stomping through a wet field, eyes shining in the flickering light as Guy Fawkes ignites and disintegrates into the bonfire.

He switches off his Head Cinema and thinks about how maybe they could have a Battle of the Somme or a blitzkrieg in the dormitory. There's a meeting somewhere down the corridor, so Dormitory Dobson is absent. The boy gropes along his chair, finds Aitkin's *Atlas of the Natural World,* and flings it into the dark.

"Aargh!" comes a cry. "What was that?"

"A shell! Say 'pax' or you're pulverized!" The boy flings a shoe the other way.

Thwang! Incoming fire hits the boy in the tummy. He flings a shoe into the darkness. Objects crash into cupboards, smash into pillars, thunk on heads. Something smacks his face so hard he sees stars. Fireworks! Shrapnel! Shrieks and bangs drown his yelp. He hurls a broken-spined book. In his Head Cinema he leaves the trenches to clamber into his triplane. He's the Red Baron, dodging enemy fire.

"Stay close, lads!" he shouts to boys in accompanying planes. "I'm Richthofen!"

"Why should you be Richthofen?" shouts Bunting. "Aargh!"

"I can't help who I am," says the boy, teeth gritted against gunfire, but Bunting stops playing anyway because his eye has come loose.

The battle rages. Items flash past like lightning. Cries split the darkness. The boy retreats to his cockpit and ponders flying home, but someone is stripping beds and yelling, Prepare and *pull!* This is what Matron McRipp says in her Scottish accent when checking if you've wet the bed. He's lying in the cold air. A heavy object knocks the breath from him. He stands on his bed and hurls it back.

"Cave!" someone shouts. Beware. But it's too late. The lights snap on.

Dormitory Dobson is there. Behind him stand Glinty, the Major, the Captain, Matron McRipp, and the Colonel, empire-pink face offset by blue eyes glinting like droplets of gin. The boy alone is bouncing on a bed. Everyone else is tucked in. The book—a *Look and Learn* annual—arcs as if in slow orbit and smashes to the floor.

"I shall see you at dawn," says Glinty. "Dobson, have him clear up the mess."

"Of all days," rumbles the Colonel, "Remembrance Sunday!"

"Have you boys no respect?" mutters the Major gloomily.

Matron McRipp stays behind. "Boy," she says, "who was in this with you?"

Parts of books lie strewn across the floor and over beds, along with shoes, clothing, and a dismembered teddy. The boy's Head Cinema shows him with his severed head stuck on the school railings. His effigy will be burned every Guy Fawkes Night or Remembrance Sunday. But suddenly he's not Guy Fawkes nor in World War I. He's Spartacus.

"It was me," he says. "I acted alone."

"You can't have hurled whole histories hither and thither!" whistles Matron McRipp.

"I was sleepwalking."

"Sleepwalking!" snorts Dormitory Dobson. "Clear up the mess and await your fate."

Then Dollaton, twiddling hoofy fingers, face longer than usual, stands on his bed. The ceiling is so high that even he comes nowhere near it. "It was m-me, Dobson. I s-started it."

"Okay. You too."

Then Aitkin stands up, face wider than ever. "I started it."

Then Bunting, hair flopping over his restored glass eye. "I started it."

Soon several boys are up on their beds.

"I started it!"

"I started it!"

"Well, all of you clear up the mess then," grunts Dobson. "It seems, boy, that you have accomplices. But I don't care. Be outside Glinty's study first thing. Alone!"

So once again at dawn the boy passes the portraits and tiger skin and stands in the study on the oriental rug. Behind Glinty is the print of elephants running at him from the stormy sky. Glinty leans against the leather-topped desk. He points to the chair with its green cushion next to the case of woodpeckers.

"Most boys learn their lesson after one threshing."

"Yes, sir." The boy knows this is probably the end for him. Glinty is quivering.

"Take off your gown. Turn, bend, and keep very, very still."

The boy does as he's told. Glinty no longer gets a cane from the walk-in cupboard. He now has a special rack. The boy watches beneath his armpit. Glinty seems upside down, as if walking along a carpeted ceiling. He pulls an ivory cane from the rack. It's thin and bent, with a sharpened tip. It wouldn't be any use for anything except thrashing. Glinty's spectacles catch the light— blank disks like twin moons.

Swiew! Glinty swishes the cane. "Your successive misdemeanors," he quivers, "deserve my finest cane." Swiew! He paces the ceiling. "Hands on chair. Face wall!"

Hands gripping the chair and facing the mildewed wall, the boy can no longer see Glinty from under his arm. Swiew, swiew! He turns slightly.

"No looking!" Warm, vicelike fingers steer the boy's head back to the wall. Cobwebs stretch to the woodpecker case. The Lesser Spotted Woodpecker stares right at him. What's a whacking, its expression implies, compared with what they did to me?

The boy switches on his Head Cinema.

Swiew!

He's—flying. That's it. Flying into a different sort of pain.

Swiew!

Flying over the garden. The sun is shining. It's a painfully sunny day.

Swiew!

The mother and father are drinking pain on the terrace.

Swiew!

The boy is kicking pain against the garden wall.

Swiew!

It's time for Sunday Lunch. Time to be carved up.

Swiew!

Step into my saucer—words from *Salad Days*, a musical the parents have an LP of.

Swiew!

And have a cup of tea.

Pain. As if his bottom has been sliced off.

The Head Cinema jams. The Lesser Spotted Woodpecker stares back at the boy, discolored yellow. There's a ringing in his ears. The room is yellow.

Straightenupboyputonyourgownandgoandgetdressedblowyournoseontheway.

The boy straightens up, reaches for his dressing gown. Glinty is yellow. The boy's body is buzzing. The stinging shoots down his legs and up into his back. His hands are numb from gripping the chair.

Ihopeandpraythatlwonthavetodothistoyouagainitisnopleasanttasknowwhatdoyousay?

The boy's hearing is returning. Glinty speaks normally now.

"What do you say? It won't happen again?"

The boy stares up at the yellow Headmaster in his yellow study.

"Play the game, boy! Slot into place or you will never get on in this world!" Glinty's forehead shines. His gums lurk like shadows in a cave of stalagmites and stalactites between which steams his fruity breath. "Off you go. Lesson learnt."

The door opens. The boy walks through it, stinging, aching, unblinking, his body a trembling volcano. His teeth hurt from clenching. The door shuts. In his Head Cinema, the Lesser Spotted Woodpecker, as if listening intently, stares at Glinty scratching a letter on his cream-tinted paper. The boy wonders why during the beating he thought of *Salad Days*. The album sleeve shows cartoon people singing round a piano. The songs make no sense to him but there's a lot of conversation because it's a stage play, and somewhere a man says, Step into my saucer, and have a cup of tea. The boy wishes he were at home and not at this old dump. He hates Glinty. He hates the masters, the officers, the school, and if he's ever an Old Boy he'll tell the truth about it. He wishes he had a flying saucer and could spin off to another galaxy. Commander to crew: There'll be no next time, Comrades. Liberty or Death!

Step into my saucer, and have a cup of tea.

5 OMAHA

From our hotel window Paris spreads before us. The golden dome of Les Invalides glitters in the sunset, and each night on the hour Tour Eiffel sparkles. At present there's also the Grande Roue de Paris in the Tuileries. This Ferris wheel disappears when the Paris-Plages close but reappears for the Christmas fair. If it's hot during these last days of summer I retreat to the tranquil garden of Musée Delacroix just off Rue de Furstemberg in Saint-Germain des Prés. In milder sunny weather I cycle Rivoli to the Marais, home of two eccentric venues that remind me of childhood, the Musée de la Magie with its spooky toys, and the taxidermy-packed Musée de la Chasse et de la Nature. From there I walk down Rue du Prévot and cross the Quai des Célestins to sit at La Terrasse, opposite where the Seine curves round the eastern lip of Île Saint-Louis. As ever, the future's uncertain, Marais casualty Jim Morrison reminds us from Père-Lachaise, and the end is always near.

Meanwhile my mind brims with images not just of boarding school but of a time when my dreams of escape to foreign lands became possible. Aged seventeen, I started a Foundation Course at Reigate School of Art, but I was a hopeless student, a student without hope. Teachers despaired of me. Drunk in class, I was finally kicked out. One said I'd regret it the next day, to which I replied, Tomorrow, sir, I'll be sober, but you'll still be old. Since in youth we consider aging to be a matter of carelessness, this felt like a clever riposte.

I hadn't a clue what would become of me, only that in creating I'd travel, in traveling I'd create. You imagine a place just as you imagine an artwork, I reasoned, then you make it real. I spent my childhood on mental journeys but now I'd add physical ones. A stranger in strange lands, I'd create strange landscapes besides. Music would aid me in this, not least that of Bruce Springsteen. I didn't see him in concert until the 1981 *River* tour but *Darkness on the Edge of Town*, especially the song "Badlands," boosted my restless urgency. At eighteen, a year after release from incarceration, I took to the road in search of an adult self. My early travels focused on the United States, so dominant in my childhood imagination, but I hadn't envisaged, when I set off, that my first adventure would bring me to as unlikely a place as Omaha. Ah, the great wheel of time! The trip began and ended in the sky, from a transatlantic flight to a Ferris wheel in Waterloo, Nebraska, at the Douglas County Fair.

Capitol Airways from Gatwick to Gander was the first of five flights to reach Muskegon, on the eastern shore of Lake Michigan, and from there Camp Jakalak. After refueling in Newfoundland and a stop in New York, I spent my first American night at the Chicago YMCA, waking to my alarm-radio playing "Born to Run." The Sears Tower loomed in mist beyond South Wabash Avenue. Ladies with hats as bright as the two-seater planes in Newfoundland stepped off a Union Baptist Church bus. From Chicago Midway Airport, I flew Northwestern Airlines to Muskegon via Milwaukee, the plane's shadow rippling across the lake. Camp Director Don Dimmerstamm sauntered into the foyer in a green Jakalak cap.

"So, hey," he said, handing me a Whatchamacallit, "how d'you like the U. S. of A?"

Dimmerstamm bumped his white Buick round a sandy bend to the sound of Bob Seger's "Against the Wind." A Budweiser sign pulsed in a bar window opposite a park with a softball diamond. The lake shone, vast as a sea. I followed his directions to my cabin in the deepest backwoods. Dust specks floated among sunbeams. Used to surviving in strange environments, like that quintessential castaway Robinson Crusoe, I dreamt an inventory. *First, health and fresh water. Second, shelter from the heat of the sun. Third, security from ravenous creatures, whether men or beasts. Fourth, a view to the sea, that if God sent any ship in sight....*

But Dimmerstamm rescued me and we joined other counselors for yams and grits before trooping to the Council Circle for orientation. Time passed smooth as the lake. I began by teaching tennis each morning with a counselor named Dougie Tout, whose jacket sported the Jakalak motto: "My own self at my very best all the time." Afternoons, I taught soccer, burdened by the help of Darius Weilschnecker of Tallahassee. Darius was a terrific sprinter but his sun-baked muscles prevented him turning corners. We devised a system. I ran up and down one side, Darius the other. The campers drifted to other sports. I taught tennis full-time. Darius took on long-distance canoeing.

Three weeks before camp ended, a squall of Summer Love blew in from Nebraska in the shape of Hungarian American Carlotta Cak. The rest of the world went on standby. We floated onto the porch, down over a fence, and deep into the woods. Through the cold night, with me shivering in a white T-shirt and red jacket—my homage to James Dean—we gazed at the stars through a gap in the trees. My youth was finally happening. All that mattered about day was that it led to night. All that mattered about night was that I spent it with Carlotta. We'd find a crater of sand in a clearing near the abandoned Pioneer Unit or stumble up a giant dune called Shifting Mountain, down through Shifting Mountain Draw to the lake. A strawberry moon rose to a bright disk, doubled in the water, and completed a circle with its reflection. The Aurora Borealis weaved across the sky. But every night collapsed too soon. The sky lightened and we slipped back to camp, footsteps quiet as snakes in sand. As the nights passed so did our final weeks at Jakalak. The present was about to become memory.

"We're like painted spheres in the Universe," said Carlotta against the rumble of the bus waiting to carry her away to Omaha. "We bump for a moment and bounce off toward distant constellations, but leave a paint mark on each other."

The counselors and campers dispersed. Darius Weilschnecker took the straight route south to Tallahassee. Only Dimmerstamm and I remained beneath the Jakalak sign, the sand dappled with a summer's footprints. Jakalak lay ready to return to its ghosts. Dimmerstamm dropped me in Muskegon before heading home to Denver. Feeling as if I were plunging off the edge of the world, I climbed aboard my first Greyhound Americruiser. The bulky driver eased into his seat. The door hissed shut.

"Let us advance," he announced over the intercom, "upon the Chaos and the Dark."

Deep at night in the deep Midwest I jolted awake. To my bleary vision, the sign seemed to read DESMOINESIA. I closed my eyes and drifted through lands beyond the rainbow. Desmoinesia! But just as I folded myself back into sleep, a large-limbed man in a brown fedora and suit worn to a shine sat in the aisle seat.

"Welcome to Des Moines, Iowa," he said. "Mr. Lundt." Through the tinted window a green moon tracked the ripened corn. Mr. Lundt coughed, a throat-scraper. "I'm long retired after thirty years in insurance. Let me tell you about my life."

Dozing to the sound of his voice, I thought of us rumbling through the prairies and how the highway would look from a plane. For the first time in my life, I seemed to exist in open rather than enclosed space. Mr. Lundt's commentary accompanied my dreams.

"We Cornhuskers don't waste time sleeping," he was saying. "We keep at it. I cycled the RAGBRAI before my hips crumbled. Five hundred miles between the Missouri and the Mississippi. No hills in the Corn Belt? Say it from a bicycle saddle! What's your age, son?"

I yawned, pulling my red jacket tight over my T-shirt. "Eighteen."

"All that lovely time ahead!"

"I don't know where I'm going."

"Like all of us, you're trying to get home. What do you want?"

"The unattainable place of inexpressible happiness."

I'd heard this phrase on a film late one night, *Les Indiens sont encore loin*, starring Isabelle Huppert and Christine Pascal.

He laughed, teeth like corn at sunrise. "Enjoy youth. I'm seventy-seven."

"What's it like being old?"

"You'll be there tomorrow."

The bus pulled into Omaha in sudden rain. Mr. Lundt shook my hand and said he was glad I'd found the heartland and not just "gone coastal."

Watching the rain, I ate breakfast in the depot Burger King. By the time Carlotta walked in, chewing Hubba Bubba, the sun gleamed on the downtown office blocks. Omaha was a Cubist cityscape of chiaroscuro angles. Cars were fleeting shadows. The sun caught Carlotta's brown legs and auburn hair.

"Today's a workday, waitressing at a diner." She pulled into a driveway on South 131 Avenue and opened the car door. "Can you handle my parents?"

She introduced her mother. "Mrs. Cak to you, Mom to me." Eyes narrowing needle-thin, Mrs. Cak pinched my hand. Carlotta nodded to her weary-eyed father. "Mr. Cak, or Pa." She went to change for work. Mrs. Cak bustled to the kitchen.

"So," yawned Mr. Cak, "you rode the Dog. You shoulda gone Big Red."

"Frank's a Trailways driver," explained Mrs. Cak. "He works the night shift, drives miles through the night. You like it, eh, Frank? But you sure get tired."

Mr. Cak yawned again. "It ain't what you'd call a vocation."

"See ya later!" called Carlotta.

"Take the money, honey," said Mrs. Cak.

We sat in the shade on the deck. The thermometer read 105 degrees. Mrs. Cak fed us spinach and bacon sandwiches and apple pie. Carlotta returned at sunset, just as her father was leaving. Mrs. Cak sat with us in the TV room. June bugs battered the screen door.

"Carlotta," Mrs. Cak said. "I'm worried about your father's soul."

"Me, too, Mom."

"And about yours."

'My soul's intact, Mom."

Mrs. Cak rose. "Your soul needs its sleep, Carlotta."

"My soul will be right up, Mom."

Carlotta gestured to go out on the decking. Soon we were on the grass beneath. Crickets clickety-clacked. Lightning bugs dotted the bushes like fallen stars.

"Tomorrow's our last night."

"We'll go to the fair," said Carlotta.

So on my last evening we drove to Waterloo for the Douglas County Fair.

"You must be looking forward to home," said Carlotta. "Your parents, your friends? I'm a homebod. This little acorn'd never fall far."

Dusk transformed the fair into a stage set. The streaky sunset gave way to stall lights. Dung odor mingled with whiffs of sugarcane. Two farmhands shut a barn door and strolled over the cable-strewn grass to watch Jerry Reed twang "Tupelo Mississippi Fish."

I picked up a leaflet. Billed in the *Omaha World-Herald* as Waterloo's entertainment package bargain of the year, the fair included livestock judging, Championship Slo-pitch Softball, the Nebraska Bantam Show, a Hog Carcass Contest, a Tractor Operator Contest, and something called Furniture Interview Judging.

"The advertised acts are Gene Watson, from Palestine, Texas; Dave and Sugar, Jerry Reed, and Dottie West, whoever they are."

"Oh, my God!" Carlotta pointed to a woman in a Stetson and spangled shirt, "Dottie West!" She ran up to her. "This guy's never heard of you."

"I ain't heard of him neither." Dottie smiled at me. "You live here, darlin'?" I said I was leaving tomorrow. "Listen later. I've a song for you."

We gorged on hot dogs, caramel apples, sodas, threw darts for pink rabbits, shot at plastic ducks, jumped onto the blue-and-red bird cage from hell. The bar clanged shut. The machine jerked forward, circling, spinning. The lights blurred. The ride ended. We tottered across the damp grass past the deserted coconut shy. Boards had gone up on the target shooting. September's shadow was creeping near. Carlotta gazed at me with her Slavic eyes.

"You're always deep in your thoughts," she said. "You go to another world."

"I'm where I want to be for the rest of my life."

"Will you come back? People never do. I'll get crowded out."

"You'll marry a farmer or grain exporter and forget all about me."

Dottie West was singing "Country Sunshine" to a thinning crowd. "This final song, 'If You Go Away', is for two lovebirds," she said. "The guy's leaving one of our country girls. Ask me he's a damned fool." There was a desultory cheer.

"One more ride!" whispered Carlotta. "The Ferris wheel!"

Risky, I thought, knowing how a girl broke the Everly Brothers' hearts on one, but I ran after Carlotta, Dottie's voice fading behind us. We'd be old tomorrow, Mr. Lundt had warned me, so were rushing to live. The only riders, we flew up into the midwestern night.

"Try to roll it," said Carlotta, rocking our cage back and forth. The panorama of the closing fair bobbed like lights from shore. Wedged as if inseparable, we rose and fell, stomachs a second behind. Then, at the very top, eyes mirroring the fair, Carlotta vomited everything she'd consumed that evening into my lap.

On lurched the ride. Time, once fleeting, now seemed eternal. Indulging the perennial summertime ride of young lovers, the operator felt no rush to remove us. Carlotta buried her face in my armpit. I sat stoically upright. When the wheel finally creaked to a halt she jumped out and ran behind the closed shooting gallery. I found her murmuring, "Mary, forgive me."

We scrubbed grass on the stains on my shirt and jeans. I scraped vomit from her chin.

"The sad thing," she sighed, "is I'll be the girl who puked on the Ferris wheel."

"You'll be the girl Dottie West dedicated a song to."

The next morning, Mrs. Cak's eyes widened at news of my departure. Mr. Cak yawned, "Take Big Red next time." I boarded the bus for New York with Carlotta's gift of a self-help book, *If You Don't Know Where You're Going, You'll Probably End up Somewhere Else.* At least I was going somewhere, I reflected, even if for now it felt like backward.

Raised in a Tennessee farming community, Dottie West got her break in 1963 when Jim Reeves recorded her song "Is This Me?" Hearing her sing for us that last summer of the seventies, I'd no idea how successful she'd been, nor could I have known she'd descend into alcohol-fueled, divorce-littered near-ruin. In 1991 she was a passenger in a car crash on the way to the Grand Ole Opry, dying later of her injuries. But here in Paris, whenever the radio plays Jacques Brel's "Ne Me Quitte Pas," of which "If You Go Away" is an adaptation, I recall the gentle sorrow in her voice. Whatever we have we lose—youth, love, life—whether down on the ground or way up high, on the Ferris wheel, wherever that wheel may be.

6 NECESSITY

The boy's Head Cinema continues to roll out its features even while he sleeps. Once again he dreams of the boat with a candle for a funnel. He's concerned it will blow out or that the boat will catch fire. How will you steer? he asks. By waving, says the mother. Soon the parents are far away. He watches them wave until all he can see is a faint flicker on the horizon. Oh well, he thinks, they'll need the light to guide them home.

The boy awakens in darkness. It's three weeks into term. He can't recall what the parents look or sound like. He needs a wee. They used to have potties under their beds but a few nights ago they filled one, tied it to a window blind, and let go. The "cascade," as they called it, was the end of potties. Boys must now brave the haunted corridor past the tiger head and skin and dead men's portraits to reach the lavatory. The boy tried it once and stumbled into the African gongs, waking the nearby dormitories and duty master. He got detention.

Now, like most others, he wets his bed. Each morning he finds it cold and damp. The Get Up Bell sets off a frenzied bustle. In comes Matron McRipp. The dormitory must strip covers back so she can check for wetness. The boys try to hide their shame with a pillow or teddy or by not pulling the cover back far enough, but Matron McRipp always knows. One morning, Aitkin fails to pull back his covers.

"Prepare and *pull!*" orders Matron McRipp.

"I haven't weed," murmurs Aitkin.

After an undignified struggle, back come the covers. Asplodge the white sheet lies a turd. Aitkin's face glows red as a teacher's pen. The other boys hold their noses at the sudden stink. Wet your bed, you have to remake it with clean sheets. Matron McRipp inspects it for proper hospital corners, a special way of tucking in the sheets and blankets. Bad bedwetters, says Matron McRipp, become brilliant bedmakers, and indeed most of the boys are experts at hospital corners. But to turdify your bed is humiliation indeed.

The boy never wets his bed consciously. Sometimes he dreams he's walked to the lavatory, raised the lid, and relieved himself. But tonight he's wide awake, can't ignore his need, but daren't chance the corridor. Everyone else seems asleep. Bunting faces him with his false eye open, but he always sleeps like that. Other boys are champion snorers so there's a night chorus. Tonight, though, the snoring competes with wind and rain clattering the windows like laughter. The boy knows he should run down the corridor past the portraits but the dead will hurl abuse at him for having a weak bladder.

He makes out the bedside chairs, stacked with strictly ordered uniform: garters on top of socks and underpants, vest, flannel shirt, corduroy shorts, polished lace-ups beneath the chairs. He squints at the cake-icing ceiling and imagines the terrace in blackness, pelted by the rain beyond the blinds. The cacophony of rain and snores increases, as if the sleepers are reacting to the noise of nature. His bed's still dry but he'll never get back to sleep. Safe against the noise, he tiptoes through the shadows to the end of the dormitory and starts to wee. Despite the snoring and the rain, it sounds as loud as a waterfall. He tries kneeling so the flow is nearer the parquet floor but wets his pajamas. Instead, he wees beneath each bed in turn, edging farther on when the occupant stirs, and quickly when one boy sits up and says, "What's for lunch, Granny?" Eventually, he tiptoes to the aisle between the beds and wees along the floorboards, then gropes his way back to bed and falls sleep.

No sooner has he done so, it seems, than the Get Up Bell clangs and Matron McRipp snaps on the lights. "Rally and rise, Troopers!" she shouts. "Goodness! Who's been sick?"

It's a rain-dark morning and the lights make outside look darker. Rain batters the windows in rolling bursts. He feels beneath his covers. For once, his bed is warm and dry. But the dormitory is in uproar and he, too, marvels at the mysterious phenomenon. Beneath all the beds up to the far end of the dormitory are roundish white patches, and down the aisle a pattern of white lines mottling the parquet floor.

Determined to find the culprit, Matron McRipp commands each boy to say if they've been sick. Finally, she's in front of him. "And you," she says. "Have *you* been sick?"

"No, Matron McRipp," says the boy, "I have not been sick."

Telling the truth sometimes avoids saying what really happened.

7 BREAKAGE

Spring arrives. Sitting on the rusty swing at the end of the lawn, the boy wears swimming goggles. He's a Spitfire pilot about to fly. The family has been to London to see *The Battle of Britain* (or *The B ttle of Br ain,* since some letters were missing from the cinema sign). He spends hours swinging back into shadow then up into sunlight as if to touch the clouds. He swoops as high as he can then plunges down and back and up again. He twists and turns to avoid flak. Hit by gunfire, he leaps from the swing at the top of its arc, tumbling to earth from the height it would feel like to hit the ground parachuting. He wears his bruises with pride.

Up he swings, and back into the shadows. Up again into the clouds, the lawn and house and trees swirling in obedience to his movement. Back then up then back then up, preparing to jump, Messerschmitt on his tail. Bam! Bam! He can't return fire. His Spitfire is aflame. He can only loosen his arms and—jump! He hurls himself into the air and lands with an expert roll. Still smoldering, he hears the call, Scramble, scramble! He grabs the twisting swing and is on again, pushing off, feet scraping the dirt beneath it. Not high yet, he seeks momentum, pushing with his feet, pulling with his arms. Soon he's airborne. House martins swirl in the sky as if part of the dogfight. Higher and higher then—jump! Crash, roll, grab the swing, push back and off again, higher with each arc, a pendulum between the bushes behind him and the sky above. Higher he swings, so high he wonders if maybe he'll loop the loop, but with his body almost horizontal he's alarmed at the energy he's created, then back and so high he faces the ground, and forward again in a sweeping arc and this time he jumps on the sweep upward. But his shorts catch. There's a ripping noise. He's not airborne but tangled, somersaulting, falling. A sickening crack.

Through his goggles his left forearm looks bent at wrong angles. He seems to have two mini elbows. He grabs his goggles with his right hand and flings

43

them off. His forearm is still mangled. He hears himself screaming. After a while he runs out of screams and gets up using his right arm and walks toward the house cradling his left arm and sits on the stairs. Slowly the arm begins to ache and swell.

"You can tell it's bad because he's not crying," says the mother.

"Also," says the father, "it looks wrong. We'd better find a hospital."

The boy wakes to find his arm up to his shoulder in what the doctor calls "plaster of Paris." The plaster is on for several weeks then replaced with one up to his elbow until July. It gets him out of cricket but he also misses Sports Day. Not that he ever wins anything. The stars this year are Helter and Kadenge. Helter is blond and Kadenge is the only Black boy in the school. He's rumored to be an African prince. Glinty calls him "the Black Pearl." He outruns everyone, but after winning the hundred-yard sprint is disqualified in the four-hundred for going too fast, leaving Helter to win, and become Victor Ludorum.

The excitement momentarily takes the boy's mind off the itching in hot weather. It's a relief when they finally cut off the plaster, even though his arm is weak and thin. On his first day home he has to go to the dentist but his thin arm doesn't lead the vicious Mr. Dixon to pity him. Trapped like the colorful creatures in the waiting room fish tank, he's summoned to the Torture Chair. Mr. Dixon is dying of heart disease, says the mother, so he's pretty cross.

"Lie back!" shouts Mr. Dixon. "Open wide!" The boy opens his mouth in an O, like the fish, or like the mother doing lipstick. "Your milk teeth should be out by now!" shouts Mr. Dixon. "I'll have to take an X-ray!"

It's not my fault, thinks the boy.

Mr. Dixon takes the X-ray and, at the next appointment, forces the boy to admit that he hasn't dissolved his milk teeth roots in the proper way.

"Can't be helped, then, can it!" shouts Mr. Dixon. "I'll have to *rip them out!*" He grabs a gas mask from his Torture Cupboard. "Nothing but jam sandwiches for you for a while! Ha! Breathe into this!" He clamps the mask over the boy's face. "Count to ten!" The boy tries to breathe. His lungs fill with rubbery fumes. "You're not trying! Breathe *in!*"

The boy becomes lightheaded. He dreams he's crawling through the holes of a cartoon Swiss cheese to escape cartoon mice. Come on! they squeak.

Nearly there! He jumps out of the cheese and flaps his arms. He's high above a field, swimming through the air toward a forest with the mice snatching at him from behind.

"Wake up!" He's back in Mr. Dixon's Torture Chair. "Spit out the blood!"

He leans forward, spits blood, and rinses his mouth with lukewarm purple water that gets sucked down an aluminum funnel.

"Why doesn't your blood clot? Eh?"

"Soyyee," says the boy. His mouth feels wrong. His tongue slides over metallic tasting holes where his upper and lower teeth once were. "Whe yar ma tee?"

"If you won't dissolve your roots we yank the teeth out!"

Recovery is slow. Driven to fury by the boy's refusal to dissolve his milk teeth roots or fall asleep by the count of ten, Mr. Dixon has taken out four front teeth top and bottom: eight in total. All the boy can do is wait for new ones to grow. He spends sunny summer days playing tennis against the garden wall. On rainy days he stays in his room and reads John Wyndham. *Chocky* aside, the best are *The Chrysalids* about children with an extra finger, and *The Day of the Triffids*, where a meteorite shower blinds everyone except a few people who aren't looking. That summer he also reads Bill Naughton's *The Goalkeeper's Revenge and Other Stories*, with a story called "Spit Nolan," about a go-kart champion who crashes and dies. His last words are, Did I win? The narrator says he did, so Spit dies happier than he would have had he known he lost.

But the most important thing he learns is that names mean a lot and that you have to be brave. Spit Nolan is cool because of his name. Bill Naughton is a good name for an author. You trust a man named Bill with a no-nonsense surname to be an expert on sport and go-karts. The boy may not have any front teeth, and his arm may be weak, but they're just bits of body. His mind's his own and can't be taken out or broken, or won't be, not if he can help it.

8 VANCOUVER

It's late August and we're in the Rue Chauveau apartment. In recent years Neuilly has been best known for Sarközy de Nagy-Bocsa, a local lawyer who became president. Other celebrities include Antoine-Augustin Parmentier, who introduced the potato to French cuisine, Duc d'Orléans Ferdinand Philippe, Alexandrine Zola, Marcel Duchamp, Ernest Hemingway, and Neuilly-born Jean-Paul Belmondo, who despite chain-smoking through Jean-Luc Godard's 1960 film *Breathless*, is still alive. Ferdinand Philippe died here in an accident in 1842, and has a Louvre portrait, a Porte Maillot chapel, and an equestrian statue, brought back from Algeria after independence. Alexandrine recovered here after Zola's death from carbon monoxide poisoning in Clichy. Duchamp had a Neuilly studio. Hemingway was treated at the American Hospital after pulling a skylight on his head. Reawakening the trauma of being injured on the Italian front, the accident inspired *A Farewell to Arms.*

The Paris heat remains. C'est une canicule, remarks a neighbor, a heat wave. Our balcony overlooks dry-leafed trees. The apartment block opposite resembles a dolls' house. A man and woman watch TV in matching dressing gowns. A father smokes on his balcony while indoors his wife feeds their toddler. An aging woman sunbathes naked. None of them know what's happening in an adjacent apartment except for the naked lady's cat, who risks the abyss to step between worlds.

I occasionally run a circuit round Île de la Grande Jatte. The views across to Courbevoie, Asnières, Levallois, and the business district of La Défense would have been more tranquil in the days of Impressionism, though Seurat's *Bathers at Asnières* does have factory chimneys much like those still on the horizon. But it remains pleasant to jog past the boats, cross to the island, and watch the canoeists sweep along the Seine.

Other days I catch the 174 bus for métro Line 1 from Les Sablons to the Louvre, or 274 to Porte Maillot for the RER C train to the Orsay. But buses charm me most since, as a boy at school or in the countryside, I almost never rode them. Other regular routes include 43 to Gare du Nord for the Eurostar to London, Montmartre's 40 up Rue Lepic, and 82 to the Latin Quarter. I take the 40 to dine at Dalida's favorite table in the Moulin de la Galette, perhaps after visiting the cemetery that holds not only the tomb of this tragic Egyptian-French singer but also that of Stendhal. With the 82, which I take to frequent a favorite restaurant, Au Père Louis, I may alight at one of Paris's obscurest museums. Above the Préfecture de Police on Rue de la Montagne Saint-Geneviève a display of murder weapons includes the blade of a Revolution-era guillotine. Either way, bus rides involve contemplating passing scenes, whether around a city, or a country, as with my early North American travels by Greyhound, Trailways, or regional carriers like Bonanza in New England. However extensive or limited, they're one of my postchildhood continuities.

In the new freedom of my teens and twenties, my footlooseness was twinged with unease about my future. By studying at night school, I finally entered university aged twenty. Imposter that I felt myself to be, I read twice the recommended number of books per assignment but still felt rudderless. Travel alone provided a sense of direction. Such had been my manic restlessness in previous summers that I only had four conterminous states left to visit: North Dakota, Nevada, Oklahoma, and Arkansas. Wearing a rollneck like Steve McQueen in *Bullitt*, I withdrew my savings and entered a travel agency.

"Any standbys to the States today?"

"Tampa," said the counter girl. "Check-in closes in two hours. The flight's at four."

I caught a train to Gatwick. The last passenger to board the plane, I slunk into my seat next to an oceanographer, one Marco de Voto from La Tour-de-Peilz off to Gainesville to study with Professor Frank Maturo Jr. Over Greenland I pondered my aim. Darius was in Tallahassee, Carlotta in Nebraska. I'd plan a route around that.

"It's hard being an oceanographer in Switzerland," said Marco. "And you?"

"In pursuit of the unattainable place of inexpressible happiness."

It was a bad time to visit Darius. He and his ex-hippie eldest brother, Todd, had deadlines, Todd's being for his thesis on the songs of Willie Nelson and Jimmy Buffett. Their rented house was a wreck. The roof sagged beneath a live oak draped with Spanish moss. The warped deck rose to complete the grimace. A basketball hoop jutted netless from the outside wall above a rusted refrigerator wedged like an iceberg in the weeds.

While they studied, I read *On the Road*. Darius joined me one afternoon and cracked open a Busch. "Still questing?" He rolled his eyes. "I have another hour's study. Then we'll hit the beach. No sunscreen if you want a tan like mine!"

"Damned limey!" he said later, as I nursed sunburn with a cold beer. "Y'all ought to visit our brother, Ben. He's taking the Sea to Sky Highway to the mountains, hiking on Vancouver Island, and wherever else."

At dawn in the depot, I had my pass stamped for Chicago, climbed aboard, and daydreamed as the red earth and clapboard houses of the Deep South slid by. Across the aisle two girls giggled at my sunburn. One was a brunette with brown eyes and a maroon dress, the other a blonde with blue eyes and a sky-blue dress. They got off in Huntsville, still giggling.

I slept through Birmingham, Chattanooga, and Indianapolis and woke with Chicago a distant haze of vertical brush strokes. We trammeled over a bridge's ribs, two beats a second, a magnified heartbeat. A coffee-colored Cadillac with a green-and-white Illinois license plate flashed by in the evening sun. We plunged through tunnels into the Arrival bays. I phoned Carlotta's house. Pa Cak told me she was at UNO in Lincoln, so the next dawn I was sitting on a baggage trolley outside the Lincoln depot. Carlotta arrived with a wary, bow-legged cowboy who wasn't her boyfriend, she confided, but wanted to be.

"My soul is safe," she said later. "But what about you?"

"Still soulless."

"I mean where are you going?"

"Vancouver, to find myself."

"In Vancouver? Well, I hope you do."

Two days later I bussed west then up into the Dakotas. North from Sioux Falls, I took Bus 162 of Jack Rabbit Lines ("Make Tracks with the Rabbit"), changing to a Canadian Greyhound through Winnipeg, Moose Jaw, and Medicine Hat. All kinds of people boarded: a bearded, pig-tailed man with a creased face; a Native American in a Montreal T-shirt carrying a plastic bag printed with "Everyday Low Prices"; two ladies who proceeded to smoke cigarettes in holders in the "rear of the coach," all of us in the hands (as the sign above his name slot read) of our "safe, reliable, and courteous" driver.

We passed a lake in the midst of flat land broken only by copses and slowed at a railroad track. The driver hissed the door open to listen for trains. Clouds stirred eerily through the green windows. A well-dressed young man handed me a note: Have you ever thought of becoming a Mormon?

From Calgary the bus sped north to Edmonton and Vancouver via Kamloops and the snowcapped mountains, fir forests, and foamy streams of Banff National Park. Time went back another hour. My eyes stung from tiredness. Maybe I should go to Alaska, I thought. But I had to come back, somehow, via Nevada, Oklahoma, and Arkansas.

"Well, y'all did come to Raincouver!" said Ben at the Vancouver depot. "They got some damned fine mountains though." He had similar tanned features to Darius but was a little shorter and thicker set. Along with his Labrador, Mr. Dog, he was here for the wedding of two friends, former classmate Dr. Calvin Krycjek and the love of Ben's life, Marlene.

"I'm here to see a friend marry my woman," he said on the (rainy) ascent to Western Parkway next to the UBC campus, chewing tobacco and spitting into a coffee flask. "Their vows will riddle my chest."

Krycjek lived in a large corner house. Willowy, with curly hair and a droopy mustache, he had a banjo, a waterbed, and Marlene, a Nicaraguan nurse with lustrous hip-length hair. Marlene made me wish I too were a doctor living on Western Parkway with a fiancée, a waterbed, and a banjo. Poor Ben. Once, in college, she told him she'd gladly marry him. But at the time Ben himself was engaged.

"What happened to your fiancée?"

"You'll meet her."

At the garden ceremony, blessed unexpectedly with sunshine, Krycjek and Marlene took their vows under a rose-covered arch. Beneath a tree, a blonde guitarist in a wheelchair sang "Kumbaya."

"My one-time fiancée," gestured Ben. "Christine Svenson."

After the service, I followed him over. Christine had wonderful green eyes.

She was paraplegic. It happened after she and Ben split. She dived from a cliff into a shallow creek.

"I hit my neck and managed to get out of the water," she told me, "but that was it. Once on the bank my body seized up. I sit in the shade because of sweat gland problems."

"We're off hiking, Christine," said Ben. "I've got school in two weeks and my friend has to get back to England."

She held my gaze. "What do you do in England?" I couldn't think what to say. She smiled. I looked down. Her hands were curled. She was thin but with a pot belly. I glanced up again. She'd been watching me look at her. "I can no longer fingerpick," she said, "only strum simple chords."

"She was as good as Joni Mitchell," said Ben.

Unsure what to say next, we contemplated the guests mingling in the sunshine.

The next morning Ben and I drove north on the Sea to Sky Highway. "What I need," he said eventually, "is clean mountain air."

We hiked up near Whistler, caught the ferry to Vancouver Island, then drove down to Oregon to hike Mount Jefferson. We saw no one, just wildlife and stunning scenery, the plains of heaven painted by John Martin. Plus the weather held. I felt heartsick about Christine. I couldn't imagine what lay ahead for her. Christine, Carlotta, and others: My God, I thought. Why not marry them all and live on a Montana ranch and father numerous children like an Old Testament patriarch? I didn't compile answers to this but lay on the grass between rocks and flowers and, trying to imagine my future, began to worry about money.

Ben was driving to Florida. "Want a ride?"

"I need to go via Nevada, Oklahoma, and Arkansas, my last mainland states."

"Hell," he said, "let's do it."

I gave him my roll of bills beyond what I needed for flight money. We left Lakeview after dusk and reached Reno before dawn. The five hundred miles to Las Vegas took us past the treeless shores of Walker Lake, through the Excelsior Mountains, and along rock-strewn hills. From Sarcobatus Flat, past signs for Chloride City via a town named Amargosa Desert, we crossed back into California. Near Twenty Mule Team Canyon we escaped the burning sun into a saloon. The paunchy proprietor told us it got its name from the mule teams that hauled borax up miles of unpaved road in the 1880s.

"Chloride City—nice place for a night out?" I asked.

"It's a ghost town." He wiped his brow. "So yes, if you like ghosts."

We drained our beers and drove off through the rocky scrubland of Death Valley. Eventually, Las Vegas shimmered on the horizon. The highway became a flat black snake winding into a city roasting in the 120-degree heat.

Vegas was a sparkling oasis of hedonism; a mirage dedicated to decadence, a town begrimed with fake jewels. A dollar bill floated along the carpeted sidewalk.

"Supper," said Ben, snatching it.

"I'd prefer food."

We exchanged it for quarters in a casino. Gambling machines stood in rows across red carpets. The tinkling fanfares of one-armed bandits punctured the piped music ("The Green, Green Grass of Home"). We fed in our quarters. Out came ten dollars.

"We've won in Vegas," said Ben. "Let's eat."

After sleeping overnight in the pickup, we drove to Flagstaff and stopped at the Grand Canyon before continuing past Albuquerque and Amarillo. Much of the time Ben chewed tobacco to keep alert, streaming juice into his flask. We hit Oklahoma City in time to catch the last rays on the Statue of Liberty outside the County Courthouse. By 2:00 a.m. we were in Arkansas, stopping around 3:00 at a Fort Smith diner. Gritty-eyed, I bought a postcard featuring a razorback hog and the word "ARKANSAS," inscribed it with reference to this being my forty-eighth state, and mailed it home. Something had ended. I was twenty-two with conflicting visions. Did I want a family, job, and pets, or to be a lonesome vagabond, trekking China, hiking Australia, barely subsisting in a bitter world? I was no longer the adolescent who arrived in Michigan, let alone the eight-year-old left at boarding school. But I hadn't yet become whoever I'd be.

From Fort Smith we took Interstate 40 to Little Rock, then 167 into Louisiana, picking up 49 to turn east on 10 for Baton Rouge.

"You've seen more of the country than most Americans," said Ben.

"There's always somewhere else." We pushed through the Louisiana heat. "From somewhere near Salinas," I said, "we're now busted flat in Baton Rouge."

Detouring to New Orleans, we drank a Dixie in the French Quarter and watched a steamer paddle by in the delta mist, then headed northeast through Mobile.

"Stuck inside of Mobile." I sipped a Coors. "With the Memphis blues again."

"Kristofferson! Dylan! You sure like your American writers. Finished Kerouac?"

"He ends by evoking the vast land rolling in one gigantic bulge to the west coast, and the fact that no one knows what will happen to anyone except the misery of getting old."

"We don't even know that," said Ben.

Marty Robbins came on the radio singing "By the Time I Get to Phoenix."

"All country songs seem to be about loss."

Ben spat tobacco into his flask. "Life is about loss. Haven't you noticed?"

Just as we reached Florida, Dottie West sang "Country Sunshine."

"I once met Dottie West."

"Sure you did."

"What kept you?" said Darius when we finally reached Tallahassee.

"Damned limey needed to touch Nevada, Oklahoma, and Arkansas. I taxied him."

"Where do you fly from?"

"Tampa."

"Tampa to Tampa via Vancouver," said Darius, "a whirlwind tour."

Sometimes, it's not about where you're going but that you're going somewhere. Sometimes, anywhere will do.

9 GARÇON

"Silly foolish naughty bloody boy!"

One February Sunday morning snow transforms the school's humdrum setting. Transfixed, the boy doesn't at first hear Madame Bouffant. Locust-sized flakes swirl against the white sky and blob onto the classroom windows. Snowlight brightens the World War II "Careless Talk Costs Lives" posters on the walls. The boys sit at rows of ink-stained, lift-lid desks in their itchy-stingy suits. Sunday breakfast is a boiled egg, a flour-dusted roll with wrapped butter, and a daub of marmalade. The flour mixes with the butter and marmalade on their sleeves and stains the writing pads their parents gave them for Christmas.

This brightness contrasts with the boy's darkening fortunes. He's more accustomed to the bonds of boarding school than to his uniform. Caning being reserved for heinous crimes like instigating a blitzkrieg, the boy hasn't had a repeat but still feels the ridges. Since October he's been whacked with a jokari bat (Mr. Croulebarbe), slipper (a half-hearted effort by Major Nott), and wire hairbrush (Captain Bullet). The Colonel has rapped the boy's knuckles with a ruler. Mr. Flat has pulled his hair and twisted his ear. Mr. Pavilion has done what he does to many boys, clenched a fist with the second knuckle of the middle finger jutting out like a mini pyramid, and punched the boy between the muscles of his upper arm. Whether for serious crimes like breaking a window or just for swapping marbles in class, he's been hit more than enough for one childhood. Many of the bruises worsen over the days after a beating. Some turn yellow round the sides and violet in the middle.

He's fed up with parading. You parade before and after breakfast. You parade before and after lunch. You parade before Low Tea, High Tea, and chapel. Sometimes the masters make you parade because there seems nothing better to do with a hundred and fifty boys on a wet afternoon Activity Time. They even make you parade in and out of the shower, where Mr. Youngstown in particular makes some boys stand until they shiver.

"Garçon Deux! You silly foolish naughty bloody boy!"
　The boy's Head Cinema jams. He's back in the snowbright classroom.
　"Garçon Deux! Réponds-moi!"
　Before the blackboard sways Madame Bouffant, a galleon harbored against a raging sea. She calls him Garçon Deux because of where he sits. Sometimes she uses a boy's surname but never his. He sees Madame Bouffant as clearly as he sees all the other teachers from those days. Childhood memory is like a flashbulb. The images burn into you forever, like those little ridges. He can even summon up Madame Bouffant's smell. Floating in a gas that seems to merge flowery perfume with sulfur dioxide, she stands before him, snowlight dancing on her purple dress. A Daddy Longlegs fusses like a handmaiden around her ornate hairdo.
　The school has two kinds of teachers. Those who are there forever, and those who sweep in at the start of a year and are swept out at the end, either because they're insane (incompetence is not a problem) or criminal in a way the school can't hide. In other words, they "interfere" with boys. The oldest is Mr. Peatle, known as Peanut because he resembles one. Peanut is never outside the netted garden of gooseberry and black currant bushes. He taught boys between the wars and has been allowed to stay in his garden until he dies, and maybe beyond. The Colonel, Major, and Captain are others of this kind. The second kind includes Mr. Youngstown, who likes to play-fight with specific boys and doesn't last the year. Glinty stands beneath the school shield and print of the man looking out over a vista, and announces that Mr. Youngstown, having stolen the Athletics cup and posted it to his mother in Yorkshire, has been asked to leave. Tell a lie so outrageous they might believe it, the boy overhears the Colonel say, but of the boys only Dollaton does.
　A new, temporary master, Mr. Rawmin, takes over History when Mr. Croulebarbe is arrested midlesson while explaining the violent death of King William Rufus. Mr. Rawmin's beard resembles a mass of burned bracken. You guess at his expression from the shape of his eyebrows above twinkling eyes. Blond, blue-eyed Hinton quickly becomes his favorite. He leaves the dormi-

tory at night to go to Mr. Rawmin's room at the end of the landing. The boys accept that Hinton has special status. When he leaves the school suddenly, Mr. Rawmin shaves off his beard and becomes a strange man with lips, teeth and a jawline. But shortly Mr. Rawmin, too, disappears.

Madame Bouffant is another who departs abruptly—except that she's just mad. She's hired to teach French not because she's a French teacher, or even a teacher, but because her dead husband was French. She uses French words in the hope that soon the class will speak the language. But she's too ugly and smelly for them to concentrate. Her powdered face is a mask. In adulthood the boy can still see not just her billowing purple dresses but that mask, part powdery, part damp. Another thing that tells the boy she's mad is the fact that she turns up to every lesson with a slice of chocolate cake. She carries this on a china plate and nibbles it piece by tiny piece. Crumbs fall from her podgy fingers when she lurches from desk to board and back, or lunges at un vilain garçon.

"Pay attention, mon enfant," she scolds the boy this snowy Sunday. "What have I just said, vilain garçon?" A seasoned ceiling observer, the boy gazes upward. This one is wooden and painted white. The snowlight shows how dirty it is. "You won't find the answer on the ceiling, Garçon Deux."

"Pay attention, my elephant."

The class titters. Madame Bouffant sneaks a morsel of cake into her mouth and draws near, dress billowing. The boy's nostrils pinch at the chemical smell. The hairs on Madame Bouffant's chins stick through a crusty patch of make-up.

"Before that, you vilain garçon," she says cakily. "And mon enfant is my child."

"I'm not your child, sir."

"Of course not, Garçon Deux!" Madame Bouffant claps her hands in a spray of crumbs and chalk. "It's a term of endearment, though heaven alone knows why I used such a term with you. But I meant before even that!"

"Repondy-me, sir."

Madame Bouffant lists toward the boy on a gust of perfume dense as cannon smoke. In pirate mode, he slips his moorings and shelters beyond his desk. Madame Bouffant's eyes widen, black as gun ports. Before she fires he feints left, gripping the desk for balance. Dress swirling, Madame Bouffant moves to head him off. He feints right. She blocks again. Just when he seems cornered, she returns to Blackboard Harbor to keep her powder dry. Having secured another victory for the English, the boy returns to his seat.

"Garçon Deux didn't pay attention. Alors, pour le benefit de le vilain Garçon Deux, I'd like someone to explain what we're about to do. Oui, Dunn-Larkin."

Up springs Dunn-Larkin with his Spock eyebrows and fringe. "Letter writing, followed by singing 'Frère Jacques,' Madame."

"Très bien, Dunn-Larkin. And thank you for the courtesy of calling me Madame. Remember that for future reference, Garçon Deux, silly foolish naughty bloody boy. From now on, Class, every Dimanche after chapel you'll write letters home, and aujourd'hui you'll also sing pour moi. The school requires choir fodder. When you were garçons nouveaux we wrote letters home for you. But from now on you'll not only have a letter sent home every Lundi matins, but you'll spend Dimanche matins writing it! Comprenez-vous?"

The class looks blankly at Madame Bouffant then lowers its eyes to write. Bunting's eye is loose so he plucks it out and refits it. Dollaton writes *Dear Mrs. Dollaton* in big round letters with his tongue out and his frayed suit sleeves up round his forearms, even though his shirt cuffs still cover his wrists. There's another sucking sound followed by a pop.

"For heaven's sake, mauvais garçon, if you keep plucking your eye I'll confiscate it!"

The snow swirls to earth. The boy yawns. He wishes they could have a snowball fight. He observes his writing paper. It's orange with matching envelopes. *Dear Mother and Father,* he writes. The rest he only imagines: *nothing happened this week except we wet our beds and Dollaton's garters fell apart. Bunting's false eye is loose. Incidents of whacking were up this month after a January slump.*

The boys have worn their nettle suits since dawn. The flour on their rolls is like the snow outside. The boy misses toast from breakfasts at home. He no longer misses the parents. But once every three weeks, sick with excitement, he looks forward to them waiting outside chapel with other parents for an exeat. The service drags ever slower as the second hand of his Ingersoll wristwatch trudges uphill to eleven. He spits envy whenever a boy faints and gets carried out. He spends chapel-time daring the altar cross to rise into the air. It never does.

The boys file out beneath Dalí's *Christ of Saint John of the Cross* to where the parents beam their latest tan. It hardly matters that the end of each exeat leaves the boy questioning whether it was worthwhile. Come the next one, he still yearns to be home.

"Garçon Deux!"

Back in the classroom, snowflakes stick to the windows. The boy squeezes ink into his fountain pen, spills a drop in the margin, and sifts it to look like a monster. He writes a sentence and raises his eyes. At her desk, Madame Bouffant tugs a mirror from her purple handbag, which is made of carpet and large enough to contain her husband's urn. She dabs her bumpy nose with a powder puff but the bumps soon shed the powder. She pulls out a purple comb and taps her hairdo. Perhaps some of the smell comes from her having raided Glinty's Science laboratory. In his Head Cinema, he lights a Bunsen burner next to Madame Bouffant's hair. She explodes in a mass of poster-paint purple splashes.

Madame Bouffant's eyes shoot up as if she's heard the explosion. "Has anyone begun their letter yet?" She looks at the boy, gnashing her jaws to make the most of her latest cake morsel. He nods. "You have, Garçon Deux? Then kindly read it, s'il te plaît."

"Dear Mother and Father," the boy pretends to read. "I don't like it here. Please take me away. Thank you in advance. Yours sincerely, Garçon Deux."

"That won't do at all!" shudders Madame Bouffant. "That's not a letter. That's a moan! You, Garçon Deux, are a moaning minnie."

The boy pictures the mother's maroon Mini, which doesn't start in the rain. Instead of an engine noise, it moans a bit then gives up.

"I've done one, M-Madame." Being long-backed as well as long-limbed, Dollaton is the only boy who can gaze straight at Madame Bouffant while sitting.

"Well?" snaps Madame Bouffant. "Read it. Maintenant!"

"Dear M-Mrs. Dollaton," reads Dollaton, stuttering as he always does with teachers. "Mr. Dollaton has passed away, M-Madame. He—"

The class murmurs. Dead? Cor! Dollaton has never let on that his father's dead.

"Get on with it. The class doesn't need to know your personal business! Lots of people are dead, not least my stupid husband, falling off a bridge on purpose! I ask you!"

"Dear M-Mrs. Dollaton—"

"No, you clot!" interrupts Madame Bouffant with caky impatience. "Dear *Mother*. Suppose she wrote you a letter starting Dear Dollaton, eh?"

"I'm Dollaton Four, Miss. I have three b-brothers in the school."

"Then it would be even worse, wouldn't it!"

"She would have to write Dear Dollaton Four," says the boy.

"Ferme ta bouche, tu garçon bruyant!"

Dollaton reads on, correcting as he goes. "Dear Mater—er, Mother—" The class guffaws. "I'm s-sorry not to be with you on Captain—on Father's birthday. I hope." Dollaton stops and gazes mournfully at the falling snow. "That's all, M-Madame. I don't know what to write next. I'm worried it might upset her."

Madame Bouffant inhales, her purple dress stretching so tightly that the boy expects her to burst like an overblown balloon. At the last moment she spews the air out again, filling the classroom with a chocolaty smell. "What *might* you say, Dollaton? Eh?"

Dollaton takes a minute to speak, between great, gulping pauses. The class quietens. The snowfall thickens, as if the flakes are responsible for the silence.

"We don't have all day!"

"I miss my . . . Daddy." Dollaton bursts into wrenching sobs, like long donkey eeyors.

Later, during lunch, Dollaton tells the boy that Captain Dollaton was crushed in a jeep crash in the army, when Dollaton One and Two were eight, Dollaton Three was seven, and Dollaton Four was five. The jeep, in which he was a passenger, veered round a bend and straight under a truck. The other occupants of the jeep survived but because Captain Dollaton was tall with a long back his head fell off. The family weren't allowed to view the body. But for now the class has to sit through the lesson wondering what happened, as well as, forever after, how Monsieur Bouffant came to fall off a bridge on purpose.

Madame Bouffant doesn't seem to wonder about any of this at all. "I can see we need a little guidance," she says, heaving herself out of her chair. She chalks "Dear" on the board. "Are you watching, Dollaton? Alors, un: *Dear Mother and Father*, or *Dear Mother*, if your father's gone or, like Dollaton's, peacefully passed away, or *Dear Father*, if your mother is, for whatever reason, no longer here. If you're an orphan, or your parents have moved without leaving a forwarding address, you may wish to write *Dear Aunt and Uncle*, or some variation thereof, such as *Dear Guardian* or *Dear Benefactor*. Or if you're writing in French, *Cher*."

Dunn-Larkin puts his hand up. "What if you haven't got anybody, Madame?"

"Everyone has someone, Dunn-Larkin, even you. Fees don't fall from trees. If you don't know who to thank, write *Dear Benefactor*."

"How do you spell that, Madame?"

Madame Bouffant billows round to the blackboard again, dress swirling to reveal ankles almost too spindly to hold her, and writes "Benefacter."

"That doesn't look right, sir," says the boy.

"Alors." She taps on the board rising perilously on her spindly ankles. "Deux: *I have had a lovely week*. Trois: *We have a) played sport, b) enjoyed the film called _____, c) learned about _____ in our _____ lessons, d) other.*"

"Madame?" says Aitkin, shifting his wide body in the desk-seat, his face reminding the boy of a television. "Do we write it exactly as on the board?"

"Non," snaps Madame Bouffant. "Fill in the gaps. Remember this is your personal letter." She sails round to peer at Aitkin's letter. "Start again, Aitkin," she says, "and this time just choose one, and don't write a, b and c." She billows back to the board. "Quatre: *Thank you for sending me _____*. Here, Aitkin, you fill in what you are thanking them for sending you. Cinq: *I do hope _____ is/are well*. Six: *Love from your dutiful son, _____*. And here you fill in your name. Oui?"

For ten minutes the boys scribble as silently as the falling flakes. The chapel roof whitens. The steps and driveway are barely recognizable beneath the piling snow. All the boy can hear is Madame Bouffant squeezing between the rows of desks scattering laboratory smells, an occasional cough from a boy as she passes, or a sigh of "Non, non, non" or "Follow the format!" and Dollaton breathing through his mouth.

"Dollaton!" she says. "Breathe through your nose! Aitkin, follow the format. Your parents only want to know what you've enjoyed."

Pop!

"Bunting, *will* you stop plucking your eye out? Last chance!"

Aitkin's moist eyes peer up at her out of his television-shaped face. "But I haven't enjoyed anything."

"Nonsense! You are in danger of being a silly foolish naughty bloody boy, like Garçon Deux. Follow the examples on the board, n'est-ce pas?"

Eventually the boy takes his letter to the front desk, where Madame Bouffant is now at anchor. Her white scrawls on the blackboard resemble waves.

"Read it," she says. The boy begins reading it to himself. "Aloud!"

"Dear Mother and Father, I hope you have had a lovely week. We enjoyed a film called *The Great Escape*. We learned the word 'Omnia' in Latin. Thank you for sending me here. I hope you are well, and that our sister is too. Love from your second son."

"Better," says Madame Bouffant. "But there's no need to write *second son*. They'll know that. You can use your first name in letters to your parents. Now put your letters in my tray for me to read, garçons. It's time for you all to sing, while I listen to each of you in turn, and help ensure you all fit together. The song we're going to sing is—?"

"'Frère Jacques,'" says the boy.

Madame Bouffant stops, one pudgy hand in midair, as if hit broadside with a cannonball. "Mon Dieu," she says, "so you were paying attention, Garçon Deux!"

"We sing it every week."

Madame Bouffant shakes her hairdo. "Tu est une énigme, Garçon Deux."

Before anyone in the class can ask what that means she launches them into "Frère Jacques" and drifts past the rows of desks, a flagship inspecting the fleet.

Frère Jacques, Frère Jacques, the boys sing, Dormez-vous? Dormez-vous?

Madame Bouffant pauses to listen along the rows as they repeat the song. Sometimes she closes her eyes and smiles. Other times she stiffens and volleys advice into a boy's ear.

"Sonnez les matines," sings the boy as she pulls alongside. "DING DANG DONG!"

"Enough!" announces Madame Bouffant. "Très bien, garçons! We'll do it one more time, but I'd like the following—Garçons Deux, Trois, et Neuf—to please *mime*."

The boy raises a hand. "What does ayneegm mean, Madame?"

"Une énigme? You're not easily understood, Garçon Deux. You have yet to settle."

The boy keeps his hand up. "What does mime mean?"

"Ah oui." Madame Bouffant claps a cannonade of chalk dust. "It means I'd like you, along with the others I mentioned—but especially you, silly foolish naughty bloody boy, because you've got the most awful voice—to look as if you're singing, to pronounce the words, raise your faces joyfully toward me and so on, but not actually to make any sound whatsoever. Ready and, the rest of you, *sing!*"

10 BUDGERIGAR

Coloring aside, all budgerigars look the same. You can't individualize them or change their habits. But the boy isn't about to say so. Clumsy, red-cheeked Luerty has enough to deal with. He thinks his green-and-yellow budgerigar, Joey, understands him. Morning, Joey, Luerty says. Did you sleep well? In the evening, he says, How was your day, Joey? As far as the boy is concerned, Joey's days must be a doddle compared with a schoolboy's.

One icy morning, before Science, the boy slides across the playground as if skating. Luerty, in clodhopper lace-ups, tries to do the same but stumbles into the pet shed, home to Joey and two rabbits, Aitkin's black one, Buster, and Sibley's brown one, Nutty.

"That'll wake them!" says the boy. "Do budgies dream?"

"Every budgie's different," explains Luerty.

"Different? They just open their eyes in the morning, hop between perches, nibble seed, make noises, then go to sleep."

"Joey sleeps with his head under his left wing. When he wakes himself by snoring, he puts his head under his right wing."

"Good grief."

Luerty looks sorrowful. If he has a sense of humor, it doesn't extend to the subject of budgerigars. He unlatches the shed door. It's dark inside with one small window, and smells of rabbit droppings and straw. "Joey," he whispers. "Did you sleep well?"

"Blimey, Luerty," says the boy. "It's freezing in here!"

Buster and Nutty scurry around in a cage.

"Joey," Luerty whistles again. "Say, Hello, Master Luerty!"

"*Hello, Master Luerty!*" the boy parrots behind him.

"Joey?"

Joey is perched upright, his green and yellow feathers silvery in the light from the little window. "I thought you said he slept with his head under a wing?"

"He's usually awake for breakfast," whispers Luerty. "Had a late night, I expect."

So black as to be barely visible, Buster chases Nutty around the cage like her shadow.

"Why not wake him?"

"He might be angry. Joey can put me in Coventry for days. He won't look at me."

"We've got Science in ten minutes."

"Okay. Wakey, wakey, Joey. Wake up for Daddy."

"Let me try." The boy prods Joey through the bars with a pencil.

"Don't hurt him!" whimpers Luerty. "Joey?" The boy knocks Joey with a pencil. He sounds wooden. Luerty breathes out. "He's moving!"

Slowly, alarmingly, beak set firm, the budgerigar topples backward and clunks onto the cage floor.

"Perhaps he's got sleeping sickness."

"He's just cold," pleads Luerty. "Joey?"

He opens the cage and prods Joey. Joey slides around the cage floor, bumping over his own droppings. For a moment half a Milky Way that Luerty left him yesterday blocks his progress but, as Luerty pushes, bird and chocolate bar slide round together, gathering droppings, seeds and crumbs.

"Perhaps we can thaw him," suggests the boy.

A squeal ricochets from the rabbit cage. Buster has jumped on Nutty.

"Come on, Joey," sniffs Luerty. "I'll look after you!"

Luerty pulls Joey from the cage and rests him on his palm. Joey looks hand-carved. The boy opens the door of the Science laboratory. Luerty stumbles in, half-blinded by tears. Other boys are milling around the tanks of snails, locusts, xenopus toads, and incubating eggs, while Glinty, in a white coat, lights Bunsen burners.

"Hold him up to the wall heater," advises the boy. "But not too close. He'll singe."

Luerty raises the frozen budgerigar in cupped hands toward the glowing bars. Tears stain his chubby face. "Joey? Come on, Joey!"

"Wake up, Joey!" encourages the boy.

"Joey? *Joey! JOEY!!*"

To other boys' amusement, Luerty suddenly howls.

"Cry baby!" laughs a spongy-haired new boy, Umber-Gristle, shoulders bobbing, teeth undulating like piano keys. "*How* old are you?"

Some boys laugh along with Umber-Gristle. He's the son of new, second headmaster, Mr. Umber-Gristle, whom the boys call Pug because he signs everything P.U-G. Also, Pug's scrunched face on huge head and shoulders suits such a name. It's not clear why the school needs two headmasters, or three if you include the Latin master, Splinter, known officially as Old Headmaster Splint-Croakham the Younger.

Glinty's voice silences all but Luerty. "Gather yourself, boy! What are you doing?"

Luerty howls on, still standing, arms up, tears falling, pleading with Joey to awaken.

"Luerty is thawing his budgie, sir."

"*Joey! Joey!*"

"The budgie's called Joey, sir."

Joey remains unmoved by the drama, or the warmth, but his feathers begin to steam.

"Is he crying?" asks Sibley.

"That's the ice melting," the boy explains.

"Give me that thing! Corpses are contraband and subject to confiscation!"

Luerty lowers his arms. "At—at least," he sobs, "you're warm now, Joey."

"Dead birds don't feel," Glinty corrects. "All in all, a veritable science lesson!" He snatches Joey and drops him in the swingbin. "Into your groups, everyone! Turn to Nuffield page one hundred!"

Luerty sniffs through the lesson. The boy does the experiments for him, letting him copy the write-up. At break time the boy pulls Joey from the bin. Luerty is standing in the pet shed by the cage, empty now except for droppings and the half a Milky Way.

"Let's do an experiment."

"What do you mean?" Luerty wipes his eyes with a sleeve.

"Let's stuff him—it's called taxidermy! He'll be like the birds in Glinty's study. We could even stick him in there. He'd be the only one with a personal name."

"Okay," says Luerty. "So long as you know what you're doing."

In the classroom after lunch, the boy comes to realize taxidermy is an acquired art. He's got straw from the rabbit cage, but his penknife is no scalpel. Thawed innards prove sloppier than expected. The lab stapler isn't designed for straw-filled budgerigars. Used chewing gum doesn't help. His original plan was to have him in flying mode like the house martin and swallow in Glinty's study, but now Joey, wrapped in place with elastic bands and Sellotape, is a sorry sight. This is disappointing but technically the boy has fulfilled his promise. Joey has been stuffed. The problem is that he won't stand up, even when propped.

"New idea," says the boy. "Let's say he's been embalmed, Egyptian-style. Instead of displaying him we can bury him. You're supposed to take the brain out through the nostril but that may be difficult with a budgie. No one will know, anyway. Later we'll build a pyramid." They find a cardboard box. "This," says the boy, "is Joey's sarcophagus."

He does some Egyptian-looking drawings on the sides and top including sideways-on budgerigars, and Luerty writes Joey's life story and a personal message of worship and memory and places it in the box. With Luerty carrying the burden, the boys climb the steps behind the chapel where there's a pet graveyard. They dig a hole in the slope one side of the steps beneath a rhododendron and make a cross of twigs by splitting the thicker one enough to push the thinner one through.

"I don't think he was Christian," mumbles Luerty.

"Nor were the Egyptians. The cross is so passersby know it's concerncrated ground."

"What's that?"

"It's where people should show concern."

A pretty, freckled woman comes down the slope in a crisp white outfit, her hair in a long, fruitgum-red ponytail swinging in stride. She must be a matron, except most matrons are old and lumpy like Matron McRipp.

"What are you boys doing?" she says in a foreign voice. "Can I help?"

"Burying Luerty's budgerigar, Joey."

"I'm Matron Radeva. It's my first day. And what's your name? Freckles?"

"You have more than I do!"

Luerty looks at her as if she's a goddess who'll resurrect Joey.

"Where are you from, Matron Radeva?" asks the boy.

"Bulgaria."

This means nothing to the boy but he notes the similarity with budgerigar.

Matron Radeva kneels by the boys on the earthy bank. "I'm so sorry." Her eyes glisten. "I hate to see animals in distress."

"He's not," says the boy. "He's dead."

"He's at peace," she smiles. "How did he die?"

"Froze solid."

Luerty stifles a sob. "He's Joey," he sniffs. "He's my budgie."

"But he wasn't in pain," says Matron Radeva. "If you get too cold you just go to sleep and never wake up."

Luerty breathes in, a sharp, double intake.

"We thawed him out," says the boy, "and now we're burying him."

"It's very kind of you to help your friend like this."

"Bad things happen to us all," says the boy, feeling like a man in a film. Thinking this would be a good line to end a scene, he repeats it. "Bad things happen to us all."

11 MOSCOW

Down a corridor of the Musée d'Orsay a sequence of rural paintings includes *Paysanne,* or *La Marguerite,* William Morris Hunt's portrait of a peasant girl holding a daisy. Elsewhere are society portraits of Madame de Loynes (later Comtesse de Loynes), Comtesse de Keller and actress Madeleine Brohan. Madame de Loynes shares her companions' social poise, but she was once herself a peasant girl. Born Anne-Marie Detourbay in Rheims, at fifteen she was discovered in a brothel by Alexandre Dumas Jr., calling herself Jeanne de Tourbey. She became a famous courtesan of the Second Empire and a salon-holder of the demimonde. After a visit, Flaubert wrote: "I took away from your dear person a kind of emanation which penetrates me, a fragrance of which I am embalmed, which makes me drunk and intoxicates me." Her mesmerizing gaze—"You again!" it implies—is hard to reconcile with the fact that this willful woman is now a decayed corpse in a dilapidated, if still identifiable, Montmartre tomb. Yet even amid that desolation, I often see a black cat eye me from the shade of a sapling that's grown through the cracked headstone. Along with the portrait, perhaps these are hints that her formidable spirit lives on.

As for Hunt's diffident peasant girl, we only glimpse her features. But her delicate touch and reddish hair remind me of Matron Radeva. Today, too, perhaps because I've also viewed Cuno Amiet's *Snowy Landscape,* where a tiny figure negotiates immense whiteness, she reminds me of Polina Odintsova, a guide who met a group of us in the foyer of Moscow's Hotel Cosmos, accompanied us on a snowy train ride to St. Petersburg, and bade farewell soon after a visit to Dostoevsky's house.

It was some years on from my freewheeling days. I'd received a BA in English and History and a boarding school story had won me a scholarship to Upstate New York for an MA. Back in England, teaching British Studies and player-coaching the soccer team at an American college in Lincolnshire, the chance arose to take students to Russia.

It was mid-December. The Aeroflot plane landed on what looked like sheet ice. Soldiers in heavy coats and bear hats escorted us into passport control. The Hotel Cosmos had black-painted décor. My room looked out over drab yellow trams trundling along Mira Prospekt. In the Park of Soviet Economic Achievement, Lowryesque figures crossed the snowy wastes between exhibition buildings and the soaring monument to the Conquerors of Space.

Polina had crinkly hair and ice-blue eyes that matched the Moscow streets. Her teeth, the color of the greenish oranges for sale on the street stalls, betrayed her poor diet. She had an otherwise lovely smile, and since this was the era of Perestroika, I like to think that, before Vladimir Putin screwed the lid back on an opening society, she managed to get them fixed. But she was pleasant to talk to, supremely intelligent, and eager to ensure that the dozen students and I saw as much as possible during our stay.

Highlights included a Bolshoi performance of *Giselle* and the Moscow State Circus, with incredible trapeze artists and vanishing acts of people walking in and out of doors to nowhere. This was too much for the man next to me—a doctor, a man of science and reason—who threw up his hands in frustrated disbelief. His temper flared again, now from compassion at the sight of bears riding three to a horse. It was obvious that, extraordinary though the spectacle was, they'd been whipped into obedience. In Red Square, soldiers goose-stepped on packed snow past Lenin's tomb as if stiffened by the winter air. In ГУМ—or GUM—the giant store off Red Square, the architecture outshone the paltry goods on display.

From Moscow's Leningrad Station, Polina and I shared a compartment of bunks on the Red Arrow to St. Petersburg. It was all very *Anna Karenina*. But any chance of sleeping while the train trundled through the snowy wastes was interrupted by a loud knock and a tough-looking lady insisting we drink her obligatory cups of tea.

"You'd like to see more of the world?" I asked clumsily, warming my hands round the mug. "With President Gorbachev's decision to open things up, might you be able to?"

She was on her bunk, concentrating on her tea. "I can't talk about this."

"Is it not safe?"

Head down, she smiled, like the first hint of sleety dawn, and shook her head. "We don't know." Then she gave me a sudden, direct look. "You're free to travel?"

I nodded. "Nowadays, yes."

With a streak of yellow across the horizon, we pulled into St. Petersburg.

Soldiers stood at points along the street. A legless man propelled himself forward on a cart, gloved fists pushing at the snowy pavement. The statues in the park had been covered for winter. The Neva along Nevsky Prospekt was white from a distance but up close you could see dark water between blocks of ice. The eggs in the street kiosks were as white as the snow. The lampposts stood caked on one side. Twilight lasted all day. Through condensation-soaked shop windows, low-wattage bulbs cast shadows on the near-empty shelves. The interior of a hair salon exuded warmth, its orange walls and seats providing a jollier atmosphere. Some of the buildings were white trimmed and painted in bright colors, including the Hermitage with its numerous roof statues.

On Monday Polina, the students, and I crunched to Dostoevsky's house on Kuznechny Lane. I know it was Monday because on the outside a sign said закрыто по понедельникам, zakryto po ponedel'nikam, or, as Polina explained, Closed on Mondays. She was hugely apologetic but it didn't matter. We viewed the paintings in the Hermitage—in particular those by Rembrandt, Cézanne, Picasso, as well as Russian artists—but also the Baroque extravaganza of the State Gala Staircase; the czars' carriages; the Fabergé eggs; the red rooms of Italian art; the Malachite Room, and the chandeliered Pavilion Hall with James Cox's astonishing, multifaceted mechanism, the Peacock Clock.

"On Wednesdays it comes to life," said Polina. "The peacock moves its neck and head, the cockerel crows, the owl blinks. But anyway, see there, the squirrels, the dragonfly which is the second hand. I love this."

The students had the next day free so she and I agreed to return to Dostoevsky's house. It contained lots of photos and objects, including a bowl and chain, perhaps the ones he had in prison in Siberia. Next to them were charcoal portraits of himself and of fellow inmates. Dostoevsky was quite the doodler.

Faces crowd the margins of his manuscripts. But what I most vividly recall was a cigarette box on his desk, turned on its side. On the underside it had some writing which Polina translated.

"Daddy died today, it says. It was written by one of his daughters."

Walking through a snowy park we passed a man selling handmade Russian dolls. I bought a *Crime and Punishment* one. The outer layer depicted Dostoevsky himself. The next doll in was Raskolnikov. Within Raskolnikov was the examining magistrate, Porfiry. Within Porfiry was Raskolnikov's friend, Razhumikin. Within Razhumikin was the doppelgänger murderer, Svidrigailov. Within Svidrigailov was the long-suffering Sonya Marmeladova, and within Sonya was a tiny, solid baby Jesus.

"We're all layers of selves like this," said Polina.

Maybe so, I thought. Proust writes of his love for Albertine that he "ought to give a different name to each of the selves" who thought about her and "each of the Albertines" who appeared before him. Yet perhaps a core self does exist in that nugget of childhood within our succession of selves. The rest of our lives those nuanced layers cover that core and shape us as we appear to others. In maturity we finally resemble, spiritually, the layered mummies lined up in the glass cases in the Louvre.

As for Polina, though we only scratched the surface in our conversation, I felt a bond that was perhaps the result of spending four days together and a night train through the snow. When it was time to fly home, I bought from a street vendor a red rose surrounded by daisies and headed for the hotel foyer where she waited in advance of the group gathering.

"I have something for you," I said, pulling them from my coat.

Her look of happiness turned to laughter.

Only then did I see that I'd managed to rip off the rose head. Its bare stalk stuck up through the daisies. Petals cascaded to the floor like red confetti.

"I will remember the gesture all the more," she said. "Also, I love winter daisies. There were lots of them on my grandparents' farm. Whenever I see zimniye romashki, which is our name for them, I will think of you."

"Perhaps one day you'll be free to visit the West."

"Perhaps," she replied doubtfully. "After all, a rose does bloom, though it also sheds its petals, and sometimes faster than you expect."

"What now for you?"

"My job is to guide foreigners, but it always starts and ends in Moscow, my home."

Thousands of miles and decades from that moment, I head back through the Orsay and, reaching Hunt's daisy-gazer, imagine Proust perusing her then turning to me. Languorous and lazy-lidded, he tells me of his fantasy of meeting "a peasant girl" on his pastoral wanderings.

"At certain moments," he says, "we believe with the profoundest faith in the originality, in the individual existence of the passing figure we desire, as if she's not just anyone but a necessary and natural product of this particular soil."

"Polina was special."

Proust raises an eyebrow. "I had a desire for a peasant girl from Méséglise or Roussainville, for a fisher-girl from Balbec, just as I had a desire for Balbec and Méséglise."

Maybe, as he suggested another time, I believed Polina had "a share in an unknown life" to which she could win me admission. What quixotic beings! But life is too interesting to pause for long. I take the escalator up to the Impressionists. Glancing through the first of the two immense clockfaces out across the Seine to Sacré-Coeur in the distance, I pass Manet's *Déjeuner sur l'herbe* with its little frog in the bottom left corner—representing la Grenouillère, the "frogpond" of promiscuous young Parisiennes—and head for Degas's ballerina paintings and the bronze copy of his *Petite danseuse*. The strangeness of the past is akin to the strangeness of the foreign, a fact distilled by L. P. Hartley's opening observation in *The Go-Between* that "the past is a foreign country." Maybe my attraction to Polina was merely to do with her existence in Russia, in a season as cold as the scenes in Monet's snowy landscapes or Caillebotte's blizzardy rooftop view, *Vue de Toits*. But still, as she said, a rose does bloom, and in such a cold, desolate place I'd felt enchantment in those words, even if the petals can indeed shed surprisingly fast.

12 STRIPE

With the arrival of Umber-Gristle's father the boys see less of Glinty. Pug is a bullish man. His huge head is combed over with strands of hair, his brow dented where he bashes it in exasperation. He quickly installs his son as captain of all teams in his age group, honorary captain of school sports, and mascot for senior teams. Aside from this lesson in nepotism, school goes on much as before. Contact with strangers from the outside world is confined to visits from tattooed barbers known as the Sergeant and the Corporal, and an old man known as the Swindler, who wears a cravat and misted spectacles, and sells the boys yo-yos and Ping-Pong bats from a rusted van. Beyond that, it's a self-contained, repetitive world. There's the compulsory small bottle of milk a day, topped in hot weather with a cheesy crust and in cold weather a layer of ice. There's summer cricket in heavy flannels, autumn soccer and spring rugby, both played without underwear in scratchy shorts and shirts. There are the long periods of working or eating in silence, and parades in the school hall, where the boys stand in lines according to their houses—Armada, Poitiers, Trafalgar, and the boy's house, Waterloo. Reading about Nigel Molesworth in Geoffrey Willans's *How to be Topp*, the boy grows used to all this, but rarely avoids punishment.

On summer mornings parades take place in the blossom-scented outdoor air. But usually they're in the high-ceilinged hall decorated with boards of house achievements. Doors on one side lead to classrooms separated by partitions and a corridor to the chapel they attend twice daily. Doors on the other side open to changing rooms and a yellow corridor off which is the masters' common room. At that end of the hall, between the yellow corridor and the chapel corridor, is a stage with windows at the back either side of a clock. Along all other sides of the room wooden seats form the lids of so-called lockers, although they don't lock. Each locker belongs to a boy for the year. They contain personal items, such as those bought from the Swindler, but the threat of a "threshing" generally ensures a theft-free zone.

The boys sit on their lockers until the duty master nods to the School Captain and Commander. These two thirteen-year-olds stand in an alcove halfway down the hall beneath the board of previous Captains and Commanders. At the duty master's nod the Commander marches out to the middle of the hall.

"Fall in!" What at first seems like a mass of unconnected bodies forms into four lines facing the same wall, sorted in terms of height. "School's company, company, 'shun!" shouts the Commander. "Company, right dress!" You put out your left arm to create the correct distance from each other. "Company, at ease!" You put your hands behind your back and part your feet. The duty master strides out then nods again. "Company, left turn!"

Each line turns from the wall to the Commander. The smallest boy is at the front, tallest at the back. Unless it's a Sunday, when they wear suits, the boys wear corduroy shorts and, in summer, a lighter, short-sleeved shirt, no tie, and sandals without socks.

Each line now facing him, the Commander shouts. "Waterloo Squad, quick march!"

The boys march in house order to the end of the hall, down the steps past school photos dating back decades, along the Glass Passage and a windowless corridor to the dining hall. This parading ritual is usually routine. But then comes the moment when, as in most areas of school life, the boy's discipline falters and he enters survival mode.

It's mid-December. Each week a different house is at the front of the ranks, and the following week at the back, with the next house moving forward. This week Waterloo lines up at the front, facing the Colonel as duty master, standing by the lockers and the Games Board. The boy is next to Whippy. Thin, wavy-haired, with a face like a fox, Whippy never has an exeat. His parents live in Bologna. But the boy is not paying attention to Whippy. He's learned the word "scrutinize" and is scrutinizing the Colonel. Yesterday he scrutinized the Major. It's a study in contrasts. The pallid Major is an insipid watercolor, as if all shades were a transparent wash across paper. The full-blooded, crack-veined Colonel is a gloporous oil painting. The Major's jowls quiver either side of a head that sits on his bulky body as if shrunk by cannibals. Provoked to fury, the Colonel's head swells volcanic red whereas the Major's goes white as apple blossom and shakes as if about to topple. He shoves his hands in his corduroy pockets to jingle keys and coins like an in-built alarm system.

The Colonel's pink face, as all the boys know, is the result of an explosion when he parachuted into Arnhem. The Major can't eat baked beans because, storming Juno Beach after breakfast, his best friend got shot and spilled guts and beans not only across the Normandy sands but also into the Major's mouth as he howled in horror. Beans, to him, mean guts. Grandma Cologne's husband was at D-Day, too, commanding a landing craft onto Sword Beach. Shock made his hair fall out. It grew back like baby hair and was still brown when he died aged seventy. The boys also know that the Major won't punish them but the Colonel will. I am not to be trifled with, the Colonel says. The boy pictures him stirred into a gigantic raspberry and chocolate trifle—only his pink face showing, like a tinned cherry.

"Company, left dress!" shouts the Commander.

Whippy's arm shoots out, punching the boy on an earlier bruise from Mr. Pavilion hitting him with his middle finger. Knowing he must retaliate, he executes a sidekick, where, unseen from the front, you kick your leg up and back from the knee to connect with your neighbor's backside. Whippy punches him again. The Colonel's sports-jacketed back is turned. The boy kicks Whippy's shin. Whippy melts wailing to the floorboards.

The Colonel turns, hands behind him, shoulders taut. "For pity's sake, get up!"

"He kicked me, sir," cries Whippy, rolling in fake pain.

The Colonel pulls Whippy to his feet. Blinking tearless eyes, Whippy points at the boy. The Colonel fixes his bayonet stare.

"Step forward!" The boy steps forward, heart pounding, hands clammy. "Silence!" the Colonel orders the murmuring ranks. "Onto the lockers!" The boy steps up onto the lockers. A hundred and fifty boys look at him. "Face the wall!"

The boy can smell the bricks. Next to him is Pug's Notice Board, pinned with rules and team sheets, mostly with Umber-Gristle central. A condemned prisoner with nothing to lose, he's outraged, defiant, ready to defend himself. Whispers ripple from the ranks behind. His heart thuds. He stamps his foot, vibrating the lockers, shuddering his breath. He wants to lash out. Crack the locker lids. Pummel the Colonel. Crunch Whippy's slender face holding up that cornetto hair. Burn down this dump. His Head Cinema reels off footage at double speed—the Colonel, Whippy, masters, twisting from the rafters, the school looking up aghast at the lengths to which this boy has gone to avenge himself. He stares murderously at the pitted bricks and imagines the notice board to his right composed of news headlines.

Whippy Cheats Innocent Boy—*Mirror.*

Boy Defies Colonel in Unfair Court-Martial Drama—*Times.*

Mass Hanging at Thornditch—*Mail.*

The boy half catches a muffled exchange between the School Captain and the Colonel. The Colonel clears his throat like cracking glass. The boy concentrates on the pitted brick in front of him, fists clenched, alone in the world.

The Colonel's warm breath brushes his ear. "You'll be sorry for this."

"No, I won't."

"I beg your pardon?"

Heart hammering, lips salty at the edges, he tries not to shiver.

"All right, Commander," says the Colonel. "Carry on!"

The boy's tummy coils into his throat. Blood laps his brain. He won't be sorry. He didn't start it. He'll never buckle. He'll fight injustice forever. Legs shaking, he kicks the wall, punches Pug's sacred Notice Board, crumpling a photograph of the Colts soccer team, as captained by Umber-Gristle.

"Wait, Commander." The Colonel's breath ignites the boy's neck. "You have bullied a fellow infantryman," he growls, "shown insolence on parade, damaged school property. You deserve a Court-Martial. One more word and I'll issue a Stripe."

The boy almost stops breathing. A Stripe—the blue piece of paper that confirms a caning—will be another victory for the enemy. He'll defend himself to the death. But he finds himself muttering *stupid arseholes.* The Colonel hasn't marched away. The school's murmur intensifies, reminding him of the sound of the metal slab in *2001: A Space Odyssey.*

"Right," says the Colonel, "a Stripe it is!"

"*He—*hit—*me!*"

"Silence!"

"It's not fair!"

The ranks murmur.

"I demand obedience!"

"It's not bloody *fair!*"

Well, he thinks, that's the end of that. I'm dead. He wonders if such a swear word has ever been uttered in the school before.

The murmuring dies. Someone laughs uneasily. Birdsong enters through the open window at the end of the hall. Decades seem to pass, as if the school has long since become derelict. He has the strange impression that those watching him defy the Colonel are ghosts forever caught in that past moment, and the hall itself merely an echoing emptiness. The day itself has long vanished. The Colonel and boys have dissolved like clouds.

But really there's no hope. The Colonel has marched off to write the Stripe. The boy itches in his shirt and sweater. The Colonel returns. The boy tenses for a slap, punch, or worse. The Colonel's voice is again in his ear.

"I hereby issue a Stripe," he says. The boy is aware of a blue piece of paper held toward him. "You are to take it to the Headmaster."

The boy scrutinizes the brick in front of him. It's not simply brick color, but actually has within it the colors of a mature bruise.

"You're making an exhibition of yourself. Take the Stripe."

The boy stuffs the paper into his pocket. "Thanks!" he shouts. "Thanks a fucking lot!"

Deathly silence. Not even a murmur now. In the corner of the boy's vision, the Colonel's lower lip moves without sound beneath his trim mustache. The upper and lower sets of regimented teeth battle one another in khaki uniformity. The senior teeth at the top crunch down. The lower ones punch up.

"Commander," he says, "fetch the Headmaster."

"Which one, sir?"

"Headmaster Umber-Gristle."

There seems to be a lightning flash but it must only be in the boy's head. As if from an electric shock, he becomes strangely detached, fascinated by the predicament of a body he merely inhabits, as if he were only observing this willful, foolhardy being. He's gone too far, and has no idea what will happen, but he does think he might be shot. He feels less frightened than sorry, without knowing what for—surely not for the Colonel? It's too late, anyway. He imagines the ranks gawping. All he sees are the colors in the bricks, like a burned and shattered rainbow. He breathes in their smell. He has no future other than this wall.

He hears Pug's voice. "Get down!"

The boy obeys. Whippy grins. Wearing his black gown as if it were the black cloth worn by a judge pronouncing sentence, Pug clasps the boy's shoulder and marches him to the yellow corridor, closing the door behind him.

The boy has no recollection of saying anything but he must have. The Headmaster is shouting at him, grabbing him with both fists. The backs of the fists are wiry-haired. The fists are pinning the boy against the yellow wall, shaking him again and again so that his head aches. Pug's thin hairs, the ones he brushes across his large head, fall over one ear to reveal a startling baldness.

He swivels the boy round, grips his shoulders. His black-gowned arms flap like the raven wings of death. He shakes the boy until the boy thinks his head will tear off and splatter against the wall. He shakes him until the boy can only hear a buzzing sound. His nose feels about to bleed. He wonders if perhaps Pug will punch the life out of him and all will go black and the boy will be dead and gone. All he can see is a shiny face rocking in front of him, hair strands down one side of the skull.

As if from underwater, the boy hears it shouting, *Don't you ever—you hear me—ever—say that to me again.* The way Pug measures out his words gives the boy the weird impression he's in a musical and Pug will break into song to the tune of "Here We Go." *Don't you dare—don't you dare—don't you dare speak to me or any adult with those words again. Do you hear? Do you hear? DO—YOU—HEAR?*

The shock of being shaken, slapped, the shock of Pug's enormous shiny face, voice vibrating with anger, dented forehead, heavy lips and jowls, gigantic hands shaking the boy—brings a sudden amnesia the boy will never lose. What words has he used? What has he said? Who is he? If he can remember such things it might be useful. But all he can hear or think is *Don't you dare—don't you dare—do you hear? DO—YOU—HEAR?*

"Do you hear?" hisses Pug again, suddenly clearly, as if the boy has come back into himself out of a strange dream. The Headmaster is still shaking him, but more slowly: like a dance, balloony shoulders, piggy eyes, corners threaded with red, pinprick pupils, and the dent in the orangutanish forehead. The wisps of hair still hang down, revealing baldness, but he can't push them back up because his fists clasp the boy's sweater. "Do you hear me? Don't you dare speak to me in that manner. I am the headmaster. *I am the HEADMASTER!*"

"I've got a nosebleed."

The boy always knows when they're coming, that familiar feeling of blood sliding down inside his nostril, sometimes right, sometimes left. Instinctively he raises his chin. Pug lets go of the boy's sweater and the boy cups his hands to his nose.

They stare at each other, the Headmaster's eyes wild and blue beneath his huge dented forehead framed between two sets of blurred knuckles. The boy presses back against the wall, certain that had Pug a blunt instrument he'd crush the boy's disobedient brain.

But somehow, perhaps because of the nosebleed, everything calms down. Fate sealed, he awaits punishment. Beyond the door he hears the bark of an order, feet slamming to attention, and, if not the words themselves, the tone he knows so well.

"Waterloo squad, quick march!"

Thud-thud-thud-thud.

"Armada squad, quick march!"

"Poitiers squad, quick march!"

"Trafalgar squad, quick march!"

Thud-thud-thud-thud.

There's a gradual sliding to quiet. The hall must have emptied.

Pug's voice: "Go in there."

The boy feels light and weak. Pinching his nose, he finds himself in the masters' common room, where perhaps no boy has ever been before. Orange-painted walls, masters' horseboxes, the smell of tobacco, an umbrella hooked on a chair, a whisky bottle on a table, a gas fire. On the desks of each horsebox, exercise books and papers compete with mugs of pens and bottles of Quink. Each horsebox has a row of pegs, with gowns and outdoor wear.

Pug leads the boy to a cracked enamel sink and turns on the cold tap. Drops of blood spatter into the stream and sluice down the plughole. The boy pulls at the flesh of the end of his nose. The bleeding has almost stopped. He splashes his face and wipes his hands on his sweater. Looking into the water-spattered mirror he rubs blood from his upper lip. Behind him, Pug's startled eyes stare back.

"Sit down."

Torn leather chairs sag beside the gas fire. Cigar smoke casts a bluish pall across the walls giving the room a grandfatherly atmosphere, though he can't imagine any of the masters being grandfathers. His Head Cinema runs a brief, supporting documentary on open fires, low beams, the sparkle of sherry, the smell of peanuts and strong cheddar served before Sunday lunch at his grandparents' house. But the pipe smoke here clings to peeling ceilings.

Pug hands the boy a tea towel. "Sit down and put your head back on."

The boy wonders if his hearing has gone wrong.

When the bleeding has entirely stopped, Pug speaks again. "The Colonel tells me you kicked Whippy, and on receipt of a Stripe proceeded to stuff it in your pocket, all the while uttering uncouth language. So how do you redeem yourself? What is the right thing to do?"

"I didn't ask to be dumped here in the first place."

"Apologize to the Colonel," says Pug, "or we expel you from Thornditch." He smooths the hairs across his skull. "*So* far from civilized!" He sighs through his nostrils. "You are a privileged boy. You will adhere to the behavior expected. You will do as you are told and become a stalwart of your social class. You will apologize. If you fail in this, the ignominy of expulsion will haunt you for life. You will be banished from the tribe!"

"Apologize for what?"

"Fighting authority and disobeying the Colonel." Pug is breathless, his tie awry, specked with blood. "A man who fought the war for you."

The boy now sees that this angry exchange has shocked a second adult. A point has been passed. These adults have nowhere to go. They are unlikely, in fact, to kill him.

"Your impertinence beggars belief."

Beggars belief.

"Also," says Pug, "you are to ask for a new Stripe. When you have your new Stripe, which will be a Double Stripe, I'll see you in my study."

Pug wipes his hands on his gown and opens the door. A vein in his dented forehead throbs. The boy slinks out beneath the extended arm, pushes through the second door, and walks through the deserted hall. Footsteps resounding in the rafters, he trots down the stone steps past the rows of whole-school photos. He jumps the final steps and skids along the shiny floor of the Glass Passage as if on roller skates. The sky has darkened, heralding a downpour. Escaping serious damage, he now feels oddly free, ready to repel the official punishment. He used to take one beating at a time. But if they try it again, he'll fight back.

By the time he reaches the end of the Glass Passage rain clatters the panes. Down the dark, food-smelling corridors, he steps into the dining hall. With a resting of knives and forks, a putting down of Duralex glasses, the cavalcade of crashing cutlery and boisterous voices slowly lulls. The terrace glistens with rain. The storm outside and warm interior add coziness to a room filled with masters and boys, matrons and domestics. The Colonel stands upright as ever, shoulders back, pink palms clasped behind his sports jacket, beneath the print of the man surveying the vista. His ruddy face reflects the pattern of rain on the windows.

The boy notes the gray stubble on the back of the Colonel's shaven neck. He sees how the Colonel's dark trousers have been neatly pressed. He doesn't regret kicking Whippy. In fact, he wishes he'd kicked him harder. Nor is he sorry to get a Stripe, or fearful of having to repel any attempt to beat him. But he's sad at the fact that all this has knocked away something that, while oppressive, had provided strange safety and certainty.

He approaches the Colonel, expecting a clip round the ear. Slowly the Colonel turns. Man and boy look at one another. Years later, the boy will wonder what kind of boy the Colonel had been, before he became a man with a trim mustache and ruddy face. He wonders if they could have been friends, and whether the Colonel ever imagined a son of his own. The look they exchange, as he recalls it, feels unlike any look normally exchanged between an aging master and a willful schoolboy. It seems to acknowledge a respect between the supposedly powerful and the almost powerless, between generations.

"I'm sorry for swearing, Colonel."

The Colonel smiles, revealing those ground-down, tobacco-stained teeth. It's the first real smile from an adult he's received at the school.

"I accept your apology," says the Colonel.

"May I have a new Stripe, sir—a Double Stripe?"

"Sit down with your friends and eat," says the Colonel, touching the boy's shoulder, as if to push him toward his friends. "Your food will get cold."

"It's always cold, sir." The boy stands awaiting the Double Stripe. "Sir?"

"Off you go," says the Colonel.

Something more needs saying. "Thank you for fighting the war for us, sir."

Without looking at the Colonel again, the boy hurries off to sit down.

On the last night of term, the boys pack their belongings and head down to the large fireplace in the hallway by the Grand Staircase to sing carols with the masters and matrons. Because they've packed their dressing gowns, they wear gray pullovers over pajamas. The tight feel of wool against cotton is oddly comforting. Across the blazing hearth, the boy, who only ever mimes nowadays, watches the Colonel sing loudly. The Colonel catches his eye and winks. That's how the boy will remember it, even though in adulthood he knows that our memories create suitable scenes. But the fact is that, although an older boy at his next school will break his nose and damage an eye, no teacher will ever hit him again.

13 LATIN

When the boy turns eleven, he begins not just to live in the constant present that characterizes childhood but to pattern the past and to imagine the future. Spring and summer, with the more comfortable uniform, are best for thinking. The less constricted physically, the freer you feel mentally. So, at three o'clock one sultry afternoon in the early seventies, awaiting Old Headmaster Splint-Croakham the Younger's Latin class, he's able to concentrate on a print on the classroom wall labeled *Relativity* by someone named M. C. Escher. Beneath a clock behind the teacher's desk, it depicts faceless people walking on stairs, but some of them are walking up and others down, even though the stairs can't be going both up and down.

Still waiting for Splinter to arrive, the boy looks down the length of a ruler.

"What are you doing?" asks Dollaton.

The boy flattens the ruler. "Examining space and time," he says. "When happening, time is vertical so it seems long—like a Latin lesson. But when passed or still to come, it's horizontal so seems shorter. That's why we can speed back into the past or forward into the future. The length of time never changes but we experience it from a different angle." Dollaton looks at him the way animals do. He can't tell if they're smarter than him or dimmer, or a bit of both. "Don't look at me," he tells Dollaton. "Look at the ruler." He holds it up vertically to Dollaton's horsey face, slowly turning the ruler horizontal. Dollaton goes cross-eyed. "See?"

"No," says Dollaton.

"I'm a Time Traveler. I can go anywhere. This morning I was home in the garden. Can't you do that, Dollaton? Go anywhere—in your mind, I mean?"

Dollaton's eyes go round and round. "No."

"But you understand how to think about being somewhere else, don't you?"

Dollaton shakes his head. "I'm always where I am."

"Never mind." The boy is used to Dollaton not understanding. At least Dollaton never tells him he's a loony. Other boys do. He doesn't mind. It's not like you live forever, so what's the difference? But it's nice to have someone listen, even if it's only Dollaton.

Across the sun-hazed classroom, in which everyone is sleepy, a pale-blue butterfly batters its wings against the dusty glass.

"That's a Common Blue," says Dollaton.

Before the boy can help the Common Blue, in strides Splinter, sucking his habitual Fox's Glacier Mint, the only cool thing in the room. "Silencio!" he bellows ferociously. Even the butterfly stops fluttering.

Splinter peers at the boys through barely open eyes beneath wiry eyebrows, and collapses with a puff of sun-specked dust motes into the chair beneath the classroom clock. Even before his chalky gown floats to rest on his thick forearms, the class stands as one, then sits.

"Sir?"

"What now, boy?"

"There's a butterfly trapped in here, sir."

"Kill it."

A murmur washes over the class. Splinter's word is final. If he ordered a boy shot for cowardice, shot they'd be. The boy speculates that Splinter was himself a boy here during the Trojan War, a junior master in the time of Romulus and Remus, and senior master through the Armada. His hair is styled after Moses, but his Roman nose and stern lips suggest kinship with Julius Caesar. The main difference is that, unlike statues of Caesar, Splinter has pupils in his eyeballs, though, dozing lion that he is, they're rarely seen.

No one knows why he's called Splint-Croakham the Younger except that a Splint-Croakham the Elder is apparently buried near the Soldier's Cave—a giant rock in the School Woods, its entrance too narrow for anyone but the smallest boys to creep into. No one has been in the Soldier's Cave in living memory, though there are rumors that once upon a time a boy named Keelan inched his way in but was never seen again. His faint screams can be heard on moonlit nights. It's known, too, that Splint-Croakham the Elder's ghost walks there when no one's looking. An oak tree has grown straight out of the rock above the entrance. Splinter is said to water it to keep alive his father's spirit.

"Boy," bellows Splinter, snapping the latest reel of the boy's Head Cinema. "Have you neutralized the insect?"

"I'll catch it, sir. Dollaton says it's a Common Blue."

"Common is all the more reason to kill it. Anyway, no time for wounded prisoners!"

"I wasn't intending to wound it, sir."

"To touch such fragility, boy, is to wound irrevocably."

Spewing the sad scent of peppermint, Splinter motions the boy to complete his mission. It's thought that Splinter sucks peppermints in memory of his brother, who was shot down as the rear gunner on a bombing raid over Berlin. He sucked peppermints on every flight out of superstition. On the fatal flight he forgot his peppermints. The boy thinks this could be proof that superstitions work, or it could be that the crew got nervous once they realized Splinter's brother had forgotten his peppermints.

"It will crash land and fail to take-off," Splinter is saying about the butterfly, holding the bluish mint up to the light between crusty thumb and forefinger. "Anyway, they don't live long. Few of us do—Immortals aside." He winks at the class—or twitches an eyelid—and pops the mint into the inner reaches of his very old mouth. "Observe the fluttering butterfly, boys."

Despite Splinter's warnings, the boy scoops the butterfly up and nudges it through the opening at the top of the window. It flutters off into the clear sky. Butterfly. Peppermint. Sky. Everything is blue today.

"Neither caught nor killed!" bellows Splinter. "Still, now that you've bade farewell to our fluttering friend, kindly repose and attend to class." Splinter settles back into his chair, eyes closing, hands clasped on a boulder-sized paunch, mouth sucking away, and bellows, "Get out yer Kennedy's! Turn to page one hundred and sixteen!"

The class all have their Kennedy's *Revised Latin Primer* open at page 116, Splinter having rejected the *Shorter Latin Primer* because every copy had been altered to *Shortbread Eating Primer*. In October, the boys of IIIA, generation after generation, do declensions and gender (pages 12 to 15) and learn that everything is either boyish or girlish to the Romans. In November, Splinter steers them along what he calls the Wild and Rocky Ridge of Substantia (16 to 36) where they get pinned down by defective and variable substantives and practically destroyed trying to master the declensions of Latin nouns. December is a comparative breeze. Pages 37 to 47 race them like charioteers across the plains with nothing but hordes of adverbs, adjectives, and numerals to block their progress. But after January revision, February to April brings the perilous voyage through pronouns and prenominal adjectives (personal, reflexive, possessive, demonstrative, definitive, intensive, relative, interrogative, indefinite, and compound, 48 to 57). Only as summer approaches do they land safely in the Juicily Varied Jungle of Verbs, including regular, irregular, defective and impersonal, pages 56 to 107. Now they've reached the famous page 116 that Splinter's intoned all winter as the Promised Land.

"You'll remember, boys, from page 62 in May, what fun we had! Sum!"

"I am!" chants the class.

"Es!"

"You are!"

"Sumus!"

"We are!"

"Splendid!" bellows Splinter, lids down over his eyes like stones. "And I have faith in you, boys. You know yer Future Simples, yer Imperfects, Perfects, Future Perfects, and Pluperfects. Fuero!"

"I shall have been!"

"Splendid! Fueris!"

"You shall have been!"

"Fuerimus!"

"We shall have been!"

"As indeed we shall, boys. Fueritis, pueris! You shall have been, boys. All of you, in the plural, note. Presently estis, but someday fuetitis! For tempus fugit, meis pueris! Time flies, my boys! Remember the Imperative! And now, at last, we have the famous page one hundred and sixteen! Look what it says, boys! Rules of Four Concords, boys!"

Dunn-Larkin raises a Spock eyebrow. "Isn't that a supersonic jet, sir?"

Splinter's lids quiver open and two twinkling eyes regard Dunn-Larkin like those of a weary lion considering whether to pounce on a gazelle.

"Boys, listen to me." Splinter's coal chunk eyes widen. He unclasps his fists and bangs the desk. "Choose any page! In a book we can go back and forth in time, but in life *never!* There is no way *back!* Yer only hope is to become part of a book but even then it's not really you."

Splinter coughs gently, reclasps his hands, and once more closes his eyes, revealing tiny pimples on the bruise-hued lids. To the boy, this outburst is a rare sign that Splinter might value unpredictability. Usually, everything moves smooth as the hands on the clock above his head. The boy wants to ask how come he's obsessed with time when he's lived so long, except maybe that's the answer. Each boy has his ancient textbook, each copy numbered to match the desk, each with its own cribs, signatures, cartoons, doodles. The boy's copy contains three caricatures of Splinter. One, faded by decades of sunny afternoons, shows him as a young man in a mortarboard, standing by a boulder-laden onager with an arrow pointing to it inscribed, *Splinter about to be hit with a boulder from a giant catapult. P.T.O.* On the next page a scribbled explosion blows Splinter to pieces, arms, legs, head, and body flying all over the page, with a scribbled statement beneath: *Just like the Hun in next week's Big Push.*

The book is full of the names of boys—Siskin, Hodson One, Merlin, Ronston Three, Redpoll—who've sat at this desk in previous years. The inside cover says the first edition was 1888 but the earliest inscribed date in the boy's copy is 1910. Probably people didn't think much about time before the new century. Siskin's name half-covers a rubbed-out string of words joined by arrows: sum → fuero → fui. I am. I shall have been. I have been.

As for going back and forth, the boy doubts Splinter even knows what century it is. As in all previous lessons, eyes now closed long-term, Splinter raises a right hand that could clasp a medicine ball, and lowers it, like God's to Adam, as if to zap the first boy (always Aitkin, alphabetically on the far-right side of the class) to life.

"Aitkin?"

"Yes, sir."

"Anderson?"

"Yes, sir."

"Aylward?"

Here Splinter's wiry eyebrows wiggle into a frown and his eyeballs flicker behind their lids like a dreaming lion's. "Where's Aylward?"

"Would that be Aylward I, sir," the boy asks, as usual.

"Do you know him?"

"He's no longer at the school, sir."

"Where is he?"

"Nowhere to be found, sir."

"Out of bounds? Then he must be expelled! Or has he a long-term illness?"

"Worse, sir. Aylward is dead."

"Dead? By Jupiter, *how?*"

"He's on your Remembrance Sunday list, sir. Aylward F."

Splinter unwraps another peppermint and puts it in his mouth as if it were information to ponder. "That's too bad. But I recall now. Yes, dead indeed, young Aylward. Gavrelle, April 1917. Aylward II died at Beaumont-Hamel on 1 July the same year. Too bad."

"Aylward P., sir."

"Hmm. Their deaths killed their parents, too. Died last year. Ostensibly the Spanish flu, but their hearts weren't up to surviving. Once upon a once upon a time, yes, yes, once upon a once upon a time." At this point, Splinter always forgets he's been doing the register and says, "Very well then. Aitkin, pro-gress."

So Aitkin begins to read from Kennedy's *Revised Latin Primer*. "Amo. I love."

"Just the Latin, Aylward!"

"Aitkin, sir."

"Oro lovi! Pro-gress."

"Amo, amas, amat, amamus, amatis, amant. Amabo, amabis, amabit. . . ."

They don't always read from Kennedy. Splinter often lumbers in with dog-eared stacks of Thompson and Craddock. ("Too advanced, really, boys. But tantum fun!") From Thompson and Craddock they learn such phrases as rara avis, reductio ad absurdum, caveat emptor, and deus ex machina, and about Romans like Agricola, Scipio, and Gaius Sallustius Crispus. ("No, he didn't invent crisps, Dollaton, although Greek philosopher Chrysippus died laughing at a donkey eating figs.") Sometimes Splinter gets carried away and brings in Catullus, or Pliny's Letters, or Virgil or Horace, and strides around booming, "Sume lege!—take and read!"

It matters little what they read. No one but Splinter understands much. He grunts at every reading. Always he starts with Aitkin and after a line or two moves on to Anderson.

"Studes an piscaris—" reads Aitkin.

[Grunt]

"—an ven-venaris—"

[Grunt]

"—an simul omnia—"

"OMNIA?"

"Sir?"

"Omnia? It's a question, dear boy! You may puncture Pliny, but you can at least recognize a question mark! Wait until Lord Kitchener gets you!"

"Who, sir?"

"Ask the Contemporary Studies master. Next!"

Aitkin lowers his blushing face, finger following every word as Anderson begins. Splinter leans back, wiggles his wiry eyebrows, and holds out his right paw, suspended in a locked line on Bunting. Bunting reduces another pillar of Latin prose to rubble just in time for Splinter's paw to swivel, unexpectedly missing boys in between, and lock on the boy himself.

"Rescuer of the Common Blue," bellows Splinter, "continue."

Writing *once upon a once upon a time* in the margin, the boy has lost the place.

"Ahem. Boy, I have enlisted you to read!" The boy raises his eyes. Sunlight flashes in his face. Splinter becomes a silhouette. "I hear you'll soon have a brother here, boy."

"He's already here, sir. I'm the younger one."

"Hmm. Where is he?"

A cloud dims the sun and the boy sees Splinter again, sucking a new peppermint, and sending its fumes out across the class. Wrappers litter his desk like clusters of crystals.

"He's not in the class, sir. He's a Senior."

"Already? Tempus Fugit! I thought you seemed a bit small, Pueris Duo. Still, pro-gress."

"Where from, sir?"

"Too late! A missed opportunity to read Pliny! Next!"

The sun brightens again, and Cribley stumbles through the sunlit page of Pliny's verbal minefield awaiting Splinter's detonation of annoyance, but reaches the end of his paragraph without being blown up. The arm shifts like the shadow of a giant sundial to Dunn-Larkin just as the butterfly flutters back into view and clings to the windowpane.

Spock-fringed Dunn-Larkin is the unluckiest boy in class. The arm always stops at him. His voice signals Splinter's nap, leaving Dunn-Larkin, eyes twitching, reading until the end of the lesson or end of time, whichever comes first. To the tick of the slowest clock on Earth, only the boy and the butterfly join him in remaining awake for the duration. On reads Dunn-Larkin, as the sun swings across the afternoon and evening shadows tumble over the desks. On he reads through such long-gone afternoons as through the years until finally the butterfly stops flexing its wings in the sunlight, leaves its grip on the glass, flutters back in through the open window, pauses on Bunting's desk, alights on the clock, and rests on Splinter's bulky shoulder.

As if by magic, the bell clangs. Splinter raises his eyelids, claps his hands, so that the butterfly sets off again around the classroom, and growls, "Homework means what?"

"Translation, sir."

Splinter heaves himself up and writes on the blackboard: Horace's Satire 2:8, lines 37–79. "Plus revision of the first conjugation of A-stems."

"Yes, sir."

Off they run, knowing homework will be easy thanks to scribbled answers bequeathed by previous generations, including some of the boys' own fathers and grandfathers, before trooping off to the wars taught in Contemporary Studies. They make deliberate mistakes—a misspelling here, a misunderstanding there—but do enough right to get Splinter's initials at the bottom. No one cares what the point of the homework is. They've survived another week.

Meanwhile, in chapel that night, as every night after Latin, they pray for the Old Boys who have left ammunition to defeat Splinter.

Our fathers who art in heaven / Hallowed be thy names
For you have saved us / From those who've enslaved us
And no doubt will do so again. / Amen.

Is it a trick of the light or the boy's imagination that produces the apparition in chapel that night? He glances up from his ink-stained hands while all around him pray. For a moment the candle-shaped wall lamps seem to have again become the actual candles they must have replaced. In their uncertain light the oak rocking chair near the altar—empty in memory of past headmasters—seems to rock. He loses focus of the cerberusic triumvirate of Splinter, Glinty, and Pug in the foreground and the empire-pink Colonel and gloomy Major behind. For beyond them all sits Splint-Croakham the Elder, smiling thinly at him from the flickering shadows.

The boy hardly has time to think before the apparition disappears, leaving behind, as if carved for a moment on the stone wall behind the chair, the word fui—I have been!

14 ROME

How well I remember that Maurits Escher print on the classroom wall more than half a century ago. Yet, while life moves inexorably "forward" (however inaccurate the spatial metaphor), the human brain can indeed go back and forth, and, for me as a child and adult, Escher's *Relativity* is a visualization of our ability, in mind if not body, to defy time's apparent linearity. I find that rather comforting this sunny November morning, given the disconcerting disappearance of certain portraits from the Musée d'Orsay.

To reprise Vincent van Gogh, all paintings are personalities. But portraits, expressing painter and sitter, offer two-for-one. Especially haunting is Marat assassin Charlotte Corday's commission from Jean-Jacques Hauer before she greeted the guillotine. What did he think as he painted? What did she think as she sat? It can be hard to believe such individuals are mere brushstrokes rather than restless to return to their living state. Vincent thought Rembrandt "almost alone among painters" in his "heartbroken tenderness" and "glimpse into a superhuman infinitude." I like to imagine his portraits in Amsterdam, Paris, London, New York, stepping from their frames and reuniting to celebrate their creator's accumulated life.

In the Orsay decades ago, I'd commiserate with Vicomtesse de Calonne (no relation) on her fate as the cover girl for the Penguin Classics' *Madame Bovary*. Then her portrait vanished. Recently, I've found Madame de Loynes's gaze a challenge. But suddenly, today, no Madame de Loynes! No Comtesse de Keller! Only Madeleine Brohan has survived the cull. Replaced by other portraits, they're probably stacked in a dark basement, their eyes—described by Stendhal as "the big guns of the virtuous coquette"—unable to intrigue.

Ah well. I've left the Orsay and taken the RER C to Passy to sit in Balzac's garden off Rue Raynouard. The author's modest house contains the chair and desk at which, through nights fueled by the coffee that helped kill him aged fifty-one, he created the 2,500 characters of his Comédie Humaine. Beyond the house Tour Eiffel pierces blue sky. This setting is appropriate for continuing to contemplate the boy I once was. Balzac, too, was a frequently punished boarder, often ending up, during his years at the Oratorian Grammar School in Vendôme, in an alcove known as the dungeon. But in fact I'm reminded of a later time: my mid-twenties in Nottingham. Perhaps this is because when I first arrived in the City of Caves I might as well have been in storage. I'd imagined Nottingham to be full of vistas and surrounded by Robin Hood's greenwood. But the reality, in the eighties, was that Nicki and I rented a ground-floor room with windows fastened against the fumes of Castle Boulevard. Beneath the cliff and castle, the terraced row existed in unending gloom.

Writing a PhD on the novels of William Styron, my mood swung between joy at being with my fiancée and dissatisfaction with our impecunity. Making the best of it, we ate candlelit meals at a table by a blue wall that stood in for night views of foreign cities. A research grant enabled me to turn fantasy into reality by tracing the narrator's trip to Ravello in *Set This House on Fire*. Coincidentally reviewed in the *New Statesman* the day I was born, this novel is only recalled because of *Nat Turner* and *Sophie's Choice*. But Styron's evocation of place was invitation enough to travel, helped by Nicki's observation that those inspired by Ravello include that visual magician of my childhood, Maurits Escher.

Nicki and I stayed at the Hotel Francesco in the Piazza San Francesco d'Assisi in Trastevere, close to Piazza Santa Maria, which features in the novel's opening. Styron's narrator, Peter Leverett, describes his final evening in the city. He's spent his days in an office facing the green banks of the Circo Massimo across the Tiber, and his nights in an apartment on the Gianicolo Hill. Listening to Tchaikovsky, he's watched the city spill beneath him, the Colosseum "aglow in the phosphorescence of floodlamps," the Forum a "ruined assembly of stark white shafts" against the urban outskirts rambling up the hills into the darkness.

I crossed the Tiber at the Ponte Palatino one afternoon to reread the novel in the Circo Massimo. Envisaging Peter's office window onto the arena, I mused about time. In the author's note of *The Confessions of Nat Turner*, Styron writes of how its relativity "allows us elastic definitions." The narrator of *Sophie's*

Choice ponders George Steiner's notion of "time relation," wherein some lives continue as normal while others enter a living hell. In the Circo Massimo I held in mind not only the era of its initiation as the first great sporting arena but also the rise and fall of Rome, and the relatively late construction and decay of the nearby Colosseum, "that tottering ruin," as Alphonse de Lamartine called it, "of human pride."

In the 1840s, Charles Dickens brings the timescale into relief. "Except where the distant Apennines bound the view," he writes in *Pictures from Italy*, "the whole wide prospect is one field of ruin. Broken aqueducts, left in the most picturesque and beautiful clusters of arches; broken temples; broken tombs." Nowadays there are entry tickets and barely a weed in sight. But we still climb to the Colosseum's upper levels, look out over the arches of Constantine, Septimus Severus and Titus, the Forum, temples and palaces, and imagine them in their prime.

After a last supper on Gianicolo Hill, Peter has a beer in Piazza Santa Maria. On our own final evening we, too, strolled from the San Francesco along Via Jacopa de' Settesoli to the shadowy piazza. Trastevere probably differs little from how it was in the time of *Set This House on Fire*. Peter drinks his beer amid air "aromatic with blossoms." When the church bell strikes, he leaves Rome and drives south toward the Amalfi Coast.

All I knew of Ravello came from guidebooks and cultural marginalia such as Styron's novel, Escher's etchings, Gore Vidal's home of Villa Cimbrone, and *Beat the Devil*, a movie John Huston was making when the Styrons visited. Written with Truman Capote, this Robert Morley–Peter Lorre crime caper, entwined with romances between Humphrey Bogart and Gina Lollobrigida and Jennifer Jones and Edward Underdown, provides a grainy record of the Ravello that inspired the novel. I felt, therefore, that we were driving not merely through an actual landscape to an actual town but also a fictional landscape to a fictional town.

Following Peter's route through the Campanian plains to the cliff country, we skirted Formia, negotiated Naples with its backdrop of Vesuvius, hit the autostrada to Pompeii, and reached the coast between Salerno and Amalfi. Always narrow, the road to Ravello spirals upward beside a verdurous gorge with glimpses of the sparkling bay. Some parts are too narrow for larger vehicles to pass one another unscathed. Reversing is unwise. Best to scratch paintwork than have your wheels spin dust into the chasm.

Just as Styron describes it, Ravello's cliff-top location sends a "shadow across the sea." Past the shadow, the "transparent blue" water is indeed dotted with tiny boats that seem "held up over the clear sandy bottom as if by invisible threads." From the summit the whole of Italy rolls eastward "in a miracle of flux and change" and, "steaming with noon far below," the Vesuvian plain sweeps toward the Apennines.

In Ravello itself Piazza Vescovado, dominated by an eleventh-century duomo, was large and busy. It was the start of a festival and the day of a wedding. The guests were gathered on the steps, the groom sweating in his suit and tight collar beside his bride in white. To the left of the duomo is the Viale Wagner, where the composer wrote *Parsifal*. I recognized the sloping lane with widely spaced steps as the one Morley, in *Beat the Devil*, marches down before turning into the Via Roma where the lane opens out into the piazza.

While Styron adapted Ravello to suit his themes, Huston and Capote rearranged it geographically. In the film it stands for Porta Bella, supposedly at sea level. Morley may stride down the Viale Wagner, and Bogart take in the scenic views from his balcony before retreating indoors with Lollobrigida, but in a piazza café he encounters Underdown and Jones as a British couple stuck "in a squalid, fifth-rate port" while waiting for their boat to sail.

Aside from discussing Escher's mathematical art, Nicki was content to enjoy the limoncello stalls, sunshine, and stunning views. "I don't need to read the novel, do I?"

"Not really."

But with lines and images from the novel and film in my head, the tangle of fantasy and reality tightened. We wandered along an alley that became a cobbled street, "the street a labyrinth winding narrowly between rows of dank, deserted houses, and the labyrinth finally a walled path" along "a dizzying precipice." A similar path brought us to Villa Cimbrone's sun-splashed gardens and spectacular terrace. Along the balustrade, weathered busts stood against the azure sky and deeper blue of the Mediterranean, and between them to the left the Amalfi Coast spread into the distance, and farther off and fainter the coast of Cilento.

Styron uses this town-to-nowhere as a metaphor for a suicidal urge he outlines in his account of depression, *Darkness Visible*. Where Peter is mostly detached from events, alcoholic painter Cass Kinsolving is central and in turmoil. Trapped by the town, he feels a growing terror that there's "nowhere at all to go." "Closer to the sky than the seashore," as André Gide put it, what seems idyllic to a visitor could isolate a resident. Visiting a promontory, Cass finds only a low wall protecting him from the abyss. Feeling "the merest wisp of self-preservation," he pitches forward in a "foretaste of oblivion."

We ended our visit in the gardens of the Villa Rufolo, once owned by the family of Landolfo, Boccaccio's lucky merchant in *The Decameron*. Bygone visitors and residents from Wagner to Vidal surrounded us. I thought of Dickens in Rome in Victorian times; of Styron there and in Ravello in the fifties; of my own youth in the sixties and seventies; of the complex interaction of life and artistic endeavor; the long-gone splendor of Rome; the unreality of Ravello "aloof upon its precipice," as quixotic as art itself. Up there against the sky with the sunless valley far below, one can fantasize a sabbatical from life but, if anything, the elevated setting heightens your awareness of time's wingèd chariot. You're the first to see the morning sun and the last to see the sunset.

On the journey back north, I concluded that to travel through the actual landscapes depicted in narratives affects what you see, whether in the setting or book. I saw Rome and Ravello through others' descriptions, and my own past and present through the lens of this Italian journey. The creation and experience of art influences both our worldview and our actions. Had Nicki not pointed out Escher's connection to Ravello, and had I not read *Set This House on Fire*, we might never have taken this trip. Art can affect what we do, and so rearrange reality. Hence in *Beat the Devil* a hilltop town becomes a port, an Escheresque twist in itself. Similarly, there's the slippery reality of my boarding school childhood and its vivid existence as semi-imagined scenes, an episodic movie I carry through the years, always seeking, or seeking to create, its elusive meaning.

15 PORTS

Turning thirteen is depressing. The boy expected childhood to last forever. Possessing a condition adults have misplaced, he's felt superior. But now he, too, is losing it. Worse still, having got used to Thornditch, he'll soon be at a new school. He's back in Wellington in what was once the unimaginable future. He feels as if he closed his eyes that first night half a decade ago and awoke as a dormitory captain. The new boys are scared he'll punish them. Whacking has stopped, and he's never sent a boy to the headmaster. He hopes Dobson met a gruesome fate. Caught talking after Lights Out, a boy named Danton-Hillier bursts into tears, but when the rule is explained he understands.

The parents are coming at Break with the boy's birthday tea. As usual, he's allowed up to twelve friends, or rather eleven and the Head Boy, Umber-Gristle, who invites himself to senior birthday parties. He'd even go to junior ones if he didn't look silly sitting among smaller boys. Instead, they have to bring party food as "tribute" to the Officers' Table.

Bunting and Dollaton are the boy's Helpers. Together they prepare the feast and sit either side of him. The table plan has friends in receding order of friendship status. Umber-Gristle is at the far end, where he always is if only attending as Head Boy. When the party belongs to one of his gang, he's a Helper and Pug provides presents for the invited boys. Umber-Gristle himself has the biggest party of all and Pug makes the school sing "Happy Birthday" and call out "Three Cheers for the Champ!"

Still a lesson away, the boy aches with excitement that the parents will arrive with the presents and food. The lesson is a strange one conducted by the Colonel and Major. After parade and breakfast, sixth-formers watch a slide show.

The Colonel has a cold and punctuates his talk with sneezing into a handkerchief that glows in the darkness.

"First, hahem," he says, knocking his leatherbound swagger stick on the first slide, which is some kind of line drawing, "can any of you young blades tell me what this is?"

"A port, sir?" suggests the boy.

"Think ships rather than ports," says the Colonel. "We'll come to them in time."

"A haggis?" suggests Bunting.

"Oh, for pity's sake!" The Colonel puts down his stick and sneezes into his glow-white handkerchief. "It is a diagram of a member-at-ease."

The class laughs nervously. The Colonel clicks the projector to a similar diagram but with a dotted line superimposed to show the journey the ship, haggis, or—as the Colonel claims—member-at-ease has taken. He folds his handkerchief and prods it into the breast pocket of his sports jacket. It glows in a thin line echoing his ground-down teeth. He picks up his stick and slaps the wall as if inducting troops into D-Day landing plans.

"You'll notice that here," tap-tap, "hahem, the member has abandoned its position of repose. No longer at ease—Position A—it has risen up, enlarging all the while and, following these dotted lines, taken up its point of attack in Position B, here. It is now at *attention!*"

Numerous pairs of eyes watch the Colonel's slideshow.

"At the end of the battle, of course, the member-at-attention retires, with the waters once again becalmed, from Position B to Position A, where it settles back into quietude. It becomes, in a word, at *ease!* Any questions? Yes, boy."

"So is it a ship or a soldier, sir? Ships enter ports but soldiers stand at attention."

"Good point, boy. These are metaphors. We use something to represent something else. The difference between you lot and girls is that they have ports while you have, say, ships. Now whether you choose to see that thing between your legs as a ship or a soldier is neither here nor there. What matters is that you have one."

"Sir?"

"Slide Three." He clicks the projector. Up springs a drawing of a man's back with a woman peeking out over his shoulder with startled eyes. "Once married, if married you foolishly decide to be, you may find yourself doing this." Here he slaps the board as if tapping the cartoon man on the shoulder. "Good, there we are then, that should do it. Time to pass you to the Major for further information. Once divided into groups of four and given a time, you have Free Play until your appointment. Five minutes beforehand you're to go to Headmaster Gladmere's study and wait outside until called."

"Sir?"

"What is it, boy?"

"Today's my birthday."

"Is that relevant?"

"I think so, sir. You're talking about how we get to be born."

"Is that what birthdays are?" says Dollaton.

"Birthdays do indeed have to do with being born," says Bunting.

"Every day is someone's b-birthday," says Dollaton mournfully.

"Well spotted, Dollaton," says the Colonel.

"The thing about it being my birthday, sir, is that my parents are bringing my presents and birthday tea. Since Bunting and Dollaton are Helpers, could we see the Major first?"

The Colonel's cold has made him soft. "Very well." He retrieves his handkerchief for one final sneeze. "Plus you, Dunn-Larkin. That'll make four."

They are therefore first into Gladmere's study. The Major sits gloomily behind the desk. The boy hasn't been in the study for a while. Gladmere is rarely at school now, and Pug uses the study but not to see boys. It seems barer, less antiquated. The rug has gone, along with the print of charging elephants, the chair the boy leant over to be whacked, and of course the ivory canes. It's no friendlier but less Victorian.

"Coffee?" offers the Major. Four white mugs stand beside a steaming kettle as if on parade. The boy has never tasted coffee. "Ahem," coughs the Major, who seems to have the same cold as the Colonel. "Headmaster Umber-Gristle normally does this chat but is away on business, so it falls to me to discuss these difficult and distressing issues. Sugar?"

They all take sugar, along with chocolate biscuits. This is a great day for food, except that the coffee is a weird drink even with sugar.

"Sex," says the Major gloomily. "What is it?"

The boys raise their mugs to their mouths. The coffee steams their faces.

"Come on! Didn't the Colonel tell you?" Silence. "Right, well, it's what brought you into the world. Now." The Major's eyes droop with gloom. "What is contraception?"

"English lessons about understanding a page of prose, sir."

"That, Dunn-Larkin, is comprehension. Does everyone comprehend that we are *not* talking about comprehension?"

"I don't," says Dollaton.

"We are talking about contra-*ception,* which can prevent boys like you arriving."

"There are a lot of Dollatons in the world," says the boy, "so maybe Dollaton's parents didn't contrahend compreception."

"Contraception!"

The boy sips the bitter coffee and breathes into it to enhance the steam fanning back into his face. He notes why the study appears so bare. The stuffed birds have gone. In place of the woodpeckers is a bookcase and a photo of the Umber-Gristles. Pug's grin practically breaks the frame. Mrs. Pug—known for whatever reason as Hedgehog—takes up very little space on the other side of the picture. Between them Umber-Gristle holds aloft a trophy.

"The best form of contraception," says the Major, "is not to do it, ever."

"Not to do what, sir?" asks Bunting.

"Anything," says the Major. "Just don't do anything at all, ever, except finish your coffee, all of you, and go away."

"Sir?" asks the boy. "Where do babies come from and why are they wanted?"

"The first question is technically answerable, though best to ask your parents rather than an aging, unmarried ex-army officer. The second question has a certain charm. Frankly, I've no idea why people want them. But clearly your parents did, so that's reassuring?"

This isn't at all clear to any of them. If they're wanted, why are they here? Also, if you're a second boy perhaps you're just a spare.

They troop out of the study in time for parade into lunch.

"Learn much?" asks Bunting as they line up.

"That adults can get embarrassed about certain subjects," replies the boy.

16 COMFORT

The boy, Bunting, and Dollaton await his presents and party food in the gravel turnaround where the mother and father dropped him years before. The parents arrive suntanned.

"Just back from Bermuda," says the father. "You really should visit one day."

"We stayed in the most splendid hotel," says the mother. "My, you've grown, and Bunting, you're taller, too! And Dollaton, surely the tallest boy in school!"

Dollaton smiles sadly. "I may be the tallest boy in the world."

The father pulls out the presents—two books and a drawing pad—and the box of food. The mother kisses the boy's forehead and smooths his hair with spit-dabbed fingers. The father ruffles it, and they speed off down the drive as if they've robbed a bank.

"They're nice, your parents," says Bunting.

"I don't really know them," says the boy.

"At least you've got two," says Dollaton.

The boy shrugs. "How do we know they're really ours?"

"Who else's would they be?"

"Any of us might have been swapped at birth, or adopted without being told."

"Gosh," says Bunting thoughtfully. "I'd better ask them."

"Best not," says the boy. "Touchy subject. I do wonder what we have in common."

Dollaton's mournful face perks up. "I have my mother's horsey face!"

"And your father?"

Dollaton shrugs. "I don't remember him. But mother says he adored me."

"Did he have a long face?" asks Bunting. "I mean, in the photos?"

"Oh, yes," says Dollaton. "All Dollatons have long faces. Tall, horse-faced Dollaton men marry tall, horse-faced women."

"Then I shouldn't worry."

Let off parades, half an hour before High Tea they lay out the food and set the places, covering the rubber table mats in foil to suggest festiveness. Maria in her blue coat and Miguel in his white jacket lay the regular tables. Portuguese mingles with the clatter of crockery and cutlery. The boy knows the word "Obrigado" means "Thank you."

"I wish we didn't have to invite Umber-Gristle. He always guzzles the Cola."

"Umber-Guzzle," says Bunting. "Let's spike his drink."

"Put spikes in it?" says Dollaton.

"Salt," says Bunting, winking his one winkable eye.

Soon the house squads march in, and the party guests take their seats.

ForwhatweareabouttoreceivemaytheLordmakeustrulythankfulAmen, says the school, then everyone dives into the plates overflowing with party food. They stick twiglets into tinned fruit salad awash with condensed milk, gollop chocolate-filled meringues, slurp Cola, munch fistfuls of crisps, gouge at individual tubs of ice cream, and gaze with candle-gleaming eyes at the chocolate cake with its soccer pitch icing, two goals, and thirteen red candles representing Liverpool players. All goes well until Umber-Gristle rises, jerks so violently that the boys on his bench all shake at once, cries, "My Cola!" and rushes from the dining hall.

Lying in bed that night, the boy thinks about Matron Radeva. An idea hits him. At first it seems silly, but the more he ponders it the more he dares himself to make it real. Later tonight he'll leave his dormitory, climb the Grand Staircase, and knock softly at her door. Now that he's in charge of the dormitory, the boys will assume he's on duty. He can calmly wander the same corridors that used to terrify him.

His heart pumps with excited dread. His exhilaration at the symbolic poisoning of Umber-Gristle is spoiled by the burden of the duty now before him. He feels an agony of agitation. If you fail in this, he scolds himself, both of you will leave and never meet again. You must do it within the hour. Tell her you'd like to be friends after you've left. She'll forgive you for visiting her. After all, it's your birthday.

Made miserable by his self-imposed task, he eases from bed and tiptoes across the hallway to the Grand Staircase. His new dressing gown trails the floorboards and the sleeves cover his hands as he slides his right palm up the banister. The idea is that he grows into the gown as he gets taller, but right now it makes him feel as if it's his first night at Thornditch. Alert as a stalking cat, he pads upward. Where the stairs turn up right to the landing, there's the stained glass window with the coat of arms. A full moon shines through it, glinting red where the sword and bat cross, and blue through the clear glass.

Up he continues, past the portrait of the woman in green, whom he now observes more daringly. The portrait hangs high on the wall to the left of the window and faces the landing. Once you're on the landing she's at eye level. He remembers her from the first night, but has hardly thought about her since. Tonight, though, everything is different. The moon shines on her face.

Matron Radeva's door looms before him. Can he possibly do this? He raises his hand, blue in the moonlight, black in shadow. He taps softly. It sounds as loud as coal spilling into a scuttle. No reply. He taps again, louder—surely too loud!—still no reply. He can't go back. Why won't she answer? He knocks, loud, it seems in the silence, as a table overturned in a fury. The noise echoes down the corridors. From the turn of the Grand Staircase, the portrait stares at him. What are you doing, boy? Go to bed! He now remembers why he avoided her gaze for years. She judges him guilty of crimes unknown.

He taps one last time.

"Go away, Horatio," comes Matron Radeva's voice. "We've been through this!"

Driven beyond fear, the boy turns the doorknob and pushes the door open.

"Matron Radeva," he whispers. "It's me."

"Who?" A bedside light flickers on and off, like indecision. "Is there a problem?"

"Captain of Wellington Dormitory, Matron Radeva. Can I come in?"

"Oh you. Close the door quietly and tell me quickly. You shouldn't be here."

The boy crosses the floorboards. His feet touch a rug.

"Sit," says Matron Radeva. The boy sits on the bed. "Are you cold?"

"I wanted to see you." He tries to discern her features in the moonlight, but she's silhouetted against the window. "It's my birthday. I'm a teenager, like you."

"You had a lovely party. But you see me every day. What's the matter?"

He tries to think of something. The outline of the window sharpens. A flicker from Matron Radeva's eyes is so faint he perhaps imagines it.

"I had a dream, Matron Radeva. Remember when we were burying Luerty's budgie?"

"Oh poor Zhoui, yes."

"Joey."

"Sorry, my Bulgarian version! Is that what you dreamed of?"

"Yes. Some of it was good but some bad."

"Well, go back to your dormitory and think about the good parts."

"The bad bits were about you, Matron Radeva. I was worried for you."

Matron Radeva starts as if to say something but seems to change her mind. "Go back to bed. You shouldn't worry about a matron!"

The boy returns to Wellington but lies awake. He can never sleep nowadays. He thinks all the next day about Matron Radeva and that Mr. Horatio Greatorex must be his rival. The next night, when the moon is up and the dormitory a choir of snores, he creeps back up the Grand Staircase, past the portrait of the lady, to Matron Radeva's door.

"Horatio?"

"It's me, Matron Radeva. I can't sleep."

Her footsteps reach the door. "You mustn't keep knocking on my door like this!"

"Can I come in? Like last night?"

"No."

"I've got something to tell you."

"Just for five minutes."

Squeezing the door shut behind him, the boy creeps across the dark room behind her until his feet feel the rug by Matron Radeva's bed. She sits on the bed.

He sits next to her. "will I see you after we leave?"

"I'm going to America. To a place called Harvard in Massachusetts."

"Massachusetts," says the boy. "What kind of a name is that?"

"An Indian name."

"Can I visit you in Massachusetts?"

"Time for you to go back to your dormitory!"

"I've something else to tell you."

Matron Radeva sighs. "What's that?"

"I'm here under an assumed name. I'm really an imposter."

Her hand touches his. "Why do you say that?"

"I'm not who adults think I am. I was swapped at birth. They mixed me up with another boy with the same name. I don't resemble my parents or brother or sister."

"You're lucky to have a brother and sister!"

"Do you have any?"

"I have cousins, Nadka and Stefan. I love them dearly."

"Why?"

"They're family. I'm very proud of them. Our hometown is Gabrovo but Nadka is now a doctor in Sofia. Stefan is younger. We want to pay for him to study law."

Miss Radeva's warm arm encircles the boy's shoulders. "Do lots of English boys think they don't belong to their family?"

"I don't belong anywhere. I beggar belief."

"What does that mean?"

"I don't know."

"You poor boys, away from home so young!"

"Don't worry. I've changed by name. I'm now 'Heighway', with an e."

"Heighway?"

"Yes, Matron Radeva. Steve Heighway plays for Liverpool. Like him I've taught myself to drag the ball past defenders—Dollaton and Luerty, anyway—while playing on the wing. When I'm older I'll grow a 'Steve Heighway' mustache and come to Massachusetts to find you. I'll walk all over America along big straight highways stopping at each cowboy town to ask for you. They'll say *weir ya fram, stranger?* I'll say nowhere. They'll say *what's yo' nayem?* I'll say, Heighway."

Matron Radeva's giggle echoes in the dark. "You'll be Mr. Heighway walking the highways. America's a big place."

"So are the School Woods, but I find my way around them pretty well."

"Any more dreams, Mr. Heighway?"

"Yes, about you."

Matron Radeva removes her arm from behind his back.

"When you're not being a matron, what's your real name?"

"My real name?"

"Your first name."

"I'm not sure you should know."

"One day we'll marry. I need to know my fiancée's name, don't I?"

"I'm your matron. You're a schoolboy."

"I'm a teenager, a dormitory captain. How old are you?"

Just then a powerful fist knocks on the door. Matron Radeva slaps an almond-smelling hand across his mouth. A second hard knock follows.

"Kalina!"

"K—" the boy begins.

"Shhh!"

"I need you, Kalina! I know you're awake. I can't live without you. I'll kill myself!"

"Horatio," says Matron Radeva. "You mustn't talk like that."

Terror digs vicious fingers into the boy's chest.

Matron Radeva puts a finger to his lips. She rises from the bed. Her slim figure edges toward the door.

"Horatio," she says. "If you don't go away, I'll have to report you!"

"I'll kill us both."

"You won't, Horatio. You will have a lovely life, but not with me. You will marry a wonderful woman and she will have your children."

"Have you got another man in there?"

"Of course I haven't!"

Hmm, thinks the boy.

"Not Peter Umber-Gristle, eh? I know about you two!"

"Don't be silly, Horatio. Go!" He must do because Matron Radeva returns. "And you," she whispers, "Men are all the same!"

So I am a man, he thinks.

"Go!"

"He might still be outside," he whispers.

"Twenty minutes," hisses Matron Radeva. "Then *bed!*" Covering his shoulders with the blanket, she seems to be shivering.

"I wish I could stop you shivering, Kalina," says the boy. Or is she's crying?

"I'm a little homesick. I might go back to Gabrovo."

"Are you still a teenager?"

"Yes, I'm nineteen," she sniffs. "That's quite old, isn't it?"

"Kalina," he says, "that's not a normal name."

"It is where I come from."

Kalina Radeva, newly christened, has her face to his. In the dim light her eyes twinkle. He can just make out her freckles.

"Kalina, will you sing me one of those Bulgarian songs?"

"Did I sing you one before?"

"Last summer, when I was in sick bay."

"Oh yes. You were ill for so long!"

He'd spent many days there, some of them delirious. He remembers a fever dream that his bed was crumbling concrete. His job was to stop it collapsing. Then he imagined he was at home on the lawn. Everything was widely spaced but got closer and closer and scrunched into a tiny ball in front of him. Just when he thought he was suffocating it opened again into a vast expanse until it again contracted. He knew Matron Radeva was there and felt something cold on his brow and concerned voices talking about whether he should be taken somewhere else. Gradually, the world returned to him.

"You sang 'A Gun Went off in the Green Forest'. Poushka something."

"Ah! 'Poushka Poukna Niz Gora Zelena', I remember!"

She sings it softly, her voice barely rising beyond a whisper.

"Kalina?" The boy wraps the blanket tighter. "Do you ever feel lonely?"

"Are you warm now?" whispers Matron Radeva.

"Yes. And I like your singing. Are you lonely now?"

"Are you?"

"I'm never lonely. I have my Head Cinema. But I'm sometimes cold."

"Your Head Cinema?"

"I watch films in the top left corner of my head."

"Oh yes, I have one of those. Is that what you call it in English?"

"That's what I call it."

"Then so will I."

"And will you see me in your Head Cinema?"

"Yes."

"And can I visit you in Massachusetts?"

"Or in Bulgaria. Now you must go."

"I'm still a little cold."

The boy drifts off, woken only by Matron Radeva's whisper. "Wake up!"
"Kalina?"
"It's Matron Radeva. You're awake at last! Quickly! It's light outside!"
"What if Mr. Greatorex is there?"
"I've checked. Up you get."
"Are you afraid of him?"
"You couldn't know about these things."
"How can I learn if not from you? The Colonel and Major won't teach me much."
"You'll get into trouble if you talk like that."
"I'm always in trouble. I haven't settled."
"You mustn't ever say anything about this. You promise?"
"I promise."
"Never. I mean it."
"Never ever. Can we do this again?"

17 ISTANBUL

December has begun with sunshine so last week, after pig trotters and frites at Bouillon Chartier, I caught the elevator up to the Tour Montparnasse open-air observation deck. The late-afternoon shadows stretched across the city from Tour Eiffel to the Louvre. The tower's long shadow fumbled over Saint-Sulpice, normally looming above you but seeming from there no more than a sandcastle. More distant to the right the façade of the Pompidou—or Beaubourg, Eric Hazan tells us to call it—stood out like a stranded ship: "Notre-Dame des Pipes," color-coded green for plumbing, blue ducts for climate control, yellow for electrical wires, red for circulation and safety features. I scanned forward from Hôtel de Ville across the Seine and the Latin Quarter to Montparnasse Cemetery low to the east, where lie Simone de Beauvoir and Jean-Paul Sartre, their gravestones sprinkled with lipstick kisses, and in the oldest part of the cemetery Guy de Maupassant, his tomb adorned with a plaque to *Bel-Ami*.

In doing so I found myself contemplating a very different city view: Istanbul from the Galata Tower. Spectacular in wholly other ways is that panorama across the inlet of the Golden Horn to the cluttered hillsides of the oldest part of the ancient city, its mosques and minarets brought to life by swirling seagulls, scudding clouds, and the lively waters of the Bosphorus. From the tower you can see the outline of the mosques and minarets as well as the quayside of Eminönü. Here stood, at the time of visiting, a small tourist information center manned by a toymaker named Zeki Kinali.

After the birth of our first daughter, Tasha, we'd moved to new jobs in the West Country. Since one of my responsibilities was to coordinate Erasmus, a scheme enabling staff and students to study across Europe, I took the opportunity to explore the city as an option. On the Sunday morning of our arrival, Nicki and I wandered through shuttered streets. The only life animating the cobbles were stray dogs and cats. In hazy sunshine we climbed steps into a courtyard behind a high wall. The Süleymaniye Mosque loomed. We removed our shoes and pondered the cavernous interior. Back down through the Grand Bazaar, we came to Eminönü and, seeing the information center, thought we'd acquire a map and advice about the city, including Kadir Has University where I was due to lecture.

Inside the building, surrounded by bare, whitewashed walls, sat an old man in white shirt and black trousers behind an empty table.

"Günaydın," I said, using most of my Turkish. "İngilizce biliyor musunuz?"

"Of course," he said, "and good morning to you. All Kinalis speak English."

"Do you have a map of Istanbul, Mr. Kinali?"

"Zeki, please. I have no maps," he said.

"Can you show us where Kadir Has University is? I'm giving a talk there."

"For most of my life I've been a toymaker," he said.

"A toymaker?"

He pulled out from under the desk a wooden top, which he spun on the counter. "You see?" he said. "Now I would like to be a teacher. I have such wisdom to pass on to the young. When is your talk?"

"Wednesday."

"Do you have a pen and paper?"

I took out my pen and notebook.

"Will you please write down the time, along with your name? I will come to listen to you. Wednesday, yes?"

Zeki told us to follow the Bosphorus and we would come to Kadir Has.

"We'll never see him again," I said.

By now the sun had fully broken through. From Eminönü we jumped on a ten-lira ferry. Turquoise in its depths, the Bosphorus sparkled, spray cascading in the sun. A woman in a blue headscarf smiled at us. The Turkish flag snapped at the stern, brilliant red in shadow and sun, white crescent and star flapping in and out of sight. Soon the minarets and domes were hazy silhouettes above the ancient port. The ferry turned round near Rumeli Fortress and the Fatih Sultan Mehmet Bridge.

Back on dry land, we ate fresh fish sandwiches and spat the bones into the shallow waters to sink between jellyfish. Crossing the Galata Bridge, lined with dark-clothed anglers, we veered from the crowds to climb a steep alleyway to the Galata Tower, took the elevator for that panoramic view, then walked down Istiklal Caddesi, packed with Istanbullu families arm-in-arm on their Sunday stroll. On our return a line of geese cut across the sun setting over the Old City. The bridge glowed orange. From the floodlit minarets, brightening in the darkening sky, loudspeakers proclaimed the call to prayer.

With a day or so before I was due to meet our host, Ray, we visited the Basilica Cistern, the Blue Mosque, Topkapi Palace, and the Harem and gardens. We peered at the Prophet's foot-cast and a lock of his hair, sat on a bench amid blossom in the garden, and walked down through a layered courtyard for lunch at a café overlooking the Sea of Marmara. After time in Hagia Sofia we made our way back down and along the Bosphorus to locate Kadir Has before crossing the Golden Horn on Atatürk Köprüsü.

When, on the Tuesday, I attended Ray's class to become familiar with Kadir Has before my lecture, it wasn't what I'd expected. An American married to an Istanbullu, Latife, Ray's job was under threat. Erdoğan's government was phasing out the study of literature. Numbers were falling. Only one student appeared, a girl named Elif who spoke halting English. But the three of us discussed Nathaniel Hawthorne's "Drowne's Wooden Image," about a ship's figurehead that seems to take on human form, a fable about the mystery of how art comes to life. In the late afternoon Nicki and I crossed the Golden Horn again and strolled the northern shore to watch the sunset over the mosques across the water.

The following afternoon Ray and Latife met us at Eminönü to take the commuter ferry to the Asian side. After a meal and Turkish coffee in a firetrap of a room, looking down at the busy streets of Ray's "real" Istanbul, we squeezed into a crowded basement to watch a rock band put on a good first set but a ragged second. It was painfully obvious, Ray advised us during an elongated version of "Another Brick in the Wall," that they'd smoked too much weed in the interval. At midnight we caught the metro back beneath the Sea of Marmara.

But I was really there to give my talk, which brings me back to the toymaker, Zeki Kinali. Surveying the audience from the lectern the next day, I spotted him at the back, wearing what looked like a brand-new white shirt.

"İyi akşamlar," I said, deploying the last of my Turkish. "It's wonderful to be here, and to meet new people. Speaking of which, I'd like to introduce you to my new friend, Zeki Kinali, the Toymaker. He hopes to be a teacher and asked if he could attend tonight."

Everyone clapped him and he stood and bowed.

The next morning we passed the tourist information center again. Zeki Kinali was talking to a woman. He had a map, or perhaps she'd brought it in. On the table was a spinning top. He got up and strode over, clasping my hand and arm with both hands.

"Thank you, thank you," he said. "You made an old man very happy. It was one of the best times of my life."

"I'm glad you feel that way, Zeki," I replied. "Did you enjoy the talk?"

"I didn't understand much," he said, "but I was glad to be there, and I can see that you are a skilled teacher. May God bless you."

Eventually, having come outside with us, he let go of my hand.

"Well," said Nicki, "we saw him again."

"We certainly did."

Only later did I reach into my jacket pocket and find a small wooden object. It was not a boat figurehead, of course, merely one of Zeki's spinning tops. But nothing is "merely." Objects hold power, as we know, and I'm well aware that, in giving me his art, which was his time and skill, he had given me a slither of his soul and of the soul of his city. Two things in Paris remind me of our visit to Istanbul. One is the Turkish embassy's flag visible, somewhat anachronously, from the garden of Maison de Balzac. The other is a painting by Jean-Baptiste-Siméon Chardin in Sully 920 that I never pass without thinking of Zeki. *Child with a Spinning Top,* painted in 1737, depicts a boy neglecting his homework to watch a top. All is still except the top, which gives the impression of spinning. The boy smiles in concentration. His books lie closed in shadow. The background's vertical lines contrast with the top's angled position simultaneously countered by the oppositely angled quill pen in its pot. Who knows, perhaps the boy learned more from this simple toy than he learned from whatever lessons those particular books held? As for Zeki's desire to teach, in my view he was already doing so. Despite the fact that he attended my lecture, it was not he who learned from me but I who learned from him.

18 LEAVING

The boy's final memories of Thornditch are not unhappy. He gets into the First Eleven because Pug's star forward jumps from a window and breaks an ankle. The boy scores once in the season's penultimate match and three in the last. He'll remember them years later. The father comes to watch. When the boy scores his first the father jumps up behind the goal. Chocolate bars fly from his pockets like sparks from a Catherine wheel. After the hat trick the father says, I thought you scored four, but the boy knows he didn't get a touch to one of the crosses. Only three, he says. He asks Pug if he can be in the team photo. Pug refuses. The boy remembers this as a lesson in how not to treat those over whom you have power.

He continues to write letters home, such as this one.

> *Dear Mother and Father,*
> *This is the last letter you'll recive from me at this school. Leavers don't have to write in the last month! My brother wrote a short untidy letter to me and I wrote a long untidy letter back. Yes, I would like to go to France for a holliday. I haven't been a broad! How would we get there?*
> *We have to go to boring old chapel before we go home, probably for hours and hours!! But I look forward to seeing Tina. She may just be a cat but I think she remembers me.*
> *The lecture we enjoyed as usual was "Air-to-Air Refueling in the Royal Airforce" by Wing Commander Doubleday.*
> *We also saw some of Shakespeare's "Henry V." The projector broke just as the French were attacking at Agincourt but we must of won or it woodn't be a film, right?*
> *Sincerely, your dutiful son.*

P.s. My best friend has been Matron Radeva.
PPs. Here is my version of the school magazine:

<u>THORNDITCH MAGAZINE</u>
<u>Editor: Peter Umber-Gristle MA JP Headmaster, Blah Blah Blah</u>

<u>School Notes</u>
We congratulate Tarquin Umber-Gristle on his exhibition to Eton. Other boys are also leaving. Some have scolarships. But this year belongs to the remarkable U-G. His family is proud of him. P.U-G.

<u>School Year, 1973–74</u>
Sports Captain   Umber-Gristle (Armada)
Music Cup   Umber-Gristle
Shooting Shield   Umber-Gristle
Squad Shield   Armada

<u>Sports Day</u>
Victor Ludorum   Umber-Gristle
Winning Squad   Armada

<u>Review of School Play, "Treasure Island"</u>
"Umber-Gristle played the part of Long John Silver with supreme maturity, showing both his extrordinary acting ability and his obvious musical talent. A performance to treasure!" (P.U-G.).

<u>Other News</u>
In addition to this year's Leavers, we bid farewell to two valued members of starff: Mr. Greatorex, whose coaching will be sorely missed, and Matron Radeva from Bulgaria, who has enjoyed a sucessful time with us. We wish them sucess and hapinness.

The boy never sees or hears from Matron Radeva again. Mr. Greatorex doesn't kill himself, or her, and Bunting says he saw them together at Sports

Day. The last day of term arrives. The boy finds himself in the empty changing room, surrounded by pegs where their sports gear used to hang. Voices outside call, See you! So long! He feels a little sad. It can't be because of memories of being whacked, or because he'll miss Umber-Gristle, or because he likes the place. Maybe it's because none of his friends are going to Grimpton. He's going because the brother's there, and likes it, which is not a good sign. He's visited once. It's high on a hill by the sea and made of flint stone towers and cloisters. From a distance the chapel stands darkly satanic. The uniform is black trousers, black-and-white ties, white shirts, and flint-patterned jackets. Instead of "Two" after his name he'll have "Minor."

He wanders from the changing room to the deserted hall with the lockers, through the double doors that functions as a goal during Indoor Play. He passes the sides where the marmite sandwiches get piled for Low Tea, along with the bottles of milk that freeze in winter and congeal in summer. He hops down the steps to the passage with racks usually full of tuck boxes, where Mr. Youngstown play-fought with boys. Down more steps he peers through the windows of the Science lab and pet shed, then goes round the new block that's now the Umber-Gristles' home, and the new music school Pug uses to show off his son. He climbs the stairs to the library where they watched films and remembers the shame of winning a spelling competition where if you got a word wrong you swapped places on a row of chairs with whoever got it right. He won with the word *integrity*. While Cribley and Aitkin were getting it wrong, Dollaton, on the third chair, asked him how to spell it and he said "e-n-t-e-g-r-i-t-y." The boy then spelled it right and won. He didn't enjoy the victory. Honesty, he learned, is best. But such moments vanish. Only the art remains. Rembrandt's lady still wades through water, nightshirt up to her thighs, and Rembrandt's self-portrait still watches the boy more gently than all those portraits down by the study Pug's inherited from Glinty.

The boy crosses the empty dining hall, past the Pigs' Table, the school shield, and the print of the man looking out over the vista, past the bread bins where they'd come down in the night for stale crusts and handfuls of cornflakes, and climbs the narrow stairs to the seven o'clock landing. Opposite the Grand Staircase with the painting of the woman in green and the stained glass window is Matron Radeva's door. He's often imagined himself in her room since those two nights. But this afternoon, with the sun bright outside, and the landing dark, his heart beats harder than ever at the thought of seeing her one last time. She's returning to Bulgaria and only maybe then to Massachusetts, but the night she sung him "A Gun Went off in the Green Forest" she promised to give him her address.

He knocks once, twice.

He pushes the door. It swings open.

The room is bare. The bed is stripped. An empty vase stands on the table. Something stirs. Standing between the boy and the window is the dark form of Mr. Greatorex.

"Haven't you left, boy?"

"I've come to say goodbye to Matron Radeva."

"Matron Radeva departed this morning." Mr. Greatorex treads forward, grim features taking shape as he draws closer and, sinewy muscles trembling, towers over the boy. His eyes are moist and red. "Good thing, too! Foreigners are bad for the country and women are bad for the school. What matters is to keep Britain British, and prep schools male. Remember when you're an adult, never trust a woman, especially a foreign one!"

With that, Mr. Greatorex stomps from the room like a disappointed superhero. The boy's left alone in a place he's never seen in daylight. It's cold and sparse. Yet on those two nights that he visited Kalina Radeva it felt like the warm heart of the world.

19 EXPECTATIONS

It's high summer, 1974. The boy's at home, aged thirteen but still very much a boy. One day he sets out his Cowboys and Indians as usual on his bedroom floor. The mother has bought him a disposable razor for when he might need to shave, which certainly isn't yet. He takes the precaution of using the razor's cover to—he thinks—block his door latch so that no one can enter. It doesn't work. The parents open the door and stand looking down at him kneeling on the carpet positioning the toy figures.

"When I became a man," says the father, "I put away childish things."

"Oh, let him have his childhood," says the mother.

After they leave the bedroom, the boy puts the Cowboys and Indians back in their box, and never sets them out again.

Meanwhile, the brother's voice has broken, a mysterious event with excruciating suggestions. Perhaps you're taken into a dark room and garroted just enough to crack your Adam's apple and crunch your voice into the correct tone. The shock brings you out in spots and makes you behave as if the world owes you something. The brother goes to "discos," where he's met the baker's daughter, Deodora Dandy. They shut themselves in his room until the mother says it's inappropriate. The boy isn't sure what's inappropriate: the brother being in his room with a girl or Dora being a mere baker's daughter.

If being fifteen means this, he wants nothing to do with it. Thirteen is bad enough, but better than being so old you're practically dead, or actually dead—like Grandma Cologne, who died after a "stroke." Some compensation has been the arrival of a color television and extra channels. On the old black-and-white one presenters would ascend into the top of the screen then reappear from the bottom. They only paused their apotheosis and reincarnation when the father bashed the television. Now there's a steady picture and more choice of what to watch, even if it's only been delivered thanks to a death.

Meanwhile, Grimpton College looms. Letters arrive to the brothers "Major" and "Minor." Before term, however, there's the rare event of a family vacation. In their yellow Cortina, they drive to the Dordogne to stay in a static caravan (a "caravilla"). The campsite is surrounded by tobacco fields. There's a pool and a trampoline. The brother, almost too big now to sit in the backseat, complains he'd rather be seeing Dora. But as soon as they arrive, he goes in search of other girls. Near the end of the holiday, the boy spots a girl with a toothy smile, slender limbs, and a pale T-shirt. They smile at each other in the pool and she says, "Je viens de Bruxelles en Belgique."

On the final night before they leave he finishes washing up in a central building and starts back to the caravilla. Girls are waiting in a line. From left to right, they go from Ingrid, a tall, short-haired Dutch girl, down to the girl who said something about "Belgique." In between stand blonde twins.

"Good evening," smiles Ingrid, teeth shining in the moonlight. "Please explain yourself to us." The boy's heart kicks. Because it's dark it doesn't matter that he's blushing but he can't prevent the crockery rattling in the washing-up bowl. "How old are you and what is your name?" say Ingrid's shining teeth.

"I'm thirteen," says the boy. "My name is Tin Ribs." The girls' teeth shoot into view like a line of nightlights.

"Tin Ribs!" snorts Ingrid. Four sets of teeth giggle.

"I am Ingrid, as you know," says Ingrid. "And these are my friends."

"I am Berthe," says the first blonde twin.

"Je m'appelle Sabrina," says the other one.

The row of teeth disappears as Ingrid, Berthe, and Sabrina each turn to the last girl in the line. Her T-shirt glows in the dark.

"Je m'appelle Karine," comes a tiny voice. "I is Karine."

"Now," says Ingrid. "You must kiss each of us goodnight." She leans down and pouts. At least the boy assumes she does because her teeth disappear. He smells spearmint. "Well, Monsieur Tin Ribs?" she says. "Oh, wait." She straightens up. "It must be polite, even in England, to lay your cups and plates down before you kiss?"

The boy backs away, but Ingrid grabs his shoulders and plunges her lips to his like a plug to a socket. The bowl of crockery clatters in his arms.

"Now me!" says Berthe.

Ingrid pushes the boy along so that he stands, washing-up bowl in his arms, in front of Berthe. Her peck on the lips feels like being attacked by an anxious blackbird. She jumps away as quickly as he does. Next comes Sabrina, then before him stands Karine. The other girls disappear. Karine's eyes shine in the moonlight. He sees only their sparkle and the outline of her teeth as she smiles at him. She leans forward.

"What's up, Tin Ribs?" comes the brother's voice. The boy feels a shove in the back and sprawls in the sandy earth. The cutlery and crockery shine dimly all around him. "Hello, girl," says the brother. "Mother's asking if you've done the washing up, Tin Ribs."

"I go," says Karine.

"No, wait!" calls the boy, but she's gone.

"She wouldn't have liked you anyway," says the brother. "Looks as if you're going to have to wash up again, though. Sand all over them!"

On the final day the boy finds Karine before they leave. He hands her a piece of paper with his address on. "Can we write?"

"Bien sûr." She smiles, pecks him on the cheek, and scrawls her address.

"I have to go," says the boy. "My parents are waiting. I'll write first, Kalina!"

"Karine," says Karine.

Back at the caravilla the mother tells the father that if she ever has to spend another night in one she'll bring a picture of their house "so these Europeans can see how big it is."

"Pin up a receipt for the school fees, too," replies the father.

All the way to England the boy daydreams about Karine and her brown skin, white teeth, and pale T-shirt. Kalina Radeva hardly gets a look in. At home he writes Karine a letter in his best French, apologizing for how bad it is.

The last days of summer involve packing for Grimpton. A chill wind rides in on the sunshine as September arrives and nights draw in. Two days before the return to Grimpton, an envelope with two lavender-colored five-franc Belgian stamps falls on the doormat.

The mother picks it up with her long-nailed fingers. "Open it, then."

"Not yet."

She takes it to the drawing room. The father is reading the *Daily Telegraph*. "Tin Ribs got a letter from Brussels!"

"Girlfriend? About time."

That night, in his room, the boy opens it. He doesn't care much what it says. He's just pleased to have this first really personal letter of his life. Every so often through his teens, and in the absence of anything from Kalina Radeva, he'll reread it, barely comprehending but happy. If nothing else, it seems she expected to see him again.

Cher Tin Ribs,

Je m'excuse de vous écrire si tard mais j'ai rescu votre lettre et j'étais justement invitée en Ardenne pour la semaine. Nous avons fait notre voyage en 1 jour. Sa date de mon anniversaire et le 23 juin. J'ai très bien compris votre très mal Français.

Au revoir
Karine

Poor boy—or perhaps lucky boy: he's still too young yet to realize that "au revoir" should not be taken literally.

20　LISBON

A giant Christmas decoration dominates the Galeries Lafayette foyer. The fairs at Hôtel de Ville, La Défense, and the Tuileries are open. On the Grande Roue last night we caught the sunset over the silhouetted spires of Basilique Saint-Clotilde and dome of Les Invalides. A Tuileries stall sells carved statuettes including a mustachioed, bespectacled figure that resembles Fernando Pessoa, the Portuguese poet whose survival mechanisms parallel those of many a boarder. "I make landscapes of what I feel," he says. "I make holidays from my sensations." Beware the outer world, he counsels, find interior sustenance.

I discovered Pessoa through José Saramago's *The Year of the Death of Ricardo Reis,* which I'd assigned on a European writing module. Reis is a Pessoa heteronym, or alternative self. The novel has him wandering Lisbon. It's a story of exile and alienation, so naturally I decided to retrace his steps and explore the Portuguese capital myself. Now the father of a second daughter, Ani, I'd long understood that my own sense of exile and alienation had nothing to do with adulthood, marriage, employment, or most importantly parenthood. But since these childhood feelings lingered, Lisbon seemed as good a place as any to immerse myself in another's artistic world while also being, once again, a stranger in a strange place.

Reimagining 1930s Lisbon from political exile on the island of Lanzarote, Saramago's conceit is that Reis outlives his creator by nine months. After years in Rio de Janeiro, he checks into a hotel, named Bragança in the novel, that's still on Rua do Alecrim by Cais do Sodré. Wearing his distinctive gray hat, he visits Pessoa's grave in Cemitério dos Prazeres—cemetery of pleasures, as it oddly translates, named after the district—and makes an equally dismal pilgrimage to Rua dos Douradores, where supposedly lives another heteronym, Bernardo Soares, author of *The Book of Disquiet.* Returning to his room, Reis encounters his dead creator, who says he's come from the cemetery to reciprocate Reis's visit. His short time before oblivion is "a question of symmetry" since "before we are born no one can see us yet they think about us every day" while "after we are dead they cannot see us any longer and every day they go on forgetting us a little more."

Ricardo Reis is a magical realist novel and the characters self-evidently imagined beings. Toward the end, one of Reis's love interests and her father "cease to exist." Another, a servant named Lydia, referred to as Anna Karenina's nursemaid, also disappears. Reis eventually exits with his original creator. Reis is reading Herbert Quain's *The God of the Labyrinth,* an imaginary detective novel by a fictional author reviewed as if real in Jorge Luis Borges's story "An Examination of the Work of Herbert Quain." But *Ricardo Reis* is also a political critique of Catholicism and fascism, and Lisbon itself so faithfully described that I arrived feeling I already knew the city. At thirteen, I imagined Grimpton and my development toward adulthood before experiencing either. Again, in Lisbon, I'd attach a physical place to a mental image, albeit one shaped by the words of my fellow exiles, the apolitical modernist Pessoa and the political postmodernist Saramago.

The flight into the Portuguese capital skirted the Tagus estuary. Lisbon Cathedral stood out, along with the maroon girders of Ponte 25 de Abril and the statue of *Cristo Rei,* the city's imitation of Rio's *Cristo Redentor.* Once in the city, I walked up to Castelo de São Jorge, which shapes the city's eastern skyline. From there the sweep of Lisbon spread from the orange-and-white Cacilhas ferry I'd catch for *Cristo Rei,* to beyond Terreiro do Paço and Cais de Sodré. In the middle distance, the various squares interspersed the churches from the startling white of Igreja de São Roque and São Domingos to the ruins of Igreja do Carmo near the Elevador de Santa Juste. In the near distance the flat shopping district of Baixa-Chiado led to the Barrio Alto. Below me swifts chased their shadows over clay tiles.

Cristo Rei's relevance to Saramago's novel is its link with Catholicism and fascism. Blow it up, said a Portuguese friend, it's built to thank God for saving Portugal from World War II. The figure of Christ with outstretched arms is a hundred feet high on a pedestal close to three hundred. It dominates the skyline even if dwarfed, seen from the city, by Ponte 25 de Abril. But, impressive though its colossal scale is, only the devout could take seriously the shop merchandise beneath: flying Christs in crystalized robes; sugar-coated Christs who seem about to high-dive off the shelf; soap Christs that obviously dissolve if used, and Christs who look like they're celebrating a sporting achievement. Likewise, there's an army of Our Lady of Fatima models and some muscular baby Jesuses. "Hold on to what is useless," Saramago muttered beside me, "you will always find a use for it." "The buyers of useless objects are wiser than is commonly supposed," replied Pessoa. "They buy little dreams."

"Only when we are dead do we become spectators," Saramago writes, but we also become spectators in a foreign city. "I am dead and wander about," Pessoa tells Reis, which could equally be, "I am a foreigner and wander about." For I, too, paused on street corners, all but invisible to passersby. Trying to follow Reis's route was, as Pessoa wrote of life, "a ball of yarn that someone got all tangled." Ascending Rua do Alecrim, I came to the statue of Eça de Queirós. Noting that the spelling could be Queirós or Queiroz, Reis stops "out of respect for the orthography used by the owner of that name" then lapses into a meditation on words and imagination. "Once language has said all that it has to say and falls silent," he muses, "I wonder how we will go on living." By the time he reaches Praça Luís de Camões, he's decided it's miraculous we don't go insane each time we speak.

I sat at a refreshments pavilion in dappled light. A 28 Tram trundled toward Prazeres, another toward Rua do Alecrim. A man in a gray hat headed up Rua do Misericórdia. I followed him across the whiteness of Largo de São Roque and into the church. I was less startled by the splendor in the interior gloom than by two glass coffins, one encasing the Virgin Mary, the other the body of Christ. Like the shroud image I viewed the other day in Sacré-Coeur, his eyes were closed, face ashen, wounds coated in dried blood. His neck hung as if broken. This was a depiction of death, no mistake, and very unlike the gigantic *Cristo Rei* preparing for ascension. As Pessoa observes, we are afraid of death, but indecisively.

Escaping the church, I crossed the square, pausing by a window as guitar notes opened a fado, followed by the voice of Mariza singing "Na Rua do Silêncio." I was at the spot where Reis contemplates this process of strolling, thinking, and associating: the essence of language in relation to place. "When one idea is drawn from another," he thinks, "we say that there has been an association. Some are even of the opinion that the whole human mental process derives from this succession of stimuli, sometimes unconscious, sometimes only pretending to be unconscious, which achieves original combinations, new relationships of thought interlinked by the species." I understand this all the more now that the process he refers to is the one that currently preoccupies me.

I visited Prazeres but like Reis I didn't linger, not least because Pessoa is no longer buried there. Just as Victor Hugo was promoted from Montmartre Cemetery to join fellow luminaries in the Panthéon, so Pessoa now rests in the splendor of Jerónimos Monastery in Belém. Instead I took a taxi back to Largo de São Roque and descended Calçada do Duque. Outside a closed shop at the turn up Calçada do Carmo toward Igreja do Carmo stood a slight, mustachioed man in hat and glasses—very much Pessoa's twin. Desculpe, I said, Fala Inglês? Of course, he replied. I asked him if the shop was ever open. Not imminently, he said. I was interested in the Pessoa items, I explained. I've been reading him, Saramago too. The man smiled and said, Saramago died rich and read, Pessoa died in virtual obscurity. He wished me good day. Obrigado, I said. Nice to have met you. He laughed. Indeed! But the very act of meeting is a nonmeeting. With that, he continued up Calçada do Carmo.

Distracted by the changing of the National Guard, strutting like tin soldiers in blue-and-green uniforms, I lost sight of him so explored the museum within the walls of Igreja do Carmo, only partly rebuilt after the 1755 earthquake. From there I headed back down to the Rossio and Igreja de São Domingos. In São Domingos battered pillars rise amid splendor, though that contrast is nothing compared to the fact that, next to some general's statuette, the do Carmo museum displays the bound, mummified corpses of two young Peruvians.

I ended the day walking to the Saramago Foundation, created by his widow in Casa dos Bicos above Roman foundations. It houses a library, a display of his books and life, and his reconstructed office. When he died on Lanzarote in 2010 people went into the streets to read his work aloud. In Lisbon, they held his books aloft by the coffin. If a painting is a personality, or a projection of one, so too is a book. Perhaps for Saramago, certainly for Pessoa, all interaction involves projection; ultimately our experience of others is our artistic construction. The important thing about Pessoa's appearance in *Ricardo Reis,* Saramago explains, is that as long as he's remembered he exists. That's the atheist's afterlife.

Weary of the city's sweltering heat, the next morning I took the coastal train to Cascais and sat by the sea to read *The Book of Disquiet*. Assistant bookkeeper Bernardo Soares lives a narrow life in all ways except in the mind. Art, he writes, resides "on the very same street as life, but in a different place." Less a direct reflection of life than a parallel universe, art is thus related but tangential to actual experience. Soares thus feels no need to leave where he is, even while it oppresses him. "We generally color our ideas of the unknown with our notions of the known," he writes. "We manufacture realities."

The most revealing moment in *The Book of Disquiet* is Soares's description of parents walking in a park "like cardboard figures" across a stage until, "finally, ever closer, and more separate," they vanish in the rain. "I am the love they shared," he says, "which is why I'm able to hear them on this night when I can't sleep." Pessoa was not simply the product of a time and place, but of the trauma of parental loss that rendered everything in life unsettled by an awareness of mortality. Yet he was too intelligent not to know this of himself, and of the mask he was donning, and his bleak self-irony is a strangely enjoyable read.

I completed my remaining tasks: to visit Miradouro de Santa Catarina and Adamastor statue, and Barrio Alto to listen to fado, which led me to miss the last bus and so meander up and down hills, lost in the nocturnal streets. Like Pessoa, I began to wonder if I existed, if I might not be someone else's dream. Al a minha solidão, came a fado from a window on a distant street. Oh, my solitude. Al lucidez que me dói. Oh, this clarity pains me! Al minha féilta de apego. Oh, my lack of belonging. Finally, I renewed acquaintance with Pessoa himself, or at least his statue outside Café A Brasileira, not—it being about 4:00 a.m.— surrounded by busy tables, but alone, staring at nothing. I sat with him a while but he couldn't tell me the way home, so I set off again into the night, glancing back only to see his brass face lit by the full moon.

Perhaps it's true that many lives, including my own in youth, are possessed, like Pessoa's, by feelings of alienation and, like Saramago's, by awareness of exile. But I'm generally upbeat and always curious. "I wander and I find," Pessoa reminds me. "I find because I wander." After Christmas at home, we're back in Paris for New Year. Aside from reports of a new, flu-like virus China is trying to contain in Wuhan, all is well. Close to midnight, with our adult daughters we'll join the crowd up the Champs-Élysées. We'll see a light show on the Arc de Triomphe that will suggest it's disintegrating and rebuilding. At midnight fireworks will burst across the sky, and 2020 will alternate with the word PARIS across the top of the arch. It will be a long walk back past closed métro stations to Neuilly, but worth it to celebrate new beginnings, a new year, our family briefly together, and to ready myself to reimagine the last years of my childhood education at another strange new school.

Art Appreciation, 2022, by Gavin Cologne-Brookes.

YOUTH & ADULT

I am often homesick for the land of pictures.

—VINCENT VAN GOGH, *Letters*

1 ARRIVAL

Any optimism the boy may feel about Grimpton is soon shaken, much like the latest family car up the driveway. A secondhand Austin Maxi has replaced the Cortina. The father complains about inflation, which means rising school fees. The siblings are squeezed in the back, the sister is in the middle, eating sandwiches. At Thornditch, the wind only rose to its height on the night of his arrival. Grimpton, the boy will learn, is prone to perpetual gales.

Both schools have long driveways, but unlike the rhododendron-lined tunnel to Thornditch, the road to Grimpton splits sodden fields scarred with dykes and treeless to the coast. Against a darkening sky, the father leaves the main road by a muddy estuary and turns left up the steepest part of the drive. Silhouetted on its promontory, the chapel looms ever larger against the rising wind, stained glass windows glinting like the portals of a moored ship. A ray of sun between rainclouds catches the wet tarmac and flashes light across the balustrades. Green storm clouds roll over the bombastic towers. By the time the father parks the Maxi on the gravel, all is dark.

"Not my kind of place," says the boy.

"What *is*, Tin Ribs?" asks the brother, who has become a rugby player and a sacristan.

"He has no idea what this is costing us," says the mother.

A spotty lout in black trousers and a wide-checked sports jacket opens the boy's door and thrusts in a salt-stained hand.

"Welcome, new man!" he says. "Grimpton anticipates you. I'm Bulsterine."

"Hear that, Tin Ribs?" says the mother. "He called you a man."

"Hiya, Bulsy!" The brother jumps out. "Bulsy's a prefect," he calls back into the car.

"Good to see you back, Mr. Big! Great summer?"

"Not to the extent that it was spent with this new squit!"

"Hiya, little girl," says Bulsterine. The sister starts another sandwich.

From the car's interior light the boy sees that the only smoothness on Bulsterine's pockmarked face is on top of unburst boils. He squirms at the sight of an especially pustular spot simmering on the prefect's neck. Is this to be his fate, too? Bulsterine's job simply involves greeting. They probably prefer him to stay in the dark when possible.

The boy follows the rest of the family up the steps to Lower Quad. Striking the hour from the flint stone above the cloisters is the white-faced clock that the boy will contemplate for the next four years.

"This is First House." The brother leads the family through an orange door. "I'll sort my stuff. Here's another mate, Pink-Chunkerton, or Chunkers. He'll tell you where to go."

Pink-Chunkerton isn't as spotty as Bulsterine but is equally tall and deep-voiced, with greasy hair, a pink jacket to offset the regulation trousers, and a nose sooted with blackheads. He beckons the boy forward.

"Heard all about you," says Pink-Chunkerton. "Your nickname is Les."

"But that's not his name!" says the mother.

"Don't worry, my good woman," says Pink-Chunkerton. "Just part of the initiation!"

The mother's expression suggests an attempt to process this.

Pink-Chunkerton opens the door to a bright hallway with stairs straight ahead and a partition into a room with mirrors, lamps, and a cream carpet.

My new life, thinks the boy, watching his uncomfortable-looking peers. In one corner a boy named Creupe with a mole on his forehead swings a key on a chain. Another boy is red-eyed because he's left his regulation Bible at home. Another, Allenby, looks like a captive planning escape. Despite his uncowboy-like, pudding-basin fringe, he stands with his weight on one hip like a gunslinger in a saloon.

There's been no photograph this time. The father long ago stopped snapping the boy because he's grown "sullen." Good word, "sullen." This has been a mostly sullen day, with a sullen sky. There's been no talk of his big day, and no expectation on his part, after his initial optimism, that Grimpton will be less than hellish. He's yet to witness any cause for joy. The school chapel especially—"the largest in Britain," beams the mother—seems designed to crush any challenge to Anglicanism. Still, at least the housemaster's hallway offers a semblance of home: carpet, lamplight in mirrors, a ginger cat padding between rooms. When I have a home, he thinks, I'll have lamplight in mirrors.

The set of parents loiter a few minutes, perhaps from politeness. The new men eye each other. The monochrome uniform seems designed to discourage individualism. Only prefects wear a jacket of choice. They've become institutionalized so pose no threat.

His attention shifts to the housemaster. Shrivel-chinned Mr. Slammer is a Chemistry teacher with twinkling brown eyes. The eyes, he thinks, are the handsome part of Mr. Slammer, and explain why he has a beautiful wife and daughter. But he and his wife must have met over a wall or fence because from the nose downward Mr. Slammer's face is a sorry sight. His chin falls into severe folds and creases, as if the lower half of his face is evolving into a giant sultana. Shaving is surely awkward. The boy twists his own jaw as he imagines Mr. Slammer pulling out the folds. It must be like shaving a cake. Perhaps he once messed up an acid experiment. Certainly his daughter—"Emma," he hears her say, "aged sixteen"—hasn't inherited this feature. Her tanned face shines smooth as a conker and, like her mother's, suggests she may be southern European or Middle Eastern.

The mother kisses the boy's cheek. The father ruffles his hair. The mother smooths it. They're ready to be off into the windswept night.

"Work hard, darling," she says. "See you soon."

"Goodbye, Mother," replies the boy, not bothering to ask when that'll be.

"Goodbye, Son," says the father. "Play hard."

The boy follows them out through rain to the top of the granite steps. The car doors slam and their red taillights disappear down this latest driveway. When he returns to the homely quarters of Mr. and Mrs. Slammer, Bulsterine is guarding the shut door. He[1] points down the corridor. The boy heads to what he learns is the Junior Common Room. This marks the beginning of a second stretch, except that they've moved him to a kind of open prison where at certain times he'll be free to, for instance, walk the several miles to Grimpton-on-Sea. *Colditz* is on TV, so he thinks worse fates exist. This illusion shatters at the sight of Matron Sandra Seton.

"New men! Bed!"

This monocled House Matron—"Call me Ma Seton"—makes Matron McRipp seem benign. A builder's forearms bulge from the short sleeves of her red-trimmed black uniform. On her chest, tucked into a white belt, shines a silver broach with her initials: SS. Her blotchy face set in an attitude of malice, she directs the new men up to the twenty-bed dormitory and orders them to prepare for sleep. The change of guard is complete. The bright moon floods the boy's bed. By the time the clock across the cloisters strikes midnight the dormitory is quiet. Well, thinks the boy, here I am, somewhere near the coast. The sea is only viewable through the south-facing windows. He'll always be aware of it. He'll smell it on the trees, taste it in the seaweed-rubbery food, and the salty wind that dries your cheeks. But on this moonlit night, he creeps from his bed for an actual sighting. The rain's been blown away by the South Coast winds. The full moon shines on the sea as if on a slab of black metal.

2 MONTEVIDEO

The new year is only partway through its first month, but anticipation of new beginnings is giving way to unease. Wandering Galerie Vivienne recently, rain clattering on the glass roof, I read on my phone that a customer who caught this new virus at the Wuhan market had died. Cases are confirmed in the States, Japan, South Korea, and Thailand. The Chinese have sealed Wuhan off. News gets daily grimmer. A cruise ship, the *Diamond Princess,* is quarantined off Japan. Now called COVID-19, the virus has killed hundreds in China, including alarm-raiser Dr. Li Wenliang. There's even been a death in Paris.

Foreboding adds to a melancholy to do with such trivia as the dismantling of the fairs. The cars of the Grande Roue have been stacked on trailers and the whole structure taken apart spoke-by-spoke and driven away. A Fun House, stripped of lights and motion, has become a gaudy skeleton. Loitering on the Terrasse des Feuillants on a blustery day, I thought not so much of Henri de Marsay encountering Paquita Valdès there in *The Girl with the Golden Eyes,* but of *Lost Illusions* and Lucien Chardon's more dismal experience of a theater after a show. The scenery, lights, and "resplendent enchantment of back-cloths" give way to "coldness, desolation, darkness, emptiness." Taking a break from Balzac, I've just cycled down Boulevard d'Iéna's cobbles past the bust of Artigas, father of Uruguayan independence. This has prompted me to counter my current bleakness by dreaming back over Montevideo, another place where I continued my search for whatever I seek.

It was June, Uruguayan winter, but the sun shone nevertheless. Well into my academic career now, I'd begun looking beyond European or North American culture. Uruguayan author Eduardo Galeano's *Soccer in Sun and Shadow* and *Open Veins of Latin America* had opened my eyes to the possibility that South America would deepen my sense of global citizenship. Such trips also, of course, further fed my addiction to being unknown to the world I entered, a desire perhaps not unrelated to the sentiments of another ex-boarder, Zola. He wrote of his "years at school" (for him "years of tears") that he had "the pride of loving natures." "I was not loved, for I was not known," he admitted, "and I refused to let myself be known." But I was now putting these matters in context. If the vulnerable child forms a carapace for self-protection, the worldly adult is wise to reckon with its legacy.

Three hours across the River Plate from Buenos Aires, the Buquebus ferry drifted into port with so eerie a quietness that we might have been docking at a space station on the moon. Once again I was arriving—not unlike at Grimpton, to a stormy sky—as a stranger in a strange land. Streaks of dawn split the horizon. The sea seemed black but burnished with sparkling light. Beyond raindrops streaming across the glass, my reflection resembled the ghost of a giant looming among the clouds. We passed a dock stacked with container crates overlooked by silent cranes like extraterrestrial robots. Outside the small terminal, I threw my bags into a taxi, named my hotel, Armon Suites on 21 de Setiembre in the Esquina Berro, and, having no Uruguayan pesos, offered American dollars.

"Fifty," said the driver. "Okay, forty."

"Eso es mucho."

"Tengo que cambiarlo." He had to exchange it.

Later I learnt that it should have at most cost ten dollars. We sped along Rambla Francia in the morning sun. Rambla Francia became Rambla Sur, then Rambla República Argentina and Rambla Wilson. We passed parkland with plain buildings set inland. The rain ceased and the sun shone on a palm-lined shore across the bay. The River Plate was chocolate brown even in the sunshine, not pollution but sediment, whipped up by strong tides in what, during my stay, was a blustery coastline. We headed inland up Calle 21 de Setiembre by a park with exercise machines, away from the spray of waves crashing in rainbows on the promenade of pink stone. Punta Carretas, Montevideo's southernmost district, seemed largely residential, with a sprinkling of shops and restaurants. Armon Suites was a mere entrance between other buildings.

My large, uncarpeted room, with plain décor, had a bar at one end and a view of buildings the other. I dropped my bags, bought a Uruguayan soccer shirt in honor of a childhood fascination that grew out of 1970 World Cup cards, and jumped on a 116 bus to Ciudad Vieja.

Little was as I'd envisaged. The passengers huddled against the wind. Sporting a Uruguayan flag on the dashboard, the curtained bus piped a succession of Sinatra songs. We trundled toward the Old Town listening to "Come Fly with Me" and "It Was a Very Good Year." The bus turned north to the Boulevard España, west along Maldonado, and north on Rio Branco. As we headed west again on 25 de Mayo, the buildings became more colorful and ornate. Curling porticoes and insets accentuated the chiaroscuro of the morning sunshine. Down a side street by the Port Market a redbrick tower, sharp in light and shadow, withstood the choppy waters. I left the bus and turned along the wave-lashed Rambla, before heading back inland through half-deserted streets. This was low season. I was seeing the real, sparsely populated Uruguay. A million people live in Montevideo and something over three million in the country as a whole. Its northern border is with Brazil, and across the River Plate is its other giant neighbor, Argentina. It's a half-forgotten land—practically unknown to most of the world were it not for soccer or rugby.

That afternoon I lunched in Las Misiones. This green-tiled corner restaurant dating back to 1907 had a fifties décor. Against flowery wallpaper, a grandfather clock stood next to a chunky cash register. I ordered pasta and Zillertal beer and wrote about the chocolate waters the color birds should be, the green and blue monk parakeets the color the sea should be, and the cerulean sky offsetting the blue-, white-, and-yellow Uruguayan flags. I wrote about the curtained buses and the Sinatra tunes; the smell of marijuana and maté, a mashed herb that Uruguayans suck from pipes attached to flasks; the fact that no parent seemed to have a baby carrier; that one or other carried the infant in their arms, just as they did in Buenos Aires; that perhaps this did something for their relationship with their children. Finally, over coffee, I wrote about the cheerful waitress and how pleasant it might have been, in youth, to have settled down to raise little Uruguayans and forget forever the far-off land where I grew up. I paid the bill at the clunking register and said I'd return. I didn't, any more than I'm likely to return to Uruguay, but I prefer to give the impression that I will.

The next morning I set off through wintry sunshine on a run of discovery. Following first the bus route up 21 Setiembre, I turned into Parque Rodo to get to Rambla Wilson and, fingers already numb, ran past the city's windswept beaches, their sand drifting over graffitied walls. Brown waves flung driftwood ashore. I ran against the biting wind a hundred wooden posts to Ciudadela, passing a coppery green bust of a Catholic priest with globular blank eyes, a graffiti head of Luis Suárez, and a sign reading Uruguay Es Tu Patrimonio. Beyond that boys were playing soccer on a dusty pitch. Perhaps, I mused, a young Suárez played here when his family moved to Montevideo. Beyond the pitch stood a bust of Almirante Guillermo Brown. ARMADA ARGENTINA, stated the plaque. 1777–1857. HEROE DE LA INDEPENDENCIA Y DE LA CONFRATERNIDAD RIOPLATENSE. Brown had quite the buccaneering life in the American, British, and Argentine navies. Irish-born, he moved to the States, got press-ganged into the British navy, and eventually became a merchant in Montevideo. There's a statue of him in Dublin, and he's buried in La Recoleta cemetery in Buenos Aires.

Inland toward Plaza Independencia, I stooped to select a red rock as a souvenir. In Libreria Puro Verso an assistant helped me choose Uruguayan music (Alfredo Zitarrosa and Ruben Rada) and suggested I seek translations of the novels of Claudia Amengual. Outside again, the streets were deserted. Pedestrian walkways sloped to tree-lined avenues of speckled sunlight. A man sporting a fedora under a handwritten "Gardel Vive!" sign was singing "Mi Buenos Aires Querido." At the end of side streets the nut-brown Plate frothed wind-driven wave caps. Above the palm-fringed plaza, the Palacio Salvo soared skyward like a thumb bandaged in concrete. Beneath the square two guards stood silhouetted by light amid gloom at the grave of an unknown soldier. La cuestión es sólo entre la libertad y el despotismo, read José Artigas's words. The question is between freedom and despotism. By the steps, three flags flapped in the sun, one bearing the phrase, Libertad ou Muerte. Surfacing from death and heroism, I ate at a restaurant named Jacinto on Sarandi, and drank a bottle of Garzón Sauvignon Blanc.

On the way back to the hotel, I hopped off the Esquina Berro bus at Avenida Tomás Giribaldi for the Museo Nacional de Artes Visuales and spent time with the paintings of nineteenth-century realist Juan Manuel Blanes. *Un Episodio de la fiebre amarilla en Buenos Aires* depicts men in a doorway observing a toddler trying to attract the attention of a mother who has succumbed to yellow fever. Next to it was the equally grim *La Paraguaya*, showing the aftermath of a battle in La Guerra de la Triple Alianza of 1864–70, when Brazil, Argentina, and Uruguay clubbed together to destroy half the Paraguayan population. A barefooted girl looks at the dusty ground. Follow her gaze and you see a rifle, a tattered book, and the outline of a half-buried face covered by a Paraguayan flag. Next to this loomed a portrait of formidable society woman Doña Carlota Ferreira, the twice-widowed, scandalous, one-time wife of a Uruguayan finance minister. But I soon came across the Uruguayans' own obsession with the national soccer team, including Carmelo de Arzadun's colorful *Partido de fútbol*, and images of the Uruguayan team in their sky-blue shirts and black shorts.

Feeling I should be making the most of my time, I walked into a packed neighborhood bar, Vasca, run by a father and his sons as a sideshow to their regular jobs. Uruguay had a match against Venezuela. They lost but the atmosphere was rowdy and friendly. I was a stranger welcomed in from the night, with all the tapas explained to me while I sat at a little table to write about my day.

"How did you end up here?" asked the dapper, pepper-haired father. "Searching for something? You are very welcome. You must return."

Giving a talk the next day at the University of Montevideo, I learned of a match at the Estadio Centenario. My route there on the Sunday started at the crowded market, a contrast to the traffic-free side streets, where my only sightings were of teenagers smoking on a corner and men burning logs to create an impromptu asado. Amid the carnivalesque atmosphere, someone—man or woman—stood in a doorway wearing a white mask and a hand-painted, multicolored raincoat. Bright scarves hung in sunlight against the shadowy windows of Colonial-style buildings. The stalls sold everything from puppies and baby hedgehogs to recycled goods. ("Recycling," a shopkeeper told me, "is very Uruguayan.") Again the smell of marijuana and maté perfumed the air. At the Port Market asado smoke decorated the sky. Couples tangoed on the cobbles to "La Cumparsita." Venturing down the churning alleys I sat at a bar between groups of friends, ordered steak and rioja, and watched mountains of meat sizzle on sloping grills.

After a second glass I set off down deserted streets toward the stadium, passing Espacio de Arte Contemporáneo, an art gallery in a former prison on Arenal Grande. Peñarol fans in black and yellow began to appear. Nearer still the sound of drums, then shouts, then a roar, then flares. Silhouettes of fans populated the upper edges of the open-air stands. I entered the venerable stadium, the only FIFA-designated historical monument, venue of the very first World Cup Final back in 1930. Armed with chorizo and beer, I wandered down to the front section of the unassigned seats.

By three, the stadium buzzed with yellow and black. Running up like gladiators from underground, the players appeared to a cacophony. This being the Southern Hemisphere, the sun arced right to left. The Peñarol fans rocked the stadium to a constant beat. Yellow flares burst in the evening air. Brightening floodlights dispersed the gloom. Despite their opponents being the minnows from Colonia del Sacramento, Peñarol went a goal behind. But by nightfall they'd become champions. Apparently they're always champions, they or Nacional. But I was there to witness the celebrations, all the more raucous, I suspect, because there's not a lot else to do in Montevideo in June, if ever.

Trudging the dark streets back toward Armon Suites, I detoured to Vasca for one more night of comradery with my new Uruguayan friends. It was shuttered, almost as if it had never been open. I left early the next morning for the gleaming, virtually empty Carrasco Airport and ate a solitary breakfast reflecting on my visit to this hitherto unimaginable land. Listening now to the music of Zitarrosa, Rada, and of course Carlos Gardel, I recall the sound of drums and sight of tango on the cobbled streets, made the more romantic by the asado haze and the Uruguayan flag flapping in the wind of a Montevideo winter's day. And I recall a street-corner exchange with a callus-fingered man named Dionisio, one of whose carved and painted lizards now hangs in the apartment.

"My lizards don't bite," said Dionisio, "but Uruguay might."

Bitten I was. You are very welcome, the Vasca father had said. You must return. And welcome I had felt, even on the other side of the Earth. I caught my Alas Uruguay plane back via Rio to Britain thinking, airborne over the Southern Hemisphere, of how I was as far away as I'd ever been from home, yet homesick, once again, for a place I'd visited as in a dream.

3 CORPS

Striding the stage in his officer's uniform, with shiny leather belt, gloves, boots, and medals, Brick Minor, known in the corps as Major Brick Minor, is addressing the assembled boys in Great Hall. He's one of those square-shaped people built to play in rugby scrums: neck as thick as his lantern-jawed head.

"Grimpton Royal Army Cadet Corps is world-beating," he shouts. "You have to sign up for a Wednesday activity anyway, be it community service, cadet corps, navy, or Duke of Edinburgh Award." He juts his already-jutting jaw and scans the audience with one eye wider than the other (too much rifle-aiming, the boy assumes). "Thus make it GRACC! Sign up, young men. Wear crisp uniforms! Canoe! Shoot! Drill!"

What the hell, thinks the boy. I'd better learn to fire a rifle before I get shot.

He ought to have known. A few pacifists sign up for community service, a few royalists for the DofE, and Creupe for the navy. Everyone else opts for the army. But this won't do. Grimpton College, after all, looks out over Grimpton-on-Sea.

"In recent years," says Brick Minor, "we've had rather less than a river of recruitment into the navy. We need to level up the forces a bit. I have therefore entered into negotiations with the head of the Grimpton Royal Naval Cadet Corps, Lieutenant Commander Butter, to press-gang the top six boys in the alphabet to set sail with Creupe."

While the majority march off in smart green berets, shoulder-padded sweaters, and shiny boots, the boy is ordered, along with Andrex, Balser-Smurt, Creupe, Cutlas, and Dripper, to a dusty shed to meet a hamster-faced sixth-former whose fingernails are bitten to the quick.

"Welcome to Royal Naval Command and Control Headquarters, RNCCH," he says. "Lieutenant Commander Butter of GRNCC. Great to have you, mateys.

I've been here alone for three years. Thank God they've decided to build us up! Who likes sailing?"

"I do," says Creupe.

"Only thing we have to source is a boat."

"We don't have one?" says Dripper.

Dripper is in a different house. The boy has never seen him before. His hair shines with grease and his dusty, black-rimmed spectacles seem smeared with gravy.

"Not as such," replies Butter.

"Could we build one?" says Creupe.

"First things first," says Butter. "Uniforms." He points to a pile of pale-blue shirts, and dark-blue trousers, sweaters, and berets. "First task. Kit yourselves up."

There are just enough to go round. The boy ends up with a thick sweater with arms that reach his elbows. The trousers—flared top to bottom—only reach his shins. The shirt engulfs him. Shape long lost, the beret lies on his head like a burned pancake.

"Right," says Butter, pointing to an ironing board. "Second task. Ironing."

"What are we ironing?"

"Trousers, matey."

At this point Butter, who appears to have gone insane from so long alone, removes his trousers and lays them out. But before ironing, he rolls them into a sausage and irons in horizontal creases as they unfold. He then holds them up to reveal seven down each leg.

"That's just stupid."

"I beg your pardon, matey?"

"Splendid," says the boy.

The press-ganged recruits line up to humor Butter's insanity. The boy is third. Like the others, he does as told and puts them on. At least they're now warm. But he feels idiotic. The creases shorten and widen the trousers still further.

"One for each of the seven seas!" cries Creupe in delight. "Can I iron my beret, Lieutenant Commander?"

Since the Grimpton navy doesn't have a boat, after ironing trousers and polishing boots, the third task, every Wednesday, is to march to the chant of IPM, Iron-Polish-March. They march down and up the drive. After that they march to the far side of the chapel and, there being no way completely round, march back. Meanwhile the wind whistles up the boy's horizontally creased trousers and threatens to blow off his beret.

"Duke of Edinburgh?" he mutters. "More like Duke of York."

"What?" shouts Butter against the sea gale.

"Nice *walk!*"

"It's a march, matey!"

After three weeks Butter promotes himself to Commodore, Creupe to Lieutenant, and labels the rest Midshipmen. "Moreover," he says. "The Grimpton navy has acquired a boat. Lieutenant Creupe will explain."

"Commodore Butter has persuaded Major Brick Minor to donate us a surplus GRACC rowboat," warbles Creupe. "Three cheers, mateys, for our commanding officer's initiative!"

"Well done, Butter," says Dripper.

"Commodore!" Creupe reminds him.

Butter and Creupe have the Midshipmen drag it up the gravel to RNCCH to construct a makeshift mast and, in the only navy episode the boy enjoys, paint everything gray with black trim. Noting the boy's unexpected enthusiasm, Butter orders him to paint its name on the side: *Ark Royal II*.

Before launching it on Her Majesty's Oceans (the muddy estuary at the bottom of the drive), Butter needs to know that all the Midshipmen can sail. He therefore instigates a course in tying knots. Supplementing the IPM pattern, this lasts until February.

Finally, just before the Easter Break, launch day arrives. They borrow an army trailer and, with Butter and Creupe marching ahead, wheel *Ark Royal II* down to the estuary. The minute they clamber in, water pours onto their polished boots and bubbles up their ankles to their ironed trousers. *Ark Royal II* almost sinks from sight.

"Abandon ship!" cries Butter.

While they wade ashore, the army canoes skim past toward the gleaming sea.

"Where's the boat?" shouts Brick Minor.

"She's a ship!" cries Butter, tears streaking his mud-caked cheeks. "*Ark Royal II!*"

But the canoes have already cut a line into the distance, silhouetted on water glittering in the late-afternoon sun.

Soon after that the boy jumps ship—or boat, or the 1PM routine, since the navy no longer has a boat—and joins community service. It happens during one of the few joint exercises with the army. Butter announces that Mr. Pedrik, a Music teacher who is also the boy's personal tutor and piano teacher, is to speak with them about a joint exercise and, for that weekend only, must be addressed as Admiral Pedrik.

Admiral Pedrik, known to the Grimpton-on-Sea Rotary Club as Alfred Pedrik, and to the boys as Alf Pint, is a little round-faced man with a red nose that sticks straight out of his red face and bulges at its tip. Like everyone else, he can't stop looking at it. Tutorials take place in his tower room—known as the turret—while piano lessons take place in a cell in the music school. Alf Pint has taught the boy piano for a term. During that time, he's never got onto the left hand, never been given a tune to learn, and spent hours alone in the cell playing scales while next door a Chinese boy, Winston Wong, plays Chopin and Debussy. In an attempt at self-motivation, the boy places a KitKat on top of the piano to save it until he can play scales. In the end he gives up and eats it while listening to Wong.

When he eventually summons up courage to climb Alf Pint's turret to tell him he no longer wishes to learn piano, he finds him on the rug with a boy named Hinckley.

"Do join us," says Alf Pint. "Hinckley Major and I were just—just wrestling."

In the boy's school report, Alf Pint advises the mother and father that, while the boy has no aptitude for the piano whatsoever, he might try a wind instrument, perhaps a bassoon. In order to consider the advice, the parents take a cruise.

So, as Admiral Pedrik—or Alf Pint—stands before the press-ganged shipmates, the boy feels no respect for this latest performer in an increasingly annoying pantomime.

"Right, Sailors," he's shouting. "Here's the show."

The show, it turns out, is that the shipmates-without-a-ship are dropped on the South Downs one icy afternoon and ordered to march three miles and set up camp. That night they walk in the rain to a village pub to order beer. The boy has never drunk alcohol before but Dripper says they easily look eighteen, even if the boy's voice has yet to break. The landlord hands them three small bottles of cider and says, "Now piss off!" They drink the ciders on a bench in the rain, and trudge back to find that the army has ransacked their tent.

The next morning consists of a seven-mile run back to Grimpton. They take a shortcut, which ends up involving an extra two miles, wading through an icy river, and clambering across muddy dykes. They arrive back after dark, shivering and wet. Mr. Slammer—or Slammer, as the boys call him—puts them in detention. The boy ends up in the Sanatorium, where he catches flu from another boy who, lucky sod, is taken away to hospital.

Time to jump ship, thinks the boy. And he does.

4 COMMUNITY

Joining the community service team means having to interact with new personalities. Its leaders are Father Honey and Father Styke, the high church clerics who teach Divinity and preside over all things Anglican at Grimpton. Physically similar, Fathers Honey and Styke are temperamentally opposite. Both have shaped beards and short legs. Years later, the boy will think of them every time he passes Cézanne's portrait of Achille Empéraire in the Musée d'Orsay, but Achille's benevolent expression is Father Honey's, not Father Styke's. Both stroll through the cloisters, hands clasped behind dandruff-speckled cassocks. Both have bushy eyebrows and sallow cheeks. Both smell stale from Mondays and bathe on Saturdays, although this leaves Father Honey smelling soapy and Father Styke sulfurous. Both have washed-out wives and numerous children. But while Father Honey oozes passivity, Father Styke spits fire and brimstone. Nice Cleric and Nasty Cleric, one invites you to heaven, the other bullies you to hell. Facial expressions and a periodic difference in smell aside, the other physical clues to their opposing natures are their spectacles; Father Honey's halo-shaped frames are mild yellow. Father Styke's are gore-red and curved like horns.

Grimpton has two identical minibuses with the school crest on the side. Father Honey drives one and Father Styke the other. Father Honey's bus seems to shake with joy and laughter. The occupants of Father Styke's bus, to which the boy is assigned, sit silent and morose in an icy, stale interior, except for a little Chinese boy who simply smiles. Chichester Wong is the younger brother of Winston, whose intimidating virtuosity ended the boy's interest in learning the piano and revived his interest in KitKats.

Every Wednesday the boy travels to town with his fellow would-be saints to find old people to help. This is not difficult. Grimpton-on-Sea is full of them. They live in bungalows on streets with names like Sea View Road and Horizon

Lane, though sea views and horizons have long since vanished behind new houses for more arrivals. Still, few of them seem to stay long. Every Wednesday Father Styke hunches at the minibus wheel grumbling into his beard as they crawl behind a hearse driven slowly to the crematorium. Once they get past "another goddamned coffin," as Father Styke puts it, he pulls up at the curb and ushers the boys out to knock on doors and ask the occupants if they need help that afternoon.

"The coffin dodgers may say no but they must be helped," shouts Father Styke against the usual gale. "If any of you return without your Job List signed, you work double time next week. Now get the hell on with helping people!"

Chichester Wong partners the boy. Wong is so short that had he been in the navy he'd have drowned, but smiling.

"Why do you do community service?" the boy asks.

Wong smiles. Soon enough the boy realizes that Wong rarely speaks. But when he does his words seem to carry the weight of the world.

"In the end only three things matter," says Wong, leaning into the wind to avoid being blown over a garden wall. "How much you loved, how gently you lived, and how gracefully you let go of things not meant for you."

They knock on a door. A wizened man peeks out. He has a bluish face and lips, one visible tooth, and almost no hair. The house smells of cigarettes and boiled sprouts.

"We're from Grimpton College," says the boy. "Would you like help this afternoon?"

"No."

"I'm afraid we must insist."

The man looks at him dolefully. "Doreen!" he calls. "Anything we need doing?"

A lady in a dressing gown appears. "Ask if they have a mowing machine, Wilf." Her voice is raspy and she coughs after speaking. Her lipstick is a different shape to her lips.

"Do you have a mowing machine?"

"No," says the boy.

"What about that push mower, Wilf?"

"It's rusty." Wilf seems to chew his tooth. "The grass is long."

Doreen coughs. "You can't use it yourself on account of your heart."

"We'll give it a go," says the boy, "won't we, Wong?"

Wong smiles.

The old man puts out a huge bluish hand ribboned with veins. The boy shakes it. It's cold, clammy, and ridged on the palm.

"Wilf Maw," says Wilf. He hobbles round to the back of the house, ushering them along as if on reconnaissance. He's wearing a thin cardigan against the biting wind. "There you are." He points over the garden gate with quivering fingers.

Wong stands on tiptoe to peer over the gate. "Long grass."

Wilf opens the gate.

"This is indeed long," says the boy.

"Grass makes me feel safer," says Wilf. "Love grass, hate mud."

Wilf and the boy head for a green shed. Wong is nowhere in sight but the boy hears a muffled voice saying, "Very long grass."

The rusty push mower is in a cobwebbed corner, behind ancient-looking shovels, pickaxes, hammers, and giant clippers.

"What are those for?" the boy asks.

"Cutting barbed wire," says Wilf.

Two hours later Wilf's wilderness has been ripped to shreds. The wind has given way to rain, quickly forming muddy puddles. Wong piles up the cuttings. The boy flattens the worst of the mud clumps. The only plants left standing are a few white flowers at the far end.

Out hobbles Wilf with an umbrella. "Come in from the rain for a cuppa, boys."

The boy and Wong sit in the dark room by the gas fire drinking tea. Their jackets and trousers steam. Wong studies the net curtains as if he's never seen such things before, which maybe he hasn't. The boy is more interested in the cockatoo in a cage above Wilf's head. Wilf rolls a cigarette and lights up. The cockatoo makes coughing noises that echo Doreen. She sinks into an armchair, picks up a lit cigarette from an ashtray, taps it, and draws.

"For me multicular cirrhosis," she coughs, smoke weaving up against the net curtains.

The boy finds this phrase rather beautiful. He thinks maybe she's talking about the white flowers but he's not sure what that has to do with smoking.

Suddenly Wong speaks, very quietly. "How do you spell that?" he asks.

"S-i-r-o-s-i-s"

"What you have is multiple sclerosis. S-c-l-e-r-o-s-i-s. Cirrhosis is liver disease."

"Hark, who's the clever one?" says Doreen.

"I hate all liver," said the boy. "It tastes like cooked boots, like the one Charlie Chaplin cooks for that big man in *The Gold Rush*."

The rain drums the window behind the net curtains.

"Father is a Harley Street doctor," says Wong. "He teaches me things."

"About Charlie Chaplin?" asks the boy.

"About disease," says Wong, "and about being kind."

"Ever been to France?" asks Wilf.

Doreen coughs, followed by the cockatoo.

The boy waits for Wong to answer, but Wong has lapsed back into smiling silence.

"It rains there, too," says Wilf.

"Not always," says Doreen.

"Always," says Wilf. "That's how I got trench foot."

The boy sips his tea. It must have about five sugars in it. The cup is lipsticky.

"Look," says Wilf. He puts his cigarette in the ashtray and holds his quivering hand under the light. It has a scar from the base of his little finger to the base of his thumb. "Got this fighting the Boche, in France, in the rain."

"The boys don't want to hear your old war stories, Wilf."

"We do," says Wong. The boy nods. He wants to hear about the hand, anyway.

"In 1918," says Wilf, "I was in the trenches. Mud everywhere, and lice, worms, corpses. We all had trench foot. We called it the Trench of Stench. The rain formed ponds in the shell holes. Some trenches flowed like rivers. You didn't know what you were treading in. Drop a knife or something and stoop to retrieve it, more likely you'd fish up a drowned rat or the remains of a face. You ever had wet feet?"

"Yes," says the boy. Wong smiles.

"They never got dry. They went soggy and fungus-covered, full of white holes, sort of died on you. Our soles resembled the top of crumpets."

"Oh Wilf!" says Doreen. "The boys came in for a nice cup of tea. They don't want to know about your feet." She coughs, as does the cockatoo. "Mind you, I might have some crumpets at the back of the cupboard."

"No, thank you," say the boys.

"Anyway, there I am in the rain with me dead feet when all of a sudden this great chunk of metal—"

"Shrapnel?" asks the boy.

"Good lad," says Wilf. "The shrapnel slices through this hand. I've never had such pain. Blood everywhere, mixing in mud. Someone's screaming in me ear."

"An officer?"

"In the Trench of Stench?" Wilf's eyes glint. "He was in a cozy one farther back, with a proper roof and a nice cup of tea like you're drinking there. No, it was me, Wilf Maw, screaming in me own ear! What they did is they strapped it up with a chunk of wood, like that." He slaps his gnarly hands together and holds them up, unquivering. "Wound string and tape round it, and off I went to the field hospital. That chunk of wood saved me hand."

The boy and Wong peer at the scar. The hand is a bit misaligned.

"It's like a dark lightning bolt," says the boy.

"Poor you," says Wong.

Wilf chortles. "Better than shrapnel ripping your face open! That was the end for me so far as the Front was concerned. Most of me chums weren't so lucky." He leans for his cigarette. The smoke curls up and the cockatoo coughs. Doreen returns with more tea, squats so her mottled thighs show, then coughs the same way as the cockatoo.

"You want to see some medals?" says Wilf.

"Cor, yeah!" says the boy.

Wong smiles.

Wilf hobbles to the sideboard, crammed with framed photographs standing on a white cloth, and returns with a row of four medals. They're the size of a new penny, each with their own ribbon, a blue-and-yellow one, a rainbow one, a green-and-yellow one and a green one.

"Who's that on the front of those three?" says the boy.

"King George V."

The other one has an angel on one side and on the other "The Great War for Civilization, 1914–1919."

"Didn't it end in 1918?" asks the boy.

"Only in the history books," says Wilf.

"Would you go to war now?"

"Hips aren't up to it. In youth it's Hip hip Hooray! At my age it's Hip hip X-Ray."

"I mean, if you were young?"

"Not if I could help it." Wilf's eyes are rheumy, ears large, head quivering. His lips have a bit of tobacco on. "But we was chums together, the Old Contemptibles, members of the regular army, the British Expeditionary Force in it from the beginning." Wilf pauses, the windows reflect in his eyes. "I've got something for you for mowing the grass, even if you've made it look like No-Man's-Land." He stands again, wavers, then hobbles to the sideboard and back. "There's sixpence in it for you."

Sixpence? The boy's heard of sixpences from the film, *Half a Sixpence*, about a boy and girl who cut one in half. Years later they meet and still have the halves. The boy is now rich. The girl is a serving maid. After a lot of singing and dancing they get married.

"How can we have one sixpence between us?" Wong hasn't seen *Half a Sixpence*.

"I'll see if I've another." Wilf hobbles back to the sideboard.

"You don't have to give us sixpence," says the boy.

"A promise is a promise," says Wilf. "But this is all I have." He hobbles to Wong and gives him what might be a sixpence.

"This is not a sixpence, sir," says Wong.

"It's a silver threepence, lad."

Wong passes it to the boy.

"Cor!" says the boy. "These are worth money!"

"They are money," says Doreen. The cockatoo coughs as if on her behalf.

"You can keep them," says Wilf.

"You want the sixpence or the threepence?" says the boy.

Wong shrugs. "You choose."

The boy gives Wong the sixpence. He has the silver threepence to this day.

They bid Wilf, Doreen, and the coughing cockatoo farewell.

"Come back next year," says Wilf. "It'll be grass-cutting time again."

"You know, Wong," says the boy on the way back to the minibus in the rain. "Maybe community service was worth doing after all."

Wong smiles.

5 SAN FRANCISCO

It's April in Paris but we've been in lockdown since March. My flâneuring has come to a brutal halt. "Ah! To wander in Paris! Adorable and delectable existence," wrote Balzac. And personally, I've enjoyed doing so all the more in rain, when wet pavements repeat the cityscape at every turn. It didn't do to ponder that a cluster of COVID cases in Codogno, southeast of Milan, had led Italy to lock down ten Lombardy towns from late February. Life in Paris continued as normal until the evening of 16 March, when President Macron announced that France would lock down for at least two weeks. What we knew of in January as a virus causing deaths in Wuhan, then as an Italian calamity, is now a global pandemic.

Wedded to nationalism in the wake of Brexit, the British government remained insouciant. It considered this a foreign business. Boris Johnson, once a boy at a school not far from Thornditch, features prominently in Richard Beard's critique of the class system, *Sad Little Men: Private Schools and the Ruin of England*. Educated, as George Orwell notes, "in a flashy, unsound way" to be superficially impressive, a certain type of ex-boarder remains unburdened by deeper thoughts or weightier interests, least of all scientific. No surprise, then, that Johnson ignored medical experts, shook hands with COVID patients, and said the British should "take it on the chin." He's now been in intensive care. Cases are surging in Russia. Donald Trump intends to stop funding the World Health Organization and wonders at the possibility of injecting people with bleach. The global economy is contracting. Flights are grounded. Our apartment is only a kind of prison if we think of it as such. We're allowed one walk a day and everything is shut, including, of course, the Louvre.

Anticipating the day we'll reach the other side, I'm pondering bridges. Paris wasn't a popular subject until Impressionism. Hubert Robert's *Demolition of the Houses on the Pont Notre-Dame* (1786) is one of few paintings of its bridges in the Louvre. Even that will return to the Carnavalet when the history of Paris museum reopens after renovation. Most have been rebuilt, replaced, renamed over time. Robert's painting depicts the fourth of the five Notre-Dame bridges. Pont des Saints-Pères, where doomed painter Claude Lantier contemplates Île de la Cité in Zola's *The Masterpiece,* was replaced by Pont du Carrousel. Pont Neuf is theoretically Paris's oldest, but nothing from the sixteenth-century original remains. It cuts through the western end of Île de la Cité by Square du Vert-Galant (described by Zola as "like the prow of a vessel eternally at anchor, straining toward Paris without ever reaching it"). A bridge in this vicinity first connected the mainland with the ancient city of Lutetia.

Even as I summon up these bridges I recall a personal favorite thousands of miles west. My attachment to the Golden Gate Bridge began when an uncle who lived in San Francisco in the sixties fired my restlessness by flipping me a Kennedy half-dollar. I'd visit several times from the eighties onward, latterly for conferences or to talk at the Steinbeck Festival in Salinas. Nicki joined me for one trip, as did Ani and then Tasha. But on Sunday 28 May 2006, I was alone. Arriving the evening before, I took advantage of dawn-to-dusk sunshine to walk to, across, and back from the bridge. That same day Barry Bonds passed Babe Ruth's home run tally on his way toward Hank Aaron's record. He wasn't initially linked to my odyssey but muscled in with the clack of a bat, and the arc of a ball against sky. I hadn't planned for it to coincide with Memorial Day Weekend, either, or the hundredth anniversary year of the earthquake, but serendipity became the wind in my sails.

I left Room 847 of the Hyatt-Regency in Embarcadero Center at 5:00 a.m. My plan was simple: a twelve-mile roundtrip, ending the day with a cocktail in the Equinox, the Hyatt's revolving restaurant. With my window framing the distorted reflection of the Bay Bridge in the building opposite, I stuffed the complementary *Chronicle* into my bag and closed the door. Muzak drifted up from eight floors below. A tiny figure clicked across the lobby. I took the elevator down, headed out to the Justin Herman Plaza, crossed the tram tracks to the Ferry Building, and turned left, away from the Bay Bridge and baseball park toward Fisherman's Wharf. Until 1991 the Embarcadero had a raised freeway but now the tracks and palms curved flat into the distance. Seagull squeals intermingled with the sound of water lapping the piers. Puddles glittered from overnight rain. Aware of an occasional jogger, cyclist, or roller skater, I walked the expanse of concrete, noting occasional odd pier numbers, the even ones being south of the Ferry Building toward the China Basin.

A cruise ship gleamed at Pier 35. I continued past the Aquarium and California Welcome Center. At the shopping area of Pier 39 I reached a mishmash of tram tracks, the narrower streets of Fisherman's Wharf, and the ferry terminals for Alcatraz, Sausalito, and Oakland. Alioto's hummed with pungent whiffs of Sicilian dishes in preparation. Yachts bobbed in the dock. The World Famous Bushman would be out soon to startle passersby from behind his leafy branches, a line of work he—or they, back then there were two, David Johnson and Gregory Jacobs—had done for a quarter of a century.

By 7:25 I was imbibing the coastal frowziness near the Cannery. Castagnola's was receiving its consignment of fresh bread. At Del Monte Square, the Mermaid Chowder House still had its doors shut. The bridge came into hazy view. The square's languorous shabbiness and paint-peeled doorways doubled in the puddles. Briefly, diesel fumes smothered the smells of bread and seaweed. An old Chinese man smoked a cigarette beneath a red hand sign telling him not to cross to the quayside. He crossed anyway.

Shortly after 7:30, I reached the cable car station and the steps to the Maritime Museum. Waves foamed against the Aquatic Park Beach. Up the tree-lined hill, I looked down on Fort Mason and across to Alcatraz. I'd been on the prison island some years before. I remember the spray, the bobbing ferry, the murder stories the forest ranger told, the sense of oppression, the rust and decay. Boarding school experience made it easy to imagine being a prisoner there, glimpsing freedom through the wire meshing of the exercise yard, even if the windowless cells look inward on each other. No window for Al Capone.

I descended past SS *Jeremiah O'Brien* and reached the Fort Mason Pier, where one and a half million troops embarked for the Korean War. A Chinese lady was doing Tai Chi in the park. The bridge shimmered against the cloudless sky. I followed the pathway down, bought provisions in the Safeway, and headed across the National Recreation Area to Marina Boulevard. With the expanse of Marina Green to my right, I passed a plaque commemorating the 1920 landing of the first transcontinental airmail plane. All was grassland, nice houses, windows overlooking the sail-dotted sea.

An Asian girl ran past in boxing gloves. Looking back to my right, beyond the yachting marina, Alcatraz stood faint against the far shore. By the harbor office I crossed Cervantes Street. A line of firs partly obscured the bridge. I took Mason Street through the edge of the Presidio to Crissy Field, and sat on a beach wall to eat. The bridge reflected in the water between the sand and sky. Solitary as the sharp-lit poppy I spotted on a dune in front of the blurry, distant bridge, I listened to passing conversations.

A man jogged toward the bridge talking into his cell phone. It pays well, he said, but is it your dream thing? Hey, guess what? said one of three girls heading toward the city, Adriana paid for everything. We didn't have to take out even a dollar. Two women jogged toward the bridge. One said, It was a collective decision to consolidate. The other replied, It was the wrong decision.

For a break from the sun, I detoured along Fort Point to where James Stewart jumps in to save Kim Novak in *Vertigo*, then doubled back through greenery to the start of the bridge. A blushing god above the foliage, it seemed too bright and real. But while officially International Orange, up close there's nothing orange about it. The longer ago a section has been painted, the more it's bleached gammon pink by sunshine. It can look orange from a distance but, color being the effect of light, sometimes the bridge can seem dark. In *Vertigo* it's sepia red. That the 49ers play in red but the Giants in orange amplifies the uncertainty. One might argue that International Orange is orange-red, but orange the bridge is not.

Noisy, though, it was. With vehicles accelerating from the tollbooth, I began my mile and a half walk along the vibrating bridge hemmed in on one side by traffic and on the other by wire netting. It was shortly after 9:00, time for rush hour but early for bridge walkers. I was briefly the lone stroller. I passed a lady in spattered overalls standing in one of the cartons that go up and down on pulleys. It was full of empty soda bottles.

"Excuse me, ma'am," I said. "What color is the paint?"

"International Orange."

"Does it look orange to you?"

"Only in the fall."

Cyclists passed. Approaching the first stanchion, I became aware of a woman in jeans and T-shirt. Moments before I'd glanced back and seen no one. The traffic noise would have drowned any sound of footsteps, but she passed silently. I thought of the numerous suicides from the bridge since Harold Wobber's in 1937. Though her amble belied speed, soon she dissolved into a passing mist that seemed to spring from nowhere and clear as fast.

Not long after the first alcove, I came across signs for the desperate. A blue metal square bellowed: EMERGENCY PHONE AND CRISIS COUNSELING. Below it was another blue square, fitting neatly into the girder. THERE IS HOPE, it urged. MAKE THE CALL. In smaller capitals on a yellow box beneath the emergency phone, suggesting perhaps that you were being drawn nearer, so could be spoken to rather than shouted at, it said: THE CONSEQUENCES OF JUMPING FROM THIS BRIDGE ARE FATAL AND TRAGIC.

In 2006 the suicides numbered 1,200 over seventy years, so about one a month. Ten million visit the bridge every year, and about forty jump, though evidently numbers have decreased since the construction of the Suicide Deterrent Net.

Midbridge, I leaned on the railing and looked back at the city to the right of the bay, Alcatraz in the middle and Sausalito to the left. The first bridge walker I spoke to appeared at my elbow and remarked on the view. Freja Sørensen, from Denmark, was studying American history in Milwaukee. Bespectacled, with well-defined eyebrows, she repeatedly curled her hair over her ear against the breeze.

"Imagine imprisonment on Alcatraz," she said. "I'm a goal setter. I'd plan an escape."

And off she went. Goal setting shapes lives. Where does time go if not into something achieved? Like John Steinbeck in *Travels with Charley,* I admire specialists. Experts tend to like their lives. Even as I write this, I think of Joseph Strauss, whose stress in building the bridge led to a fatal heart attack in 1938. F. Scott Fitzgerald wrote that you should write a book as if you'd die the day you finish it. Well, since we do die, and nothing remains of the individual, what have you created or contributed? Why was your life worth living? Even if it killed him, Strauss, like many creators of all kinds, left something solid.

By 10:00 the second stanchion loomed. On the nonpedestrian side a cloud drifted across the open sea and the green hills toward Muir Woods. At the second alcove I talked to a sporty Oakland lady creating a trail map, and a fireman who retired after 9/11.

"Were you involved?" I asked.

"We're all involved."

"Were you there?"

"We were all there."

"I saw it on TV."

"I swallowed the dust of my buddies."

"But you still live in New York?"

"My commitment is total."

"And what does the bridge mean to you?"

"I'm walking it to remember a friend."

At the end of the bridge a motorcycle cop in khaki uniform, a name badge (Torres), mirror shades, and leather boots aimed her hand-held traffic camera at the bridge.

"May I ask you some questions, Officer Torres?"

"Sure," she replied.

"What do you like about your job?"

"To catch people speeding."

"That's it?"

"Oh no," she replied. "Don't you think it's pretty the way the clouds drift through the bridge? I don't know how to explain. It's awesome, constantly changing. You see so many different things. I mean, look at that helicopter, swooping round and up over the bridge."

When I began my journey home, Officer Torres was posing for photos with a Mexican in an SF baseball cap. They were talking about Barry Bonds.

"Has he overtaken Babe yet?" asked Officer Torres. "Has he hit 715?"

"Not yet," said the Mexican. "If he does, you'll hear it."

I set off back along the bridge. By 2:00 it was busy with strollers, joggers, and cyclists. The wind was up. Waves decorated the azure sea. Multiple yachts tacked across the bay. At the alcove nearest Fort Point people crowded round a radio. Bonds was up to bat. Then the roar. He'd done it. The radio went dead. The ghost of Babe Ruth wasn't happy. A yelp went up over the expanse, as if even the bridge were pleased. Thinking back, I feel that we heard the roar itself, carried from the ballpark across the bay by a sudden breeze.

I had plenty more walking left even after the bridge so now kept conversations to a minimum until, in the gift shop, I handed the Vietnamese attendant two small T-shirts.

"For your children?" she asked. "No payment required. Good luck to you."

Buoyed by benevolence, I began the long walk back, asking myself what this mini-adventure had brought. One answer was sunburn. My flushed face made me part of the flushed scene. The sunset silhouetted the bridge to the sound of Lou's Blues at Pier 47. By Embarcadero my feet hummed with pain. I could barely walk, as if I'd started the day young and ended it old. But, honoring my uncle's half-dollar, I now felt part of the Bay Area, part of the bridge's story, one more of my self-constructed homes.

I'd next visit the city in 2008, with then twelve-year-old Ani. The spring morning before we traveled, I was with my father at my mother's deathbed, the windows open to chirping house martins unaware of mortality. The day after we returned, I read "Because I could not stop for Death" at her funeral. I'm aware that the bridge's uncertain color echoes that of her skirt-suit the evening we drove to Thornditch.

But back in 2006, forsaking the Equinox (a regret since it closed as a restaurant in 2007), I took a cable car up California Street to the Top of the Mark, the restaurant in the Mark Hopkins Intercontinental, to drink a martini, not to Alcatraz—too close to the bone—but to the distant bridge, to my uncle, to the city, and to the uncertainty of color. For color is never simply itself. It's always the effect of perspective, of juxtaposition, of light.

6 FOSSE

This young man does not concentrate with sufficient intensity, reads the boy's latest report. *He has to be forced from daydreams to the subject at hand. In order to mature, he must wake up.* Not so easy! Daydreams are one thing, nightmares another, and these, too, continue. One relates to the 1974 deaths of two divers who sought the source of Fosse Dionne, a deep karst spring in the French town of Tonnerre. He's in a confined space underwater. He mustn't panic. If he could get into this place, he can get out. He had to squirm to enter but it seemed larger only minutes ago. Now the ceiling seems barely to allow wiggle room. There's almost no light. He feels the sensation of weight—the oppression of half a mile of rock.

He edges back on his stomach with the walls closing in on either aside. The ceiling scrapes his head. He can turn enough to see the entrance but it seems too small to have squeezed through. It's no longer as wide as his shoulders and too deep, like a sluice hole in a medieval castle. His only way out is to pull back into a tunnel in which he's wedging ever tighter. He'll be crushed or starved of oxygen or drowned. But there's no way to turn now. The ceiling is pushing down. He gets one arm and shoulder and his head through, but his other shoulder is stuck. His face presses into the back of his hand. He's suffocating.

He wants to call for help but his hand muffles his words.

Then he knows he's in bed, but the dream is continuing. His body won't move.

Help! Help!

He's like a living corpse, hand tight against his mouth. No one can hear him.

HELP!

He's ready to explode. He strains every sinew to groan.

OOARGH!

And then, with a roar of terror, he bursts awake, from his own efforts, it seems, though even this cry seems drowned out by his own panting.

Oh my God, he thinks. I was dead and now I'm alive. Alive! Even as he thinks this, a voice comes from across the dormitory.

"You woke us again, you little git!"

"Sorry."

"You will be," says another voice.

He's too exhausted from being buried alive to worry about threats. He has this dream often and will have it long into adulthood. But he's alive! True, he's still at Grimpton with weeks before the Easter Break. But he's alive, and it's night. He's free to think. All he need do is stay awake. Or is it that he's been granted a hint of hell? Maybe hell is being crushed in a place without escape, trapped for eternity in a coffin-like space, but with a tiny window to glimpse the world of free movement. Perhaps it's to die, over and over. Yes, he's experienced hell. Buried alive to die, then to be resurrected only to be buried again.

He cools his arms above the covers. His heartbeat slows. He ponders his dissolving childhood. He'll remember this period, a year into his time at Grimpton, as the start of friendless years. He begins to withdraw. He's finding that the most rewarding relationships at this age are in his own mind. He suspects that what appear to be actual interactions with others are merely dramas in your own head. He can't see how it can be any other way. People fool themselves that meaningful relationships exist. In fact, he thinks at this age, it wouldn't be an ideal scenario, anyway, to bare your soul, even if you could. True friendship is the last thing he needs. The key is self-reliance.

His body is the problem.

He hates it.

He hates his lack of height. He's the smallest of the new men, and when the next intake arrives he receives, not the respect of smaller boys, as he'd hoped, but the mockery of a group of foul-mouthed, spotty postpubescent giants with gravel voices who, like everyone else, call him Les. His own face, too, has surrendered to acne. Spots fester on his forehead, cheeks, chin, and on the back of his neck where he can only feel them. Some are undersurface boils like pulsing volcanoes, tender as bruises. He has successive mouth ulcers, is terrified he has BO, gets greasy hair within a day, and has become shortsighted enough to need spectacles. He feels trapped in a body that's betrayed the child he once was.

Indeed, betrayal is a daily occurrence. He blushes constantly: when anyone speaks to him, at the thought of Kalina and Karine, at the thought of blushing. Then he wonders if they think he's blushing about something embarrassing so that doubles his blush to deepest red.

It's no good being different. He must try to be normal. He has years to survive in this place, so he'll fade into the background. He'll be no one, with no attributes, attitude, or affiliation. He'll escape being noticed. He'll merge, in his monochrome uniform, into the flint stone walls, into the cloister shadows, catch nobody's eye, be substanceless as empty space.

Then of course it happens. Other boys begin to notice that he never says anything and never courts attention, and that becomes his perceived abnormality.

"You're peculiar, Les," says Pink-Chunkerton one morning in the washrooms, peering into the mirror to press a paper clip against his nose and watching cross-eyed as a blackhead within the perimeter of pressure sprouts dry pus like a stalk of watercress. "You have absolutely no personality whatsoever."

From this point on the boy is regarded as an outsider. It's no joke being singled out. Hallington, a skinny boy with a blade-like nose and pebble spectacles, gets in a fight with a younger boy. Twisted into submission, Hallington rolls on the Junior Common Room floor.

"My spine!" he screams in pain. "I think I've broken my spine!"

The boy helps him up and retrieves his spectacles. Hallington isn't pleasant to look at and has sour BO. His shirt hangs out. His nose drips. His spots have yellow heads that burst spontaneously. The boys call spots "zits" so start calling him Zit. But spottiness hardly makes you abnormal so they seek another name and the fight provides it. He becomes Spine.

That's the beginning of the end. Hallington is hounded daily by cries of "Spine! Oi, Spine, you've broken your *spine!*" Whether senior or junior to him, boys prance around him in twisted postures. Hallington never regains face. He can't do or say anything that's taken seriously. His every appearance is greeted with "Spine!"

One day Hallington goes to the dormitory and lies fully clothed on his bed. He misses lunch. He misses classes. He misses evening school. At Lights Out he stays on top of the covers, staring at the ceiling, his blade-like nose silhouetted by the moon. It isn't until the next day that a prefect tells Ma Seton that

Hallington's been behaving abnormally. Ma Seton barrels into the dormitory and says, "Pull yourself together, Hallington, rise and shine." Hallington just lies on his bed in his uniform, barely blinking, staring upward. Ma Seton ushers the boys out and calls Slammer. What happens next is only rumor. The boy never sees Hallington again but others laugh about him being carried to a waiting car.

Slammer doesn't even make an announcement. It's as if Hallington never existed. Perhaps the view is that going mad is bad form, letting the side down, the wrong thing to do. But in a way, the boy thinks, Hallington was brave. He sought escape so feigned mental illness, except maybe the feigned illness became real. Meanwhile, with Hallington gone, and the Lads—as they call themselves—seeking new victims, the boy opts for opacity. He drops the portcullis and pulls up the drawbridge. People think he's in front of them, when all they're seeing is a barrier. The boy watches them from a shadowy interior. Incommunicado with home, he now isolates himself at school.

He's hardly alone in feeling alienated. Allenby hates the place from the start. But, armored with the experience of leaving home at eight, the boy knows that, unlike Hallington, who was perhaps a day boy at his prep school, or Allenby, who suddenly leaves, he'll endure. The price, however, is the carapace that grows around him, as if his very skin is thickening. His mind detaches from his body and wanders inside him like a small animal exploring the dank corridors and stairwells of an inner world.

Personal space matters hugely. In the first year, you just get a chair at a table in the Junior Common Room. In the second year, you get a horsebox seat with a shelf. In the third year, you have a curtained booth in the Senior Common Room. Finally, you get a "pit," a tiny room where you can at least shut the door. But until then there's virtually no privacy. The toilets have spy holes. Often these are stuffed with paper, but this can be pulled out. You're confronted, on the toilet, by an eye. There are only two ways the boy finds privacy. One is cross-country running. Especially in wind and rain, he sees no other soul in the fields and country lanes. The other is by staying awake at night, when he can ponder without interruption. Lying there, he thinks of Bob Dylan's "All Along the Watchtower": "'There must be some way out of here,' said the joker to the thief." Some way, indeed, and he must find it.

7 CHAPEL

Opting for community service over the corps means that Fathers Honey and Styke target the boy as potentially saved. They believe his choice signals religiosity, and that the spring he turns fifteen is the time for it to blossom. In his second Grimpton autumn, the boy began art lessons in a classroom off Great Hall not because he felt he'd learn anything from dour, trim-bearded, tweed-suited, elbow-patched Mr. Gurney but because he could sit with Anooshka Tiger-Desert, one of ten girls introduced to the school of four hundred boys. He also escorts her to the weekly Bible Group. This has further encouraged Honey and Styke.

As a result, chapel, which has always been purgatory, becomes more frequent. Boys usually have to attend three times a week. Now Honey and Styke regularly call on him for duties. They consider him a trainee "Shepherd." The brother has already been made Head Sacristan, so must now be addressed in chapel as Brother, which is weird given he actually is a brother. He wears white robes trimmed with gold. His processional duties include carrying crosses and swinging incense lanterns. The Fathers' joy at the brother's piety blinds them to the possibility that the boy might balk at following in the brother's slab-pounding steps.

Through the autumn, the boy endures not just the misery of increasing myopia but also Sunday-to-Sunday weeks from the doggedly labeled Fifteenth Sunday after Trinity up to the Twenty-Fifth. He wades past Saint Michael & All Angels and Saint Simon & Saint Jude's Day, and All Saints' Day, and the other flotsam that clutters the darkening river of autumn. The only period he enjoys through that melancholy season is Advent, because it heralds Christmas and the end of term.

Autumn finally fades along with the first half of winter. That's Christmas over for another year, says the father as usual after the presents are opened.

The decorations are packed away. Snowdrops appear, then crocuses, followed by primroses and the first shoots of daffodils in clumps along the banks of the driveway. But while the seasons change, Grimpton stays much the same, chapel even more so. The only comfort for the boy is a shift in the quality of light that even affects the chapel's interior. As Father Styke drains the communion chalice, pulpy lips stretching gustily from his beard, the sunlight brightens on his purple cassock and catches the halo of dust motes like fleas around his head.

Outside, the change feels dramatic. There's always a transition at the height of spring that the boy designates Blue Light Day. On a certain day, usually in May, a bluish sunlight entirely routs the ochres of autumn and winter. High summer sees the yellows and reds return, but on that balmy day the wintry sogginess is vanquished and, along with the smells of spring, blue light predominates.

On the boy's designated Blue Light Day this current year, Father Styke asks to see him in his rooms at the top of the tower next to Great Hall, in the far corner of Upper Quad. The boy climbs the winding stone staircase, and knocks.

"Come!" says a voice doubly muffled by door and beard.

The boy enters to a chill he's never experienced indoors before. Despite the sunshine outside, the room is freezing. A mottled mirror looms above a mantelpiece on which stands a cloudy glass containing spent matches. Two wooden chairs face each other on floorboards beneath lead-lined windows open to a breeze that must turn icy as it enters. In one of the chairs Styke is nibbling his beard from within. Dandruff smatters his cassock like frost. His trousers shine from wear. Sitting down he's an even odder shape than usual. Because his legs are short but his body is long, he sits in a distorted way, pale hands on small knees close to his belly, lace-ups barely touch the floor.

"You wanted to see me, Father Styke."

Styke's eyebrows wiggle like hairy caterpillars on his red spectacles. The boy sits on the other chair, detecting now that familiar sulfurous smell. He wonders what warped view Styke has of the world from behind his beard and spectacles.

"Young man," says Styke sulfurously.

"Yes, Father Styke."

"Do you know why I keep windows open, through weathers clement and inclement?"

"No, Father Styke."

"My body odor," he says without changing expression, "is a treachery." His caterpillar eyebrows now slumber on his spectacles. "A damned treachery of all we should hold dear about our human selves. But I have forsaken mortal vanity and will remain unwashed on weekdays until the Second Coming."

The boy is glad the windows are open. In truth, he's noticed increasingly nauseating smells in Styke's vicinity, far beyond the mere sulfur. He wonders what Mrs. Styke thinks about it. Perhaps she's taken the same vow.

"Anything else, Father Styke?" asks the boy, sure that even a chaplain won't summon a boy to his study just to confess his lack of hygiene.

"If you, too, find that you smell, contrary to Victorian Christian teaching you may find yourself closer to God. Cleanliness, young man, is not necessarily closer to Godliness."

"I'm sure you're right, Father Styke," says the boy. Bonkers, more like.

"But it leads me to the subject of our meeting. Father Honey and I have discussed you. Do you want to know what interests us?"

The boy nods, evidently the required response.

"Community service is for religious boys."

"Is Wong religious?"

"Wong," says Styke, "is Chinese. But we're not talking about Wong. Are you religious? In your heart and head?"

My heart and head, thinks the boy, are my business.

"You hesitate," probes Styke. "Can you recite the Nicene Creed?"

"The thing where everyone turns sideways in chapel and says they believe stuff?"

"How about the Te Deum?"

"The tedium? I know it has to do with chapel."

Styke gets down from his chair and paces the floorboards, beard ruffled by the breeze. He pauses, sighs, paces. His shiny lace-ups squeak as he puts down first his heel, then sole, then toe-tip. He paces to a cupboard one side of the fireplace and pulls out a book.

"I give you one week to learn three of these, of your choosing," he says, handing the boy the book. It's *Poems with a Purpose* by R. G. Turner. The boy leafs through and reads:

> Pioneer work for JESUS!—
> Above all, His LOVE,
> To comfort and sustain us,
> Till *all* shall rest, above!
>   HALLELUJAH!
>   AMEN.

He closes the book and holds it out. Styke shows no sign of accepting it back. "Why would I want to memorize these?"

"They will feed your scrawny soul."

The boy turns a few pages:

> Crucified—He hath died—I have died with Him!
> Crucified—I have died—justified from sin!
> Crucified—justified—satisfied is He!
> Crucified—satisfied—glorified, to be!

"Who was R. G. Turner?"

"Ronald Turner was a parishioner some years ago of a colleague, Reverend William Clark in Exmouth."

"He sounds mad."

"To the faithful, it's the unbelievers who are mad. Why risk eternal damnation for the sake of a little pride? The delusion of personal autonomy is poison. Behold pride and anticipate petrification!"

"Personal what?"

"Autonomy—the belief you stand alone, emotionally, intellectually, and physically."

"But I do."

Styke's eyebrows wiggle on his spectacles. "Don't try to be clever. I'll see you here next week to recite three poems. One more thing. As a Christian Gentleman, would you mind giving elderly people a chapel tour on Saturday?"

"Do I have a choice?"

"Hell no!"

"It won't work. Your religion preaches simpleminded obedience." Boy and priest eyeball one another. The boy's heart pumps red mist into his brain, like that time years ago with the Colonel. "Since I was eight I've had adults tell me to stand, sit, kneel." He hears the words as if they're floating across the breeze-blown room toward the astonished Styke.

"In attempting to inculcate your impertinent soul with High Church principles, I now conclude that you may be possessed." Styke's eyebrows wiggle madly. "Good God, young man. What next? Will you deny the reality of Monarchy? As an Anglican subject of the realm, you must show the visitors round the chapel. Saturday at three. Meanwhile, memorize the poems. Then we'll think about an exorcism."

But Styke isn't finished. He tells the boy to see him once a week for the rest of term. May passes into June, yet Styke's arctic room remains impervious to the warm wind that presages what will become known as global heating, bringing with it a burning of large swathes of the planet. Back in the seventies nobody, except perhaps Styke with his sulfurous breath, brimstone vision, and icy demeanor could imagine a world set on fire.

One June day, the boy stomps from Styke's room after another misery session. It's the start of the hot summer of 1976, a heat wave lasting nine weeks until the storms and floods of late August. It has nothing on the baking summers to come but breaks records that will last until 2017. The boy has discovered music. The Stones release "Fool to Cry." Along with the guitar riffs of Thin Lizzy's "Jailbreak" and Lynyrd Skynyrd's "Free Bird," it provides a soundtrack to the blazing summer. The Lads mock every disco track played on TV or radio. "Keep Britain white," rants Eric Clapton during a concert later in the summer. Upper Quad bakes in sunshine. Everyone stays in the shade of the cloisters. Either Styke is so Godly that heavenly cool surrounds him, or he's a cold bastard who, like a freezer with the door open, emits dry ice into warm air. Furious at Styke's ongoing attempts to bully him into religiosity, the boy crosses Upper Quad and takes the steps to Lower Quad and the gravel path by First House to change for a run. The breeze will calm him.

Nothing is going well but life is made worse by prefects led by Pink-

Chunkerton. Ever since Spine was taken away, they've targeted the boy and now await him on the path.

"Let bygones be bygones," says Pink-Chunkerton. "After all, I'm your bro's pal." The boy doesn't see how this is a plus. "My fellow prefects and I," says Pink-Chunkerton as more of the group come out from the bushes like an assassination squad, "have decided that, as an apology for past beastliness, we'd like you to accept this." He holds out a five-pound note.

Bulsterine, perm and thick tie-knot framing his spotty face, nudges Pink-Chunkerton.

"Okay, Les," said Pink-Chunkerton, "since you're smart enough to know you can't get anything for free in this world, here's the deal." The boy backs away. A big-jawed prefect known as Piltdown grabs the boy's left arm and twists it back and up in a half-Nelson. Pink-Chunkerton bends closer. His pupils are pinpricks. "We break two eggs on your head, and you get not five quid, but ten!" He pockets the five and pulls a ten. "What do you say?"

The boy sees no way out. "Give me the money first."

Pink-Chunkerton and his cronies smile. One, Squire, has a middle parting and an equally stupid tie-knot. The other has a face that makes you assume his name is Cantaloupe.

Pink-Chunkerton hands over the ten. "Do you want to remove your glasses?"

The boy folds it into the top pocket of his jacket. "Just do it."

"Egg," says Pink-Chunkerton, gesturing to Bulsterine, as if to a nurse for a scalpel.

Bulsterine holds out the two eggs. "Maybe he should take his jacket off, Chunkers. He'll get egg all over it."

Conceding that it would be better not to get egg on the jacket, the boy shrugs it off. Pink-Chunkerton takes the first egg and cracks it on the boy's head. The white and yoke slides coldly onto his scalp, over the left side of his spectacles, down into his collar.

"Second egg, Bulsters."

"Oops," smiles Bulsterine, dropping it on the gravel. "Sorry, Chunkers."

"Oh dear," says Pink-Chunkerton, gazing at the boy's hair. "I'm afraid the deal's off."

The boy grabs his jacket, pushes out under Piltdown's elbow, and runs toward the changing rooms. "I've got the money!" he shouts. Without looking back, he thrusts open the door, slams it behind him, and turns to the clothing hooks.

There stands an older boy, Muscle Milford. Milford is changing for Athletics. His parents live in New York, so he only goes home out of term. He has enormous muscles and a very small head with a tiny nose. The boy suspects that he has a muscly little brain no larger than his nose. He also habitually blows that nose into his sleeve, rolling it up a notch each time. He wears the same shirt until he's rolled both sleeves up over his gigantic biceps. Only then does he put the crusted article in the laundry.

"Hey, Les," says Milford. "Hey." This is how he talks. His conversation rarely goes further. Unfortunately, today something catches his basic focus. "What's in your hair, Les?"

"Pink-Chunkerton and his cronies broke an egg on my head for ten pounds. But I've got the money." Even as he says this, the boy feels into the top pocket. He feels in all the pockets. The money's gone.

Milford guffaws. "You're such a prick, Les."

The boy sees red. "Fuck off, Muscle, you tiny-brained twat."

Milford slams him against the wall, his clammy hand already on his throat. "Say that again and I'll thump you."

"Tiny-brained twat."

Milford's fist slams into the boy's face, smashing the left lens of his spectacles. Again, he sees red, but literally. Blood spurts over Milford's fist. Milford lets go of the boy's throat. The boy drops to the floor, sliding in his own blood, nose pulsing with pain. He doesn't remember much for a while, except Slammer leading him to Ma Seton, who gives him a cup of tea and tells him off.

"What did you do to deserve this?"

There's a rumor that the brother will avenge the boy but nothing comes of it. Even if vision isn't fully restored, the black eye eventually fades and he feels lucky the punch didn't flatten his nose. It just makes it a little crooked and stays that way for the rest of his life.

8 NAIROBI

The weather since May has been balmy sunshine. The world began to ease lockdowns in June but impatience to open up belied the dangers. France, Britain, and many other countries are back in lockdown. Millions have been infected. Hundreds of thousands have died. With bars and restaurants shut, and exercise restricted to an hour a day, I've found solace in Julian Green's *Paris*, a collection of essays mostly from the 1940s when he was absent from the city. Green explains how, not unlike Saramago with Lisbon or anybody with their past, he rebuilt Paris inside himself. "A map of Paris pinned to the wall would hold my gaze for long periods," he writes, enabling him to discover that the city is "shaped like a human brain." For many of us, now, it's largely "a Paris of visions" in which we take our walks, one that, "though intensely real," is "imperceptibly migrating from flesh to spirit."

For now, therefore, past and present must share my imagination. I'm recollecting the city I'm in even as I recover schooldays and pre-COVID travel. Accustomed since childhood to going anywhere in my head, I can imagine myself in the Louvre. Indeed, I've been contemplating the half-Nelson endured by Michelangelo's *Rebellious Slave*. Or I can fantasize savoring grenouilles at l'Absinthe, filets de harengs with pomme a l'huile in Brasserie Lipp, bouillabaisse in Le Dôme, a Chardonnay in Le Procope, or a simple noisette in Les Deux Moulins. Or I can rebuild that sunny afternoon of Friday, 13 March when, hours before closure, I took the elevator up Tour Eiffel. But I choose here to revisit another place that, thanks to Glinty's print of charging elephants, I first imagined in childhood.

In my preoccupation with education as searching and searching as education, our weeks teaching in Kenya, truly for us another land, is wholly pertinent.

It gave me greater understanding of what it means to subsist, let alone to be a child sent from home. Nicki and I flew to Nairobi near the end of the Long Rains. The Crane Academy, a rural school that provides education mostly for girls, is in Kitale, in the northern Rift Valley near Mount Elgon. We took two days to get there. Our driver, Danny Kyalo, met us in drizzle outside Jobo Kenyatta Airport and drove us along a bumpy clay road to the Troy Hotel. Sprayed with DEET, we slept beneath a mosquito net then took the A2 toward Uganda and checked into a Lake Nakuru hotel. Nakuru is a saltwater lake famous for flamingos, but global warming has damaged their habitat. Heavy rains have engulfed the original shoreline. Left like grotesque corpses from a catastrophic battle, the skeletal shards of dead trees stand stark against the sky. For all the wonder of watching, say, a leopard sprawled in lazy majesty high on a fallen branch, it's the environmental destruction that stays vivid. As we drove away, the Nakuru sunset silhouetted these bones of foreboding surrounding the somber shore.

Apart from further evidence of flooding, the freshwater Lake Baringo several hours north is entirely different. Our accommodation, Soi Lodge, was down a shack-lined road. Livestock nibbled the verges in a circumference allowed by the ropes that tethered them. The gates opened onto a cultivated area of paved pathways and polite staff. Between our balcony and the lake, ostriches scuffed and wallowed in the dust or ponced about splatting streams of shit. Swallows swooped into our eaves. Crested cranes called "Raowool!"

The next morning a malnourished local boy named Augustine, yellow eyes beaming, sped us by motorboat along the dead-tree shoreline. There are no flamingos on Baringo, despite the rhyme, but plenty of bee-eaters, kingfishers, sunbirds, and weavers with their distinctive nests. Farther out, a fisherman paddled his raft in circles. Crocodiles had broken his bulging net. His only remaining booty was a catfish, which we kept for him while he retrieved the net. Storm clouds gathered. A final ray of sunlight brightened the wavelets. Hippopotami peered pink and brown from the waters around a hotel abandoned to the rising lake. A fish eagle observed us from a dead tree. Augustine, who absorbed all there is to know about Baringo and its wildlife from his older brother, threw a fish into the water. The eagle swooped to snatch it and flew up to gobble it on a branch.

I wanted to ask Augustine what happened to his brother.

"Dangerous," a bird seemed to say as it flew past.

We motored around the approaching storm to an island that belonged to a man with five wives and twenty-five children. The children who ran to the shore to see us spoke no English but called out "Jambo, jambo!"

Augustine chuckled. "It's the only Swahili word they know. Their language is Maa, like the Maasai."

We left just in time. Our little boat bucked and bridled. Augustine slalomed the waves and dips, the horizon bobbing beyond the spray. Reaching shore, we scrambled up the beach to Soi Lodge. That night the thunderstorm threatened to knock out the building's generator. Power cuts punctuated the evening, reminding me of those we'd had at school during the miners' 1973 industrial action. The lights flickered off and on to the storm's percussive rhythm. Splashing back to our room, we slept fitfully through torrential rain.

The morning drive across the mountains toward Eldoret became a continuity of climbs and descents through verdurous vistas. On the dusty crossroads past the main building of Moi University we turned right through a packed street of vehicles and bustling Kenyans calling through the open windows, "Mzungu!"

"Tell them Sasa Wasai?" laughed Danny, "How are you doing? That's what Barack Obama was told to say."

We reached Kitale on a red clay street, and pulled up at the gatehouse of the Kitale Club, where they swept a mirror beneath the car. The club was a one-story complex with a veranda, sports bar, and large pool. Monkeys scampered over roofs and fences and sprang among palms and across the golf course. Sudden heavy rains arrived from nowhere and quickly dissipated. The grass steamed dry. Between veranda pillars aglow in the sunset, waiters served bottles of Tusker beer. This oasis of wealth next to roadside poverty was typical of Kenya. Beyond the club, and aside from the ubiquity of cell phones, there was a relative lack of technology. One had the sense of going back in time, of life lived just above minimal subsistence. Along with the tethered roadside goats and sheep, cows lolled in the road. A girl passed clutching the legs of two live chickens in each hand. A traffic intersection was a vegetable garden. Women wearing colorful dresses and homemade jewelry carried bundles on their heads. "Polepole," they counseled with regard to work and life amid the heat. "Slowly."

Margaret, a member of the school management, met us the next day and a driver sped us to the school. As part of the Belt and Road Initiative, the Chinese have built a new road with British-style green road signs with white diagrams, and B2 (A2) in yellow by the words Kitale and Eldoret. They're laying infrastructure across willing countries. It helps the countries but also means Chinese influence.

The new highway was anachronistic against the dilapidated shacks and fruit stalls. People walked along the curbs for miles. A boy led three donkeys, water containers slung across their backs like saddlebags. To overtake in Kenya is to assume the opposing traffic is slow enough to allow you time. Motorcyclists are often bareheaded, sometimes sporting idiosyncratic additions, such as an umbrella attached to the handlebars. The motorcycle taxi drivers wear yellow helmets on fast roads, if not on the dirt road into Kitale, where one evening a motorcyclist skidded to a halt beside me because he'd never had a white passenger. We sped off, fanning dust, bouncing over hillocks and swerving potholes.

"Yahee!" he yelled. "Me got me a mzungu!"

After circling the main area of mismatched buildings, he slid to a halt in one final dust cloud. I paid him for the ride.

"Anytime, man." He shook my hand the multifaceted Kenyan way and sped off.

The Crane Academy was down an earth road off the main highway. Crudely painted metal gates opened to bungalows amid greenery. Staff and students wandered between sun and shade. Smoke drifted from the roof of a mud hut where a lady cooked the infants' food on a stone fireplace. The classrooms shimmered beyond the chicken coup. Extensive washing lines steamed with student clothing against the blue sky. Farther still, a man chopped wood to heat the cauldron where they cooked chickpeas and maize for the older ones. Next to him, a woman washed the pots looking out over the soccer pitch, lined on three sides by maize. At each end stood basic posts with a branch as a crossbar. The sounds of children and birds mingled with the thack-thack of axe on wood.

The earth-floored classrooms were dim. Glassless windows framed sunlit foliage, dazzling rectangles on dark walls. A cowman, eyes so dark I could see no white, herded cattle through the grounds, sometimes between the washing or past the toilets, sometimes—even during matches—just behind the posts, beating errant cows with a stick he otherwise cradled crosswise on his shoulders.

The school treated us like celebrities. The mzungu were here. Children stared. Maybe the adults felt some resentment. Who were we to intrude upon their lives? But there was excitement, too, not least from headmaster Angulu Kennedy, who repeatedly clapped his hands, saying, "Karibu sana—welcome," leading us to his office curtained against the sun. I gestured to Margaret. She laughed. In Kenya men go first. I taught comprehension, something I'd not given thought to since Grimpton. We read passages about food, about sickness, about the role of undertakers. The girls whispered answers, accents sometimes hard to understand. Their faces were dark in the dark room, expressions inscrutable, eyes shy, expectant. Then, each afternoon, came soccer, on a field of ditches, mounds, and holes.

Marking books beneath a mulberry tree I was conscious of the afternoon echoing to the sound of clothes- and dish-washing. Periodically, I used the fly-buzzed privy with Management on the door. Like the huts either side, it was a hole in the ground, except this one had a hook with a roll of toilet paper. Beyond the children the maize stretched to distant trees. On a pole in the center of the mud circle used for morning assembly the Kenyan flag rarely stirred. Now and then a child approached with a question.

"What is a hamburger?" asked a girl.

"Compacted meat, made of beef not ham, and sold with chips and fizzy drinks."

"What does the sea look like?" asked another.

"Like a lake with no far shore but with waves crashing toward you."

"Is it cold?" asked an albino girl, vulnerable to persecution without the school's protection.

"In England the sea is cold," I replied, "while in Kenya it's surely warm." Kitale is miles inland, though. Few at the Crane Academy were likely to experience the sea.

"What about snow?" a boy asked.

"Snow is frozen water," I said. "It falls from the sky but not like rain and not like ice, though it does that too. We call that hail. Snow is soft, fragile, and silent. It drifts down and settles. You can scoop and throw it, or build it into a mzungu. We call this a snowman."

The children laughed. More joined them. "Mzungu! Are you made of snow?"

"I'm stardust, like all of us," I said, "and so is the snowman, really. But when you build snow it compacts. He lasts several days. You give him pebbles for eyes, and maybe a hat and scarf, and a carrot for a nose, and twigs for hands. The snow around him melts, and slowly he too dissolves, leaving only the pebbles on the grass."

"And the nose!"

"And the twigs!"

"And his hat and scarf!"

I realized after I'd told this story beneath the mulberry tree that a dozen children had crowded around. Our worlds were mysterious to one another. We were learning together.

"Do you like being here?" I asked. "I too was once a boarder."

"We love it," said one girl. "It is a privilege. They protect us, at least until we leave."

On our last night in Nairobi, I lay awake and pondered the mingling of past and present, my own life and that of Kenyans. I returned to Africa another year with colleagues for talks with universities in Nairobi, Windhoek, and Pretoria, but a larger part of me is still at the Crane Academy. Literally, some of my possessions are still there. My shoulder bag is broken, the soccer captain said one day. Do you have a spare one? I gave him mine. I need money for university, said the science teacher. I didn't give him money.

"Rafiki, friend, how will I remember you?" asked Jasper, who'd come to the school from a remote northern village. I recall him picking up a boy who'd damaged a knee, knocking him into shape and standing him on his feet. The boy ran off, evidently cured.

"The goals," I replied, "the memories!"

"Something more solid," said Jasper. "How about your watch?"

I gave him my watch.

He grinned, high-fived me. "Sasa sis ni marafiki milele. Now we are friends forever."

We remain in touch with the school, ever aware of the fragility of their existence. Many schools shut the next year during especially bad rains. There's also political instability, and general danger. What effect will COVID have? Always close to the abyss, perhaps it will be easier for them to peer within. It will hardly curtail their travel plans. And what is the fate of the children when they leave?

Visiting the Maasai Mara on the way south to Nairobi took me back to being a child again. This was not just because, as Alex Renton notes in *Stiff Upper Lip,* British colonialists in Kenya compared the boarding school tradition to the Maasai custom of sequestering adolescents to live together to learn to become warriors, or morani. I also felt as if I'd been placed in the very print that once hung in Glinty's study. Even now, I imagine waking at dawn to travel across the dry grassland in search of elephants, and coming across a cheetah watching its cubs feed on an impala corpse up a tree, vultures looking on from treetops, hyenas prowling below. I imagine us driving alongside zebras, wildebeest, lions sleeping through the midday heat. We're always expectant, always seeking that elusive moment, the lone bull elephant, even a herd, charging toward us, like the future, through long, pale grass against stormy skies.

9 ZILCH

So begin the months of bullying-interspersed monotony. Pink-Chunkerton continues to reaffirm the unattractive character denoted by his blackhead-sprinkled nose. Evidently, he nicknames younger brothers Les because of Les Delver, a member of the kitchen staff whom Pink-Chunkerton and his mates mock. Having suffered shellshock during World War II, he lacks hair and eyebrows and grins forlornly. His most onerous job is to hand out bananas. Domestic staff are called "prols." Another prol they make fun of is short, scraggy Dennis Rattle, who bleaches the bathrooms and toilets at 6:00 a.m. in blue overalls and cloth cap. If you're up at that hour, Dennis literally doffs his cap in deference. The boy thinks maybe he should get a cloth cap of his own and doff it back at Dennis.

But the references to Les do weary the boy, especially in the perennial prelunch riots. The dining hall is at the top of a stone staircase. If you're early you might get in before the crowd, but if the doors stay shut you risk being crushed. Go later, though, and you get caught on the stairs with boys in front as well as behind. It's another chance to intimidate: kicking, punching, toe-cracking with a shoe heel. The boy often has black-and-blue feet. The pain adds to the difficulties of trying out for the Second Eleven soccer team.

His decision to withdraw from the school's social world comes only after attempting other approaches. A possible escape route is to adopt different personalities. One day he speaks only in monosyllables. Another day he laughs at whatever anyone says. Another day he offers only gnomic utterances. But all such roles are doomed. There's a boy in his German class called Copeland. He's always thought Copeland an affable sort, maybe only because he resembles Robert Redford. Unkind though they are, the boy has laughed at Copeland's jokes about Herr Frischfahrt spitting out his eager German pronunciations.

One morning in marches Frischfahrt with what looks like marmalade on his bald patch, as if he'd smeared that English substance on himself to counter what Copeland calls his "Krautness." Only years later does the boy guess that the patch is psoriasis. Frischfahrt is probably stressed out by these teenage boys, stir-crazy from incarceration and brainwashed into believing themselves superior to prols and foreigners. During that same lesson, the boy has what seems a pleasant surprise. Copeland greets him by his first name.

Touched, the boy breaks his vow of silence. "You know my name?"

"It's common knowledge," smiles Copeland. "You have a brother, plus I have friends in First House." Copeland's smile fades. The boy feels foreboding. "Should I call you Les or by the secret name they have for you?"

The boy blushes. "Secret name?" He thinks of Spine. "What do they call me?"

"I'll give you a clue," says Copeland. "How come, Les, you're so boring? You come to class day after day but never speak. You add nothing to our Grimpton community. You amount to no one. You're a complete and utter nonentity, a zero."

"Zero?"

"Everyone in First House agrees. They've never met anyone so boring and worthless. You're a waste of space. Maybe we'll have you shot."

The boy leaves the class in a daze. Such nastiness is unexpected from someone he's rarely spoken to, even though he knows he, too, has been nasty in the past. He's still ashamed of joining others in taunting a Catholic and a Jewish boy at Thornditch, singled out for not attending school chapel. He'd not have done so had he known what it's like to be the victim.

He wanders up the stone steps to Upper Quad, and along one of the gravel paths that meet at the central monument to Grimpton's Glorious War Dead. It's a sunny day, so he sits and writes some words in the back of an exercise book. Horrid, he writes. Horrible. Nasty. Zero. Nonentity. Boring. No one. Les. Little Shit. But is his secret nickname Zero?

He finds out the next day. In the storage room someone has put his tuck box on the pipes near the ceiling. He has to climb to get it. The padlock is broken. When he pulls the box out it crashes down. The contents fan across the concrete floor. Scrawled on the lid in ballpoint pen is the word ZILCH. He leafs through an exercise book used for his thoughts, and drawings of masters and boys. Scrawled across several pages again is ZILCH. The boy frowns at the strange word. He's hardly even insulted. Not that this compensates for the broken padlock and invasion of his privacy. He flicks to the back of the book, and finds:

Hello, Zilch. We're REALLY *impressed! Your drawings and writings are* SO GOOD. *We've pinned one of your poems on the Notice Board. Love & kisses, the Lads.*

The boy blushes. He had no idea anyone even disliked him. And the notice board! What's on it? What have they taken? He examines the book. A page is missing. He refills the box, shuts the lid, and shoves the box into the stacks. Still on his haunches, he surveys the other boxes from his year and the year below. Ventrin, Tudor, Pusey, Difflin Minor, Smeary, Creupe, Hock, Enderson Minimus. Who did this? One of them? More? All of them?

Remembering the notice board, he jumps up, slams through the door, and skids down the cloisters back toward the Junior Common Room. Out steps Mr. Slammer.

"If you've that much energy, you can run a three-mile. Off you go!"

This is Slammer's stock punishment. It's a sports afternoon. The boy's bruised feet are too painful for soccer but this excuse won't impress Slammer. On his way to change he finds pinned to the notice board, torn from his book, his poem, "The Human Stray":

> As he walks his lonely way, nobody speaks to the human stray.
> There's no one to care. They're all unaware
> Of the plight of the human stray.
> They'd care for their dog. They'd care for their cat.
> They'd care for a mouse, maybe even a rat.
> But there's no one to care for the human stray
> He's much too low for that

ZILCH is scrawled through the poem. TEN OUT OF TEN! The boy tears it off the board and walks down the drive to a wooded area. It's begun to rain. He sits and watches foraging ants weaving past one another. An hour later he remembers Slammer's order. Now he's really in trouble. In the meantime, he's ripped up the poem and buried it.

Later, Slammer calls him into his study. He sways gently in his leather chair, wrinkled chin catching the light from his desk lamp like the craters of a half moon.

"Why didn't you run? Dawn five-mile, young man. Report to my study at six. Be back by eight. I'll be at the halfway point to be sure you're there. What's your first class?"

"Mathematics, sir. Mr. Lettich."

"I'll inform him you're five-miling. He won't expect you late, but needs to know."

"Yes, sir." The boy makes to leave.

"One moment," says Slammer, swiveling in his chair, his facial ridges and craters waxing and waning in the lamplight. "Are things going okay?"

"Yes, sir."

"Nothing wrong?"

"No, sir."

"That's the spirit! Oh, by the way. Your mother called to say they had to put down the cat. Evidently she was very old."

"Put down?"

"I'm sure they'll get a new one."

10   CRYPT

The boy quells his potential distress about Tina, who being only a cat probably didn't recall him anyway. As for his own life, all will surely come right in time. These years are the nadir before the release (he pictures an Apollo launch) that will propel his rise into adulthood. But first he must deal with the present. Much time has passed since Father Styke began their weekly meetings and the first of regular chapel tours for visitors. With the months of bullying that followed, he's neglected to do anything about his discovery, while showing the old people the chapel, on the lower level leading to the shadowy crypt. They took time to get down the winding steps. He went ahead, and to the right of the entrance found a door labeled SENIOR ART SCHOOL, with a note taped to it: *I'm not here but I'll see you soon.*

For months he thought no more of it. He gave up the art classes in his junior years with Mr. Gurney in the room off Great Hall. Gurney, with his trim beard and tweeds, only allowed them to paint in acrylics or glue together bric-a-brac. The boy almost lost interest in art. Only now, in November's misery, does it occur to him to return to the door by the crypt.

It's early evening. The chapel is lit with gloomy sidelights. He crosses the paving stones diagonal to the central aisle, at the top of which is the stained glass window depicting the schools that form the Stonebrain Foundation. At the end of the corridor, he descends the winding steps and finds the door ajar. Through the gap, he glimpses a green-faced man with a shock of white hair offset by a dazzling blue suit. The man appears to be talking to a class hidden from view. All the boy can see is a human skull against a black cloth and lit from one side by a bright light. It must be a life- or perhaps death-drawing class.

Late the next afternoon he finds the white-haired man on his own. He's wearing a lemon-yellow suit with matching shirt and tie, and white shoes that echo his shock of hair. His face, which looked green yesterday, is in fact a swarthy, pale olive—perhaps Hispanic, but evidently lacking in exposure to sunlight. A bone-white pipe sags from his shiny lips.

"Hello." The man closes an eye as the smoke rises. "Have we met before?"

"No, sir."

The man's scowl darkens his face. Although his hair is white, his eyebrows are black above blue eyes. He holds out a long-fingered hand. "Popjoy," he says. "Tom Popjoy, Art Master Emeritus. Ça va? How's it going?"

The boy shakes his hand. It's icy cold.

"How do you do, sir?"

"I do rather well. But don't call me sir. Hadn't you better tell me who you are?"

"Nobody." The boy contemplates this leather-skinned troll and his subterranean cavern. "I thought Mr. Gurney was the art master, sir."

"Please. Mr. Popjoy." He takes a box of matches and pouch from a pocket, rustles some tobacco, packs the pipe, places it between his slug-like lips, and strikes a match. He puffs the pipe and pulls it away. "I've been brought back to provide zing. I retired three years ago but Gurney hasn't coped well alone. You've taken his classes just off Great Hall?"

"Surely he's pleased to have the benefit of your experience."

Popjoy shakes his head. "Ever heard him so much as mention this Senior Art School?" He leans forward in conspiratorial fashion, sharing his tobacco breath. "Mark my words. If Gurney sets foot here, he won't even acknowledge me. He pretends I'm not here. But his appearances are rare. He sees it as empty space."

The boy surveys the room. A step down to the left is a carpeted area and shelves of large-format art books, including Vasari's *The Great Masters,* Stuckey's *French Painting,* Gaunt's *The Impressionists,* Wilson's *Surrealist Painting,* and books on Cézanne, Toulouse-Lautrec, and Picasso. Along to the left is the area for life drawing. The skull is still against its black cloth, but now has a statuette beside it of a headless winged figure about two feet high.

"That," says Popjoy, "is the *Winged Victory of Samothrace.* The real one is huge. It's in that greatest of museums, the Louvre."

The Louvre? The boy has never heard of it. Surrounding the skull and statuette, like wagons circling a campfire, stand a dozen sketching benches. Each has a stick of wood where a horse's head would be. Sketch boards sit against them. Behind Popjoy is a step down to an area with easels, some with paintings on, and beyond them small, square windows, high up because the room is below ground level. To the right is a step up, with more easels and a washbasin cluttered with jars of brushes.

"You've come to help undermine the foundations," says Popjoy. "I always know. By the way," he continues, pointing to a low table with a chessboard and pieces on, "do you play chess?" The boy shakes his head. "Pity. Let's see if you can draw." He nods to the benches facing the skull and statuette. "Start with the skull." Passing the chessboard, stopping to move a white pawn as he does so, he opens a door into a separate office and flicks a switch. Half the skull is floodlit, casting the other side into shadow. "Show me what you make of this reminder of mortality. Try a little chiaroscuro. This means the interplay of light and dark. It's the key to much pre-Impressionist composition: lightest light against darkest dark. Balance the two. It's not unlike the ying and the yang. Everything is intertwined, including good and evil. Laughter is one letter from slaughter. You'll learn, and will remember all this long after I've ossified."

The cloudy sky through the small windows has darkened to cobalt blue. The boy pictures the wintry dusk and adumbral chapel set against this bright, warm space. He sits astride the bench and observes the skull. The light catches the edge of an eye socket, giving it the appearance of observing him back. Gumless, the crooked teeth seem larger than in most living beings. The skull has a zigzag line across it, as though sawn open and repaired.

"Is that zigzag line where they took the brain out?"

"Good! Strive, as Henry James put it, to be one upon whom nothing is lost. Whoever the poor fellow was, he'd have had a right old gueule de bois, no?" The boy must have looked perplexed. "Hangover," explains Popjoy, placing a sheet of paper on the boy's board and hands him a 2B pencil. "Always 2B," he says. "2B or not 2B was Hamlet deciding what to sketch with. He was an artist, as we all are, creating the world around us. But remember, where Hamlet was indecisive, you must not be. Own your strokes, and the viewer will be more convinced, and always 2B not HB."

The boy hasn't really drawn since Thornditch. A boy there, Fernley, drew fabulously realistic fighter planes taking off from detailed airports with hangars and people, everything the right shading, and a sense of the three-dimensional. He was so good he put you off.

Beginning with the eye sockets, the boy moves on to the stub where the top of the nose would have been, then the large front teeth, then the lower teeth and jaw. Meanwhile, the smell of pipe tobacco, rather more pleasant than tobacco breath, weaves through the Senior Art School like inspiration. Popjoy stands in the shadows, pipe smoke curling up beyond his blue eyes, ivory black eyebrows, and white hair. The boy thinks of the souls of the Dead. Pipe Dreams, he thinks. Pipe Smoke.

"How are you getting on?"

"Okay—I think."

"Look not at me but at Yorick, there. Perhaps he too went to Grimpton. Perhaps his parents had grand hopes for him. He surely had hopes of his own. But whether his life was a success or a series of calamities concluding with catastrophe, he's now the Grim Grinner of Grimpton. The skull mirrors your own mortality, reminds you to learn fast, for skill, young man, is one letter from skull. Art will change you. Look hard at something, struggle to capture it, and you'll develop a new groove in the brain."

The boy tries to deepen the shaded areas to enhance the light. Meanwhile, Popjoy extends his commentary, puffing away in the shadows.

"Next time you're listening to the sermon and hymns in chapel remember who is down here, waiting to be drawn. In all that you do, keep him in mind, propped here beneath the chapel that reaches so self-importantly to the icy skies."

"I think I'm done."

Popjoy strolls over, his yellow ochre suit bursting into the light.

"You're not done," he says, "but you have begun."

11 KYIV

It's a hot September with constant blue skies. COVID is escalating again. France has yet to introduce reciprocal measures, but quarantining remains if you travel to Britain. Complicating travel to or from mainland Europe seems designed to camouflage the effects of Brexit. Yet new cases in Paris number over four thousand a day, the highest since May. Masks are mandatory, though many wear them on their chins. Worldwide infections total over twenty-five million.

Perhaps it was a sense of mortality that led me to imagine creeping into the Catacombs through a tunnel on the abandoned railway, the Petite Ceinture, to wander the dark corridors of the dead beneath the City of Light. I prefer Père-Lachaise, where one has open air and a sense of personalities, not least the Comtesse de Demidoff whose posthumous offer of her personal fortune in return for spending a year in her spacious tomb seems to me to sum up what Léon-Paul Fargue called "the bitter faithful softness of the dead." The jumbled bones of the Catacombs lack any such individuality. Rabelais and Robespierre are irretrievably dispersed while, as Graham Robb observes, the victims of the Saint Bartholomew's Day Massacre intermingle with the Catholics who killed them.

But Paris will one day be "Paris" again. Much depends on an idea, embodied in a word. Few cities provide such a vivid image before you visit. Kyiv, in contrast, was a mere name on a map: a flat, featureless city. But sometime after the Revolution of Dignity I visited Taras Shevchenko National University, and discovered the city's vibrant beauty, including its own catacombs in the caves of Lavra, and something of the traumatic history of Ukraine.

Like her city and country, my guide, whom I'll call Olena Petrenka, was a mixture of optimism and pessimism. Proudly Ukrainian but with a Russian grandfather, she was as sharp in demeanor as in her observations. Her quizzical eyebrows met as if in echo of her dual but decisive nature. She knew her city thoroughly, and was as fiercely independent as her country. Her approach to English epitomized her character. For instance, she told me of her red cat. He was ginger but she called him red because we call ginger-haired people redheads. Her logic was remorseless. Unfortunately, English is not always a logical language.

"If a person is ginger we say red," I explained, "but if a cat is ginger we say ginger."

"Because cats don't care," said Olena. "Not like people, or me anyway. I do care. During our Revolution of Dignity I walk-ed to the park and was went to the march."

"You can simply say I went. And I walked is only one syllable."

"But you say, mark-edly."

Olena's son, Bohdan, a student pianist, joined us some of the time, stopping near the funicular to play a street piano. But mostly it was just me listening to Olena. We meandered for hours through cobbled lanes, up and down hills and steps, past business blocks and czarist palaces, round parks, along the Dnipro River (not the Russian term Dnieper, Olena instructed). All the while she explained the significance of streets and buildings.

We met in the City Hotel on the first morning and walked down Kreshchatyk Street to ЦУМ Київ—TSUM Kyiv—the Harrods of Kyiv, she joked. From the rooftop coffee bar I scanned Kreshchatyk to Independence Square, not yet knowing its significance. In contrast to the drab brutalism of its Soviet architecture, many Kyiv buildings are brightly painted. In the red TSNUK administrative building we met Petro and Andrii of the International Office. As we left, graduates tossed mortarboards in the air and a girl threw a red scarf that merged with the pillars. We crossed Volodymyrska Street to Shevchenko Park.

"Did you noticing anything about the Shevchenko statue, such as what he wears?"

Shevchenko's statue shows him wearing as well as carrying an overcoat. I suggested this was either a catastrophic error or a clever way to portray Shevchenko's versatility when it came to Ukraine's extremes of climate.

"Not one or two of those," replied Olena. "Understand only that Shevchenko have complicated situation with Ukrainian clothes. As boy he wear-ed all the time same dirty clothes and sometimes no hat or boots in summer or winter. He says one time he be gifted a belt for reading the psalms but the teacher steals it for his own."

"So he wears a coat and carries a coat to be sure he has one?"

"That might be. Or sculpturer Matvey Manizer pride himself on carving overcoats."

Past the gateway to the medieval city and Saint Sophia Church toward Mykhailivska Square and Cathedral, Olena pointed out the equestrian statue of Cossack leader Bhodan Khmelnytsky. From the funicular that connects Volodimirska Hirka Park to Poshtova Square and the waterside neighborhood of Podil, we followed the edge of the park with its view across the Dnipro to the commuter belt where Olena lived. As the park bent southward, into sight below came the statue of Saint Volodymyr, holding a cross and looking out over the Dnipro. Lower down, in Podil Raion at the foot of Mykhailo Hill, stood the column celebrating the return of the Magdeburg Rights to Ukraine, granting self-government.

From that vista we took the path down to Triokhsvyatytelska Street and Evropeyska Square. Ukrainian flags flapped in the breeze, the blue and yellow representing sky and wheat. Interspersing with these were EU flags. Olena explained that Ukraine wished to join. Prime Minister Cameron had only announced the referendum on EU membership in May so Brexit was still some way off. We knew of what Nicholas Boyle refers to as the "English psychosis" of Europhobia, the right-wing nationalists' "trauma of lost exceptionalism, the psychic legacy of empire" that fueled their distaste for "collaboration with equals." But we underestimated their determination to end Britain's membership, reduce workers' rights, retain forms of tax evasion the EU intended to outlaw, and twist the dial toward plutocracy. Ukrainians in contrast, Olena stressed, saw membership as a way of ensuring continued independence. They always had to assume that Vladimir Putin, described by Annie Ernaux in *The Years* as "an icy little man of fathomless ambition," would seek more of their territory.

"When you has your referendum on membership," she said, "be sure to stay in EU, where we would like to be. Russia wants nothing more than to break up EU. They will try to influence your choice."

Along more paths we reached the memorial arch to Russia's claimed friendship with Ukraine, and another view of the Dnipro. From there we climbed steps to the Puppet Theater.

"This is known since 1927," said Olena, "but is famous, too, because Dina Pronicheva work-ed as an actress here. She was survivor of Babi Yar, you know the ravine where the Nazi Germans shot many Jews. She jump-ed before they shoot her and play dead in the corpses. Then, after they cover them in earth, she find her way out."

From the Puppet Theater we came to Lovers' Bridge, and the statue of Luigi Pedutto and Mokryna Yurzuk, an Italian prisoner of war and a Ukrainian forced laborer who fell in love during the war but were separated in 1945, only to be reunited decades later.

"Is Babi Yar far from here?"

"It's a distance but anyway there is only memorials to see. Hundred fifty thousands died there. It's a sad place. The Jews had to gather by the cemetery at Dorohozhytska Street by eight in the morning. They think-ed they was being given a new place but they was shot, pile on pile, then later Russians, gypsies, Ukrainians, dissenters. Lots of women and children, as well as ordinary people, lots of talent is destroy-ed there, like the bandurist Mykhailo Teliha and his wife, poet Olena Teliha, as well as writer Ivan Rohach. There's a monument to him where I live across the Dnipro on Melnykov Street. The Telihas was executed twenty-one day of February nineteen forty-two. Aged thirty-five, Olena wrote on her cell wall, From here goes to her death Olena Teliha. Rohach died the same day."

We passed various sculptures, including an elephant head jutting from a wall and a man with an upturned face splatted with what looked like a globule of gelatine. ("Splatt-ed is right," I told Olena, "as is gift-ed and execut-ed," adding to her skepticism). She pointed out the Roshen chocolate shop, owned by then-president Petro Poroshenko, a chocolatier (as opposed to comedian Volodymyr Zelensky, who, having portrayed a Ukrainian president on TV, subsequently succeeded him). By the time we reached a giant building unused since the 2014 president, Victor Yanukovych, fled to Russia in the wake of the revolution, the gold domes of Pechersk Lavra, Kyiv's Monastery of the Caves, gleamed in the afternoon sun. We walked along Dniprovs'kyi Descent past the Monument to Eternal Glory and the Memorial to victims of the Holodomor, the famine of 1932–33 brought on by Soviet policies. A woodland path led to Lavra, where cobbled streets sloped to Kyiv's catacombs.

"The mummified monks date from the eleventh century," Olena explained, "but there is also the head of Pope Clement I of Roman days. Once on a time if a monk arrived he never left. As you see, this is truth. You know of Marie Bashkirtseff? She is Ukrainian painter who live to only twenty-five. She was consumptive so come to pray at the open coffins. She write that her parents pray, too, but it bring no miracle. So she go back to Paris to die."

Outside again, we passed rose beds and a fountain of spring water to the Metro Bridge by the Dnipro and made our way back to the City Hotel on Khmelnitskoho Street.

"Have you a good night," said Olena. "Tomorrow afternoon, when I'm finishing with teaching and you've done your talk, I'm showing you my other Kyiv."

In the Kyiv History Museum the next morning, I was struck by the poignancy of photos of Kyiv children in 1910, oblivious to the future horrors. I gave my lecture, after which Olena, Bohdan, and I visited the Lobanovskyi Stadium in Mariyinskyi Park, lunched at Mafia off Evropeyska Square, and walked down to Poldil and along the waterfront to the funicular back up to Mikhailivskyi Cathedral. We entered a park near the history museum, passed the foundations of a church destroyed in 980 AD, and followed Sightseeing Alley to a view of Bald Hill—Lysa Hora. Saying goodbye to Bohdan, who had a piano lesson, we left the park where we entered, near Saint Andrew's Church at the top of the Adriivskyi Descent.

"You see that church?" said Olena. "It's Russian Orthodox, Pyrohoshcha, the Church of the Mother of God of the Sign, where very different people to me is worshipping."

We walked down the wide cobbled Adriivskyi to the orange house once inhabited by Mikhail Bulgakov, author of *The Master and Margarita*. Farther down was the Museum of One Street. We ducked inside and spent an hour with items from a previous era, including some belonging to Bulgakov.

"But he is not popular," said Olena. "His novel, *The White Guard,* is anti-

Ukrainian. He was loyal citizen of the Russian empire and liked by Stalin, which may be why, unlike many artists, he was not shot at Sandarmokh." After a visit to the Olympic Stadium we made our way to the National Art Gallery. "During the Revolution of Dignity there was a violent confrontation near here, on Hrushevskoho Street," Olena explained. "People fought the Berkut riot police and the paid, pro-government supporters, the Titushky. One February night graffiti appear at number four. We call it Icons of the Revolution."

The art gallery itself was an austere, pillared building guarded by decaying lions. Religious paintings were plentiful, in keeping with the city's air of devoutness. (Olena crossed herself whenever we left a church.) In general the paintings matched the seriousness of the Ukrainian sensibility. In particular I recall Fedir Krychevsky's 1930 self-portrait. Exuding self-belief, leather-booted legs apart in a John Wayne pose, hipped hands holding back his white coat to reveal a blue smock, he resembled a youngish Hemingway. Loved by students and peers, Krychevsky's Jewishness was kept secret and he survived the Nazi occupation only to starve to death in 1947. Other notable portraits were Mykhailo Bozhil's *Hospital Nurse* from 1955, a striking depiction of a nurse whose pocketed hands suggested a casualness at odds with her concerned smile, and Oleksandr Murashko's *Girl in a Red Hat* of 1903, comically translated as *Portrait of a Girl in a Red Cartwheel.*

Another room was devoted to the Avant-Garde and the Boichuk school of the early twentieth century, including Aleksandra Ekster, who eventually left Kyiv for Paris, and Oleksandr Bohomazov and Viktor Palmov, both of whom, given their death dates of 1930 and 1929, may have been victimized as members of the school of Ukrainian Monumental Art. Another held work by the Sixtiers, a group formed during the Khruschev Thaw before further prosecutions in the seventies. Olena and I discussed Tatiana Yablonska's *Life Goes On.* It merely depicted a girl with a baby, sitting next to an old man, but the authorities took exception to the title. As elsewhere in the Soviet bloc, many artists worked on ideologically acceptable forms—figurative work with Soviet themes—but secretly experimented with forbidden abstract forms that only surfaced in the nineties.

Out of the gallery, and those periods of Ukraine's history, we took Hrushevskoho Street from Evropeyska Square to the Mariinsky Palace and Parliament House, then doubled back to Bankova Street to see Horodecki House, or House with Chimeras. The architect of this startling building, Władysław Horodecki, became known as the Gaudi of Kyiv.

But now, as we returned to Independence Square, it was time for my history lesson on why Ukrainian Independence was top of Olena's agenda.

"Here is Maidan Nezalezhnosti," said Olena. "We just call it Maidan. Nezalezhnosti means Independence, a fact we don't need to spell to you. People congregate here, but I only come with visitors or for special reasons. The place is a cemetery to those who die in the revolution. They shot into the peaceful protestors from up there, see, Hotel Ukrayina, before puppet-president Yanukovych fled to Russia."

For a minute or so Olena said nothing more.

"These people, my countrymen, my friends," she said eventually, "they is the victims of January and February. We call them the Heavenly Hundred. They was murdered by snipers. A million of us was in the streets and Maidan. They shot who they could."

She showed me the columns naming individuals who died, pointing at the top of a column to the first person killed, Roman Andrusyak, on 22 January 2014. Below it was a statement about Yuri Verbytskyi and Ihor Lutsenko, activists kidnapped from a hospital on 21 January and beaten by government forces. Lutsenko was freed. Verbytskyi's mutilated body was found in a village on 22 January. Thousands attended his funeral. The official report referred only to death from exposure.

"And then, in the February, they shot the Heavenly Hundred here in Maidan." Olena sat on a low wall and looked at the crowds of people enjoying the sunshine. "We are at war even now," she said. "Today our soldiers are being kill-ed in the eastern province of Donbas. People elsewhere in Europe don't know much about what is Ukraine. You take freedoms for granted. We don't. None of our freedoms is being tak-ed lightly."

"Grant-ed is right," I said, "in more ways than one. We take too much for granted."

From Independence Square we walked up Mykhailivska Street past a blues club, then away from the cathedral past Saint Sofia and along Volodymyrska back to the Golden Gate, from where I made my way back to the City Hotel.

So in a handful of days I learned a great deal about Kyiv and Ukraine. Once again, a few days' focus on a new city and culture, especially with such a knowledgeable guide, left me with a sense that my mind, and so my life, had altered. As I write, the war in Donbas is ongoing, as is the Russian threat to Ukraine in general. Putin, who annexed Crimea in 2014 in the aftermath of the protests and the extrication of the Russian-backed president, will always seek to prevent Ukraine from becoming part of the EU. It's a matter of debate as to whether this has anything to do with Brexit and the self-image of Britain (as independent of mainland Europe) that my education tried to instill.

In seeking connections, my experience of Kyiv also has me thinking about heroism and bullying, violence and accommodation. Maybe history and culture are merely what I experienced in my schooldays but writ large. Either way, to travel is to see newness and so to see anew. Russian Formalist Viktor Shklovsky wrote that art is about ostrananie, a phrase for "making strange," and perhaps travel shares a similar function. All travel is mental travel, Saul Bellow wrote. Strangeness alters the mind, a fact not unrelated to Popjoy's advice, all those years ago, that to draw, paint, scrutinize, creates a new groove in the brain.

Equally true, I reflect now, surveying from my Louvre "office" the numerous tiny beings traversing the Tuileries, is that all that's left of Ukrainian hero-victim Fedir Krychevsky is his art. I'm now reaching the years where the boy discovered what I still believe: that art, but especially for me painting, and above all portraiture, is more than just a powerful way of expressing the present, and preserving the past. Life and art are inseparable, or they are at least for me.

12 RECLUSE

This is the final period of the boy's time at boarding school. His exam results, taken a year early to reduce fees, have disappointed the parents. Reading the results, the mother goes quiet. Not having boarded himself, the father mutters that what parents achieve children squander. *No other school would have considered putting this young man forward for exams a year early,* reads his report, *but we understand your financial concerns. He must work exceptionally hard. Far from spoiling the fun of Grimpton, it will make him all the happier.*

Winter turns to spring 1977. Seeing a performance of *Swan Lake* brightens the dull March days. Popjoy persuades him to attend the ballet because in Art History—which the boy alone has opted for in the sixth form—they're studying Edgar Degas.

"To appreciate Degas's ballerinas," Popjoy tells him, "you need to witness ballet. It's hard, skilled work. Degas is portraying workers."

The boy is transfixed. Through the first half his shins hurt from kicks he's received in his latest try-out for the Second Eleven. But when the ballerinas float like swans across the misty stage, and he counts upward of twenty spinning to the music, his own mind spins: real Russian ballerinas, Tchaikovsky weaving patterns in his mind.

At the interval he retreats to another part of the theater to avoid hearing others in the group laugh about the performance. He wants the lights to dim again so he can immerse himself in the imaginary lake. Out spring the dancers, with unbelievable feats of athleticism. He watches the ballerinas' legs and waists, and the taut muscles in their necks, and how they spin clockwise easily but only anticlockwise a single twist, more only if helped by hands on the waist. He sees how their collarbones protrude above flattened chests. But their eyes are dark, their hair up, and one resembles Kalina, or perhaps the Belgian girl, Karine. He watches her each time the chorus returns.

The ballet ends. The ballerinas remind him of circus animals trained to work in unison. They force smiles. The audience applauds. One old man stands and claps furiously. Half the audience join him. When the curtain falls, the principals are still this side and continue accepting applause. He fantasizes that his chosen ballerina will seek him out. But eventually even the principals retreat behind the curtain, the lights go up, and his adolescent peers guffaw. On the coach back to Grimpton he decides he mostly hates the real world.

Only in the Senior Art School is he left to do as he wishes. He and Popjoy seem to be its only inhabitants. Gurney appears once and asks why the boy is there.

"I'm studying Art with Art History, sir."

"Are you indeed," replies Gurney, giving him an odd look. "You do know that Art as a main subject is to be closed down at the end of the year? There's no call for it at Grimpton, not the old-fashioned kind. Technology's the thing."

"It's a disgrace," says Popjoy, seated in the corner, framing one of the boy's drawings. Today's suit is Prussian green. As Popjoy predicts, Gurney ignores him, and soon leaves. "The man's à la noix, as the French say. Not up to much. He's let the department go. He's into so-called conceptual art which is all too often foutaise, bullshit. They'll probably reopen it but should be rid of him first."

The boy is shocked to hear criticism of another master. But Popjoy is irreverent with regard to school etiquette. The boy never sees him take part in any school function. He arrives on his rainbow-painted moped by the backdoor and leaves when done. But he indulges the boy, giving him keys, including to his office. The boy can take anything he needs. Popjoy seems not to care. After all, he's only back from retirement to help out.

One day Popjoy gives him a paint board and lets him try oils. Even as he mixes the paint and applies his first strokes, there's no turning back. He paints a landscape that imitates Cézanne. It dawns on him that all he needs in order to be happy are painting materials, food, sleep, and time.

Popjoy puffs his pipe. The aroma permeates the Senior Art School. For the afternoons the boy takes to paint it, Popjoy busies himself without seeming to do much, occasionally moving a chess piece on one or other side. Every now and then, he offers advice: avoid using black. Pure gray is the enemy of painting. Make it from other colors. Don't try to show everything. Concentrate the interest on essential points.

Then, on the Thursday, he says, "Do you think you've finished?"

"Maybe."

"Mon oeil! Who are you kidding! It's a set waiting for actors. You might like de Chirico. Check out *Gare Montparnasse,* which he subtitles *The Melancholy of Departure.*"

"May I have a canvas?"

"They're expensive." Popjoy puffs his pipe. "Study the books and paintings."

"Suppose you test me on Monday? If I do well, I get canvases."

"You strike a hard bargain." Popjoy raises a black eyebrow. "I'll test you on Monday at four. No promises. But it'll be good for you to study painters, let's say up to Cézanne, whom you obviously admire. Aside from a glance at de Chirico, you can leave everything after that for a later date."

From Friday afternoon through the weekend, instead of listening to sport on the radio, he studies in the Senior Art School. Art History lessons have made him familiar with several painters. Others are new to him. By Saturday afternoon he's memorized major Italian Early Renaissance painters just as he used to memorize soccer teams, positioning them as Molesworth does with historical figures in *How to be Topp,* but with as many teams as necessary. In Team One, Cimabue is goalkeeper. Giotto, Duccio, Pisanello, and Masaccio are the back four. Fra Angelico, Uccello, and Pollaiuolo make up the midfield. Botticelli, Ghirlandaio, and Piero Della Francesca are the forwards, and Bellini the substitute.

He soon knows every painting of the period in the library books, yet this is nothing to what he's committed himself to learn, so he flicks through every book, even those beyond Cézanne. By bedtime he's unable to get the images out of his head. Falling into a wakeful dream state brought on by overconcentration, the dormitory, Senior Art School, and world of art merge. He floats in and out of paintings as if they're landscapes, townscapes, roomscapes you could enter, often with the painter or subject as guide. He roams through the Renaissance of Northern Europe, the later Italian Renaissance, the Baroque, the Rococo to Goya, Romanticism to Impressionism. Van Dyck, Dürer, and Holbein shake his hand, pat him on the back. The welcomes are equally warm when Raphael, Caravaggio, and others crowd round to congratulate him on some triumph he can't quite remember. He meets, in no logical order, Parmigianino, Veronese, Corot, Memlinc, Watteau, Canaletto, Tiepolo, Gainsborough, Goya, Jean-Jacques Henner, and Louise Le Brun.

Plunging down through a tunnel of skulls, he meets Fuseli, Blake, Turner, Constable, the English Pre-Raphaelites, Ingres, Géricault, and Delacroix. In woodland, he meets Daumier, Grigorescu, and other painters of Barbizon, then Courbet, Monet, Renoir, Degas, Seurat, Whistler, Gauguin, and Vincent van Gogh.

Snapping awake, he stares into the dark but falls asleep again to find he's Saint George fighting a dragon in Albrecht Altdorfer's forest. After a brief encounter with the humanoid lamb of Jan van Eyck's *Ghent Altarpiece*, he descends into Bosch's hell and surfaces amid hunters in Brueghel's snowy wastelands. He crossed the River Styx with Patinir's Charon, creeps among rocks to peek at Leonardo's *Madonna*, takes a spare seat at *The Last Supper*, is judged decisively by Michelangelo's thick-torsoed Christ, runs from the gaze of Andrea del Sarto's *Sculptor* and becomes Cupid, entwined with Venus in Angelo Bronzino's *Venus, Cupid, Folly and Time*. Just as he's relaxing, Giorgione's *Tempest* cracks a thunderous warning. He wakes to Titian's Philip II of Spain at the foot of his bed, black breastplate glinting in moonlight, hands over his ears to keep out the artist's plague-riddled death moans. But soon, hurtling skyward, he's squirted in the eye by Tintoretto's *Origin of the Milky Way* then mobbed by multiple El Grecos haunting the lanes of a Toledo dawn.

On goes the now whispered, now deafening, now bright, now dark menagerie of safety or damnation. He feels innocent, guilty, broken, mended. He feels eaten alive, washed in healing liquid, shot with arrows, burned at the stake, dismembered, spat on, clapped, stretched on a wheel until his wrists and ankles, in excruciating slices of pain, snap.

And just as unexpectedly he's strolling through a gentle Veronese landscape listening to Artemisia Gentileschi's pretty lute player, eating with Louis Le Nain's peasants, placing his fingers in Christ's gaping sword wound in Guercino's *Incredulity of Saint Thomas*.

"Hello, Thomas," says Christ. His knowing smile reveals unexpectedly ground teeth.

The boy wakes again. His teeth hurt and he confuses his own teeth with Christ's, and thinks maybe it's stressful being the son of God, quite a burden being sent to save the world. But when he opens his eyes he thinks at first that blue water is pouring down the walls, except that what he actually sees, beyond the dark vaults of the dormitory, is the blue sky and robes of a Poussin painting, then a sunset by Claude Lorraine. A sea breeze sprinkles his face as he accompanies Rubens to watch a queen's arrival at the port of Marseilles, except that he's now clomping with Rosa Bonheur through a ploughed field toward oxen and then with Mary Cassatt sitting in a Parisian apartment with Berthe Morisot, who rises to meet him not with dark eyes, as painted by Manet, but with ones the same pale green as his own.

"Come find me in Passy Cemetery," she whispers. "Marie Bashkirtseff is here, too, in a much larger tomb."

"It's sad, but I have no friend," says Bashkirtseff, appearing in the doorway of her furnished mausoleum. "I love nobody, and nobody loves me."

"Whereas I'm with the Manet brothers," says Morisot, "together forever."

A man taps him on the shoulder. It's Diego Velázquez. "I'll paint you," he says in a Spanish accent. "Step this way, por favor."

The boy enters *Las Meninas,* and tiptoes past the babble of the children in their finery, through a door to be met by the shadowed face of a young Rembrandt.

"Come and see my life," he says, "such as it is." Suddenly old and kindly, Rembrandt leads him, hobbling through room after room of easels to an autopsy. "We're all just flesh," he says, "mere meat."

"I once won a spelling contest in a room full of prints of your paintings."

"Extraordinary!" says Rembrandt. "Have you seen my *Anatomy Lesson?*"

Turning away as the bearded pathologist, Dr. Nicolaes Tulp, thrusts his knife into the corpse, the boy finds himself staring at the tile-floored studio of Johannes Vermeer.

So it continues through the night, though it seems like traveling through centuries. Then, after a bout of feasting that ends humbly with the boy sharing an apple with Cézanne ("We can only eat this one, or we'll spoil the composition"), he chokes awake. The clock in the quad is chiming. It's ten minutes from the end of breakfast. He dresses and races across the gravel to the canteen for the last congealed spoonful of watery scrambled egg and last rubbery slice of toast.

But even Grimpton can't stop him now. It's a mere backdrop, less real, in the long run, than the world of painting. What matters is the power of his own mind, where realities can be made that are more permanent than the days he spends in these physical surroundings. What are the beings of Grimpton to him, compared with what he can conjure up mentally and create through paint? In what sense are they—or his ideas of them—any more real?

After Sunday chapel, he hurries to the Senior Art School to finish his reading and continues studying through Monday until the time comes to be tested. Popjoy runs a slide show and fires questions. The boy, somewhat to his astonishment, gets everything right.

Popjoy nods approval. "You look as if you haven't slept," he says. "Get some rest."

"I need to paint."

Popjoy sucks on his pipe. "Interesting."

13 LOVE

The boy's latest report illustrates his general withdrawal from much of school life: *rarely shows sparks of animation* (Mathematics); *I would welcome a more vigorous attitude* (German); *is the boy actually able to speak?* (Biology). But, beyond painting, his one social interest is in that rare phenomenon: girls. His latest crush is on raven-haired, green-eyed Melanie Dragonfly. At a barbecue party she's standing alone in a corner of a barn open to moonlight. A fence curves past the silhouettes of horses against the blue mist. He asks if she'd like to go outside with him. They stand by the fence. The horses snort beside them.

"Do you play tennis?" he asks.

Snort.

"As a dancer," she says. "I can't risk my arms or legs. I've even given up riding."

Snort. Whinny.

"May I have your address?" Like a cub reporter, he fishes a notepad and pencil stub from a pocket, and holds the pad against the barn door. She seems a little startled but agrees. Her address is Tring Park School for the Performing Arts. "I love you passionately," he says.

Melanie snorts. "You don't even know me!"

The next morning the boy's stomach aches with emptiness. He feels emotionally punched. He sends Melanie a letter on three sheets of paper: red, yellow, green. On the yellow sheet he draws a diagram of his house, indicating where his room is. She responds with a drawing of a horse. That autumn, they exchanged illustrated letters, getting as far as diagrams of their dormitories. Then disaster strikes. On an exeat, the brother announces in the car to the whole family that Melanie no longer wants to "go steady" with the boy.

"How do you know this?" asks the suntanned mother, applying a fresh layer of pale lipstick, and pouting in the passenger mirror.

"The girl whose party it was goes to the same school," chortles the brother. "Melanie told her, and she wrote and told me."

The sister giggles.

The boy won't, of course, reveal his devastation. He mourns for weeks. He's kept all her letters, and even a long black hair he found in one of the envelopes. Eventually, he throws them all out, and plunges back into his paintings of the sea. He tells Popjoy about it.

"Se tu non mi vuoi bene, non mi meriti!" responds Popjoy, today in a suit the hue of pink champagne. "If you do not love me well, you do not deserve me. Read Stendhal's *De l'Amour* to understand love, but there's also the joy when it releases its grip on your heart."

The boy has always sensed something distressing happened in Popjoy's life, and Popjoy now recounts it. In Paris he'd been in love with a French girl but she'd left him for a professor. He was sad for a long time. Then it vanished.

"The strange thing," says Popjoy, "was the unexpected way it all stopped. It was just as William James describes in *Varieties of Religious Experience*. I'd left Paris and begun working here. Riding to work on my moped one spring morning, up that track between the fields, I was as usual thinking miserably of her. But then, as if grabbed by some outside power, I skidded round, raced home, retrieved everything that reminded me of her, took it all into the garden and had a bonfire. That was the end. I've rarely given her much thought since. I repossessed myself, returned to sanity, and have never been trapped again."

"But you're married?"

"Love and marriage are different things. There's the madness of love—insanity, unhappy if unrequited—and the sanity of companionship. One may lead to the other, but only the latter is a sound basis for marriage."

The boy wonders why Popjoy has so much to say. He thinks perhaps Popjoy sees his own younger self. He seems to know what the boy's pondering and provides the answer.

"Adults don't usually talk so freely," says the boy.

"I tell you about myself to help you understand yourself," replies Popjoy. "You're an adolescent misfit. You won't always be an adolescent but may always be a misfit. You'll learn to behave mostly as society expects of you, but meanwhile, as Stefan Zweig writes in his masterful and poignant memoir, *The World of Yesterday*, 'isolation enhances your powers'. Your worldview is being formed.

My job is to help you shape your restlessness productively. Listen to your inner voice, find mentors, gain confidence, grow happy and balanced, and adjust to the wider outlook. Any questions?"

The boy thinks a moment. "Actually, yes. Why do you play chess against yourself?"

"I don't have anyone to play against. Mrs. Popjoy loathes the game. She sees herself as being as much of a chess widow as Marcel Duchamp's first wife, who got so fed up with his obsession that she glued his pieces to the board. They divorced. For that reason, I keep my set here rather than at home. But I play to remind myself that, in life too, you're your main opponent. I should know. I had great fortune in youth—as in luck—but I burned through it."

Much that Popjoy says invites questions but mostly the boy prefers to paint while Popjoy talks. He has plenty to say but painting becomes his voice. It centers him like the still point of a seesaw. His Outer World self rises and falls. His Inner World self stays motionless. One day his Outer World self is apathetic and melancholy. Other days he's on a high and looks down on the tops of people's heads. Not quite there, he's embarrassed by the being who moves among his peers. Inside, he's discovering who he is. He feels much changed from that little boy in the itchy uniform who tried to avoid being left at school by saying he didn't know where to put his fruit. But even as he seeks identity, he feels all the surer he's not alone in his mind. Others are there, too, more real than the beings in his physical life. Painters—or the spirits of painters—surround him. He hears their greeting: you belong with us!

The Outer World is one of make-believe unacknowledged as such—not least custom and hierarchy. He tells Popjoy this. Popjoy puffs his pipe and regards the boy with concern.

"The final belief is to believe in a thing you know to be a fiction, and to believe in it willingly, there being nothing else. So wrote American poet Wallace Stevens. But not all is fake. Bridges are real, as is the incredible imagination, engineering, architecture, that goes into creating a city. Trees, rivers, even relationships, are real. It's a wondrous world. Don't let the bullshit blind you to the best."

The boy absorbs such comments but for now painting is what he has and does. When he's painting no one can touch him. All his meaning resides there.

"And remember," says Popjoy, standing behind the boy so that his voice seems to come from within, "what is said of painting is usually said of the human mind. You project yourself outward, but also pull inward what you've painted. It's an extension of yourself and a building of yourself. Painting and religion are linked. Both create meaning."

"Religion!" The boy points through the ceiling to the chapel above. "If there's anything like the God they worship up there, I'm hellbound. God doesn't like defiance."

Popjoy grunts. "God may well like defiance."

"He likes obedience."

"You'll have to debate that with Fathers Honey and Styke!"

A vision of hell comes into focus. He'll be stuck in Grimpton's windy cloisters forever. The Virgin Mary will turn out to be Ma Seton. Jesus will be Pink-Chunkerton. His eternal punishment will be to debate obedience with Honey and Styke.

To the soundtrack of the Sex Pistols' "God Save the Queen," the summer of 1977 sees change and a dramatic event. The brother leaves Grimpton. A new friend of the parents, Dr. Mortby, gives him a car to celebrate. There's not much to celebrate given the brother is destined to fail his exams, even if he'll be given a job "in the City," but it's not much of a car. In particular, it has poor brakes. The brother belts along the lanes and is notably excited at the approach of "The Queen's Silver Jubilee." He spends hours "fixing" the car, though it's never clear what he's fixing. It seems to go—if not stop—well enough.

June 7—Jubilee Day—arrives. The mother has bought Union Jack napkins for the after-parade lunch party with the Mortbys. The father has hoisted the VE Day flag the mother's parents had in London at the end of the war. (The father's father remained in Germany for months after hostilities ended—which annoyed Grandma Cologne no end.)

When the boy wakes it's raining. It rains all day. It rains on the parade. The mother has set out the lunch party in the garden but they have to eat indoors. The windows mist up so you can't see the flag. There's cider, beer, and a wine called Piat d'Or. The boy has beer. The brother drinks all the cider then, before pudding, speeds off in his car to see Deodora Dandy.

"I think it will stop," says the father, looking out at the rain.

"I doubt it," says Dr. Mortby.

"It will," says the father.

The only people there are the mother, father, the Mortbys, and the vicar. Reverend Billiout is always up for a party. His huge, pitted nose looks as if it's been pulled from the bowl of strawberries in the middle of the lunch spread. He's been in the pub and is swaying. He's meant to make a speech but doesn't.

"Piat d'Or! Ijis adore Piat d'Or, anyou, my lufferlee," he says to the mother, "I adore you! You're my Piat d'Or."

The father says, "Drink something British!"

"Gracious," Reverend Billiout addresses a potted plant. "Ishit shtill raining-a-ling?"

"I said it wouldn't stop," says Dr. Mortby.

The father seems not to like the Mortbys. Whenever they visit, which is regularly, he says, "Another Mortby Day." Dr. Mortby seems to threaten him. Mrs. Mortby is too ugly to look at for long. Her face seems to have lost all conviction that it can make it as a face, so has deflated into her neck. When she talks to you her eyeballs roll into her head. Still, Dr. Mortby's mushy visage suggests that the same botch-prone creator is responsible for both. Dr. Mortby always insists on helping the mother with the dishes. The father therefore has to sit and talk to the deflated head of Mrs. Mortby.

As time passes the adults drink more and talk louder. At about five the doorbell rings. Through the small window the boy sees two police officers, their caps glittering with raindrops. Finally, they've come for me, he thinks. But opening the door he finds they're standing either side of the brother, who is holding a handkerchief to a bleeding chin.

"Are your parents in?" asks the female officer.

The father comes to the door. "I'm sorry," he says. "We're celebrating Jubilee Day."

"We understand, sir," she says. "This young man's car is embedded in a tree. He misjudged a corner in the rain. He's cut his chin and gashed his hand climbing out through broken glass. We think he's all right but please look after him. We haven't breathalyzed him because it's Jubilee Day. He's a lucky fellow. But you'll need to remove the car tomorrow."

The mother appears. "Officers are standing at the Piat d'Or!"

That night there's a party up the road. The brother drinks more. The father takes him home. The next morning they locate the car. It's buckled and strewn with shattered glass. Wilting from the aerial is a limp, dripping Union Jack. Good God, thinks the boy, I really do need to escape.

14 KRAKÓW

Hulking away like Goya's *Colossus,* 2020 has at last turned its back on us. We're now in March 2021. Autumn was dismal. COVID swept the globe. Travel remains complicated. Depending on your destination, it can involve quarantining, statements of honor, PCR or Antigen tests, even phone calls from surveillance teams. Only essential travel is allowed between Britain and France, where mask wearing is mandatory and there's a night curfew. In Britain, 175 people in every 100,000 have died, 120 in every 100,000 in France. Meanwhile, those in 10 Downing Street, from Johnson down, have been caught out in Partygate as having flouted the lockdown laws they imposed on everyone else.

There's some positive news, including the imminence of mass vaccination. Parisians have reclaimed the cafés, restaurants, and museums. Cycle lanes introduced by Mayor Anne Hidalgo during lockdown are now permanent. This, at least, is positive unless you're a commuting motorist and see her as a champion of what David Brooks termed bourgeois bohemians—so "Queen of the Bobos." Along with much of the Rivoli traffic, gone too are museum crowds. In the Orsay, I pass Monets and Renoirs to the sound of my own footsteps. In the Louvre, I view the *Venus de Milo* and *Mona Lisa* almost alone. Indeed, on one occasion I momentarily felt that *La Joconde,* in imitation of the death mask known as *L'Inconnue de la Seine,* had kept her smile but closed her eyes. Pessoa suggests she'd be far more beautiful if unseen, but beauty for her might come from resting her gaze. Ah freedom! Perhaps she could even evade the Salle des États guards and, cheered on by David and Delacroix, run like the threesome in Godard's *Band of Outsiders* through the Grand Gallery and down Escalier Daru to escape.

With less panic in the air, I've felt inclined to paint again. The smell of oils lingers unless, as today, I open the balcony doors. While painting, I'm reflecting on the Louvre's Leonardo exhibition. The star of the show was *La Belle*

Ferronnière. Often ignored in the Grand Gallery, this portrait of either Lucretia Crivelli, a mistress of the Duke of Milan, or of his wife, Beatrice d'Este, featured on the poster so drew the crowds. Nevertheless, she kept her steadfast focus on me, resurrecting an intimate moment I had in Kraków with a Leonardo portrait thought to be of another of the duke's mistresses, Cecilia Gallerani.

Knowing that, during renovations to the Czartoryski Museum, *The Lady with an Ermine* was in Wawel Castle, I walked up from Kazimierz and bought my ten-zloty ticket. The attendant directed me to an armed soldier who opened a door to a cell-like room. Unlike *La Belle Ferronnière*, Signora Gallerani kept her gaze well to my right. Whatever caught her attention also caught that of the ermine. Fine by me. I studied the brushwork, the contours of her face, her oddly masculine hands, and strange headgear, not a ferronnière, the jewel-centered band worn by her Louvre counterpart (a fashion designed to hide the mark of syphilis), but still a band, holding a full hair covering. Of course, had she and the less than cuddly ermine suddenly swiveled toward me I'd have been disconcerted. With some portraits, the viewer is a voyeur, with others, the viewer is viewed.

This dynamic came into dramatic play when I left Wawel Castle for the National Museum, an altogether more disturbing experience, exacerbated by the context of my visit. I was on one of successive trips to Poland and Germany with a colleague and students from her module on Literature and Evil. The previous day we'd visited Auschwitz, the day before that the *Kraków under Nazi Occupation 1939–1945* exhibition in the former administrative building of Oskar Schindler's factory, after which I'd walked to the snowbound site of Płaszów. No doubt, too, my solitude—the only visitor to the gallery that late afternoon—had an effect, as did the way the rooms brightened as I entered and dimmed as I left. But it felt like a stroll through a nightmare.

That private moment with Cecilia Gallerani galvanized me to brave the thickening sleet northward to the museum, but the benevolent legacy of witnessing Leonardo's painting dissolved when, on the right as I reached the top floor, I encountered Gustaw Gwozdecki's *Głowa chłopca*, or *Boy's Head*. It was all black except for the head, slightly to one side, downlit so that the eyes were in shadow. But the horror of this painting deepened on closer inspection. The eye sockets were congealed paint like blackened blood. Dated 1902, the painting not only anticipated those I'd shortly witness but also the dreadful events that would unfold through that century.

I moved on to some relatively benign paintings, only unnerved by the otherwise deserted gallery and the brightening, dimming rooms. Among the paintings that drew me were Josef Pankiewicz's *Woman Combing Her Hair* and *Girl in a Red Dress.* If these exquisite portraits were in Paris, people would—COVID permitting—crowd in front of them. They were among nineteenth-century paintings that included Olga Boznańska's rather spookier *Girl with Chrysanthemums,* Władysław Ślewiński's *The Combing,* and Wojciech Weiss's *Melancholic.* I'd heard of Weiss, but as a state-sponsored socialist realist painter. These were very different paintings, revealing a bleaker vision related to his acceptance of the political hijacking of his talent.

From here on my unease increased exponentially. Described as a self-portrait, Leszek Sobocki's *Pole,* from 1979, depicted the sinewy bare shoulders and arms of a contemplative elderly man. Against a dark background, he appeared to be leaning on a blue-lit table as if more spirit than body, the light rising to brighter blue where his torso would be and seeping under his arms to his clasped hands. Then it dawned on me, even as I saw how the hair resembled a white skullcap, that I was meeting the gaze of Pope John Paul II. Sobocki had circumvented the severe censorship of the time by merging himself with the new pontiff.

Nearby were more of Sobocki's *Coffin Portraits,* eerie heads on different materials, including a road sign, a metal dish, a piece of wood, and a door. They resembled the Roman coffin lids displayed in the Louvre, but each was either dismembered or insubstantial. Next to confront me were Zbylut Grywacz's gruesome images of women. *Rozebrana (Orantka X),* or *Demolished (Orant Woman 10)*—"Orantka" being the Polish term for a praying figure, symbolizing the soul's salvation—showed a woman trying to present her best self but, like the Poland of the time, distorting that self to meet the world. Her face was half in shadow, her rib cage so dark as to suggest it had been hacked away. She was knock-kneed, swollen-bellied. Clattering with in-bent elbows, her hips were skin and bone. Across her upper chest, below and between her collarbones, three horizontal red marks like suppurating scars suggested the skeleton beneath. The point seemed to be the attempt at a beautiful surface betrayed by rottenness within, a comment perhaps on communist kitsch. "On the surface, an intelligible lie," Sabrina says of her paintings in Czech novelist Milan Kundera's *The Unbearable Lightness of Being*, "underneath, the unintelligible truth."

The next nightmarish visions were by Andrzej Wróblewski, including the most startling in the museum. Seeing the painting before the title, I'd registered at first what I took to be two standing figures. Attracted by the vibrant foreground and muted blues behind, I'd drawn closer. A boy with his back to us clung to a pale woman in blue. His arms were around her waist. Her right arm was across his back. Her left hand, palm outward, was by her side. The boy had warm-colored skin and a tank top of black, orange, and red rings. The woman's blue dress complemented her bluish skin. But stepping back I saw the title, *Syn i zabita matka*, translated as *Son and His Killed Mother*, and experienced sudden vertigo. They weren't standing figures after all. The woman lay dead, the boy lay on her corpse. He'd put her arms around him but one had fallen flat on the slab. The source of such a disturbing painting was, as with others, a combination of personal and Polish history. As a child Wróblewski saw his father die of a coronary when Nazis searched their home.

A corridor off the main gallery contained equally harrowing photographs. These included Katarzyna Kozyra's stark portrait of an elderly lady with a black ribbon round her neck. Naked and toothless, breasts flat to her stomach, thin legs together above tiptoed feet, she gazed at me with a dignity that echoed those of the life-sized photographs of starving women, naked and exposed, on the walls of Auschwitz I. A second image was of a young woman receiving cancer treatment, stretched out on a hospital bed, wearing the same neck-ribbon. She, too, observed the viewer, defying you to view her hairless body. The explanation for the ribbon and title became clear in a further photograph, where the same patient had arranged herself to mimic Manet's *Olympia*.

Art may build on art but, as Oscar Wilde noted, life builds on art. As a teenager I assumed my obsession with painting was escapism, and I suspect that's how my parents viewed it. They hoped I'd one day see sense and settle down as a lawyer, which I might have done had it not involved wearing a suit and tie, thereby echoing the schoolboy captivity I intended to escape. But cities such as Moscow, Lisbon, Kyiv, and Kraków, each a witness to totalitarianism, reminded me in adulthood that artistic expression is a reaction to entrapment. While I can hardly claim that my own artistic impulse was a response to oppression on that scale, I'm aware that I was only a child. In adulthood, I've come to understand why I might have sought such an outlet.

Literally pinching myself to see if I'd awaken from the nightmare, I decided to leave this silent gathering. But one final painting beckoned. Jerzy Nowosielski's *Egzekucja,* from 1949, is an unobtrusive, cartoonish painting, like something in a children's book. A suited man is onstage, attending to four women—one half out of the picture, suggesting more beyond the frame. The women's backs are to the audience, which includes the viewer. They're in underwear, the middle one bra-less, the one on the left in heels, stockings, and suspenders, the one on the right in knee-length blue stockings and red shoes. The middle woman has turned to the man, showing a glimpse of profile. She looks calm, as do the audience, attentive to a show reminiscent of the magician's trick of sawing a woman in half before miraculously restoring her. One might almost think the women are his assistants. But other oddities are the black squares behind the stage, suggestive of prison windows. The dreadful subject jars with the painting's seeming banality and cheerful colors. You might mistake it for a pleasant picture until you register that "Egzekucja" means "Execution." The man is checking nooses. He's about to hang women who fraternized with the Nazi occupiers.

The nightmare continued into the armory. I entered rooms so dark they seemed closed. But each time I neared a display case, faceless cohorts in uniforms from Poland's wars lit up like souls stirred from the grave. A display of flags included one, dated 1862, with a cross bound in barbed wire. A similar cross marks Hujowa Górka, a notorious execution spot in Płaszów where, to quote Myra Sklarew about a Lithuanian massacre site, "every hill is suspect." As at Auschwitz and Płaszów, and at a photography exhibition in Kraków's Jewish museum of rural sites across Galicia, I thought of more of Sklarew's words. "I am trying to remember something I couldn't possibly know." I trudged back to Kazimierz, snowfall sparkling in the light of bars and cafés. Awaiting the dawn bus for Berlin, we found Kazimierz's cobbles covered in a new whiteness. The snow thickened as we sped toward Germany and the capital of the worst crimes of an atrocity-stained century.

Museums, memorial sites, artworks themselves, are all acts of emotional connection. We re-create and preserve what we care about, but also what horrifies us. In Berlin our hotel, the Michelberger, was a haven of friendliness.

Down Warschauer Straße, toward what was once West Berlin across the Spree, remains a mile-long section of the Berlin Wall. I walked along it to the Ostbahnhof one morning in brilliant sunshine. Beyond the west wall, blinding white snow met the blue river. The Gothic turrets of the Oberbaum Bridge stood in sturdy redbrick warmth against the cloudless sky. Yellow U-Bahn trains trundled on the upper tier against the sparkling coldness of the water beneath. But the east side, seen by the captive people daily, was in shadow, brightened only by artwork that spoke to their anger and ultimately triumph. Boarding the double-decker train to Schönefeld Airport, I reflected on contemporary Berlin's benign bohemianism. Perhaps it was a reaction to the viciousness recorded in the Topography of Terror on the site of the Gestapo headquarters, and the oppression documented in the Stasi Museum, and symbolized by the wall itself. Perhaps we assert decency to counter every urge toward evil. Perhaps, I thought, art plays a part in this. Meanwhile, the train wound through snowblue fields at dusk.

15 CANVAS

Is he perhaps more able than he admits? To have done over thirty oil paintings in a term is astonishing. It is hard to get him to talk but perhaps painting is his language? The boy drops this latest report on the kitchen table. Turning seventeen was a grim milestone. Worse than the ongoing discomfort of spots and ulcers is his humiliating new height. In six months he's grown nine inches. From one of the smallest in the school, he's now among the tallest. His shins are exposed between his trousers and socks. Tin Ribs or Knobbly Knees at home, he's also Beanstalk. At school, when not called Les, or Zilch, he's Giraffe.

Before the spring term, the mother lays everything on his bed and checks the list. A gale lashes the oak tree on the hill. Crows gabble amid the field's ploughed furrows.

"One gray suit. Number sent: one. Number returned: where's your suit, Tin Ribs?"

"Stolen."

"Any idea what suits cost? Two jackets, standard pattern. Sent: two. Returned: one?" The mother carries on down the list like a raindrop down a window pane. "Overcoat, pullovers, V-neck, monochrome, tick. Scarf sent: none. Returned: one."

"I found it in Lower Quad."

"Pajamas, briefs, tick. Vests: none sent. Twelve handkerchiefs, tick. White shirts, suitable for laundry, dark socks of unostentatious shade, school ties, tick. Two pairs of black or brown shoes, tick."

The boy turns from the window. The mother looks older. Her once-long hair is now curled short.

"Still making the most of Grimpton?"

"It's okay."

In a way it is indeed okay. He's spending more time in the Senior Art School. Only there is he called by his first name. In the windswept Outer World of gravel, quads, glutinous food, bigots, and bullies, the boy has befriended the actual Les, the shell-shocked veteran who serves in the canteen. But the veteran's mind has gone, and probably never arrived in Grimpton, so the boy's only real social interaction is in the Senior Art School. Partly this is with the multisuited Popjoy, but partly with the paints and paint boards, and the subjects they allow him to explore.

Month by month Popjoy's advice, and the boy's efforts, provide the education lacking in the Outer World. Popjoy is a frustrated man of letters. He's a painter who gives titles to his paintings because he wants "to tell stories" (though the boy never sees him paint). He also tells him, one February day, while the boy sketches daffodils, that he has several homemade publications in his office.

"I type the pages and make the covers. Mrs. Popjoy sews the books together."

"Why not get them professionally published, sir?"

"I said don't call me sir." Popjoy puffs his pipe. "Only intellectual and moral hierarchies are meaningful. But the addresser must decide the hierarchy. Nothing is more idiotic than insistence on rank. Social labels are arbitrary. Albeit situated in a nominally 'United Kingdom', the Senior Art School is a republic."

The boy draws a curve for the shaded side of the daffodil stem. *Own your strokes. Everything has a thickness.* He draws a lighter curve representing the lit side of the stem. *Nothing in nature is straight. Drawing is seeing. Seeing is the effect of light.*

"I've one goal in life, Mr. Popjoy. To become someone."

"Everyone is someone. A better goal is to get laid, if easier said than done. I visited a prostitute at your age but ended up asking for a cup of tea. Maybe just listen to jazz."

The boy pictures himself years hence as a penniless artist in a room near a train station. In the late winter afternoons, the setting sun sends shafts across the shadowed platform and gives way to rain. He walks the streets alone, observing people through pub windows sipping pints. In another version, Kalina Radeva is his companion. These daydreams mingle with the smell of Popjoy's pipe. Perhaps one day he, too, will smoke a pipe, and he and Kalina will sip pints in a pub looking out at passersby in the rain.

Such fantasies also merge with his awareness of the strip lighting in the Senior Art School, and the darkening day, deep blue through the high-up windows. Often the boy is alone but when Popjoy arrives, leaving his rainbow moped outside, they might almost be a father and son on a fishing trip: silent concentration and awareness of the proximity of someone else caught up like you in thought.

Other afternoons, Popjoy doesn't turn up. Perhaps he knows the boy will leaf through the self-made books. One, *Eats of Eden and Other Typos: Reflections on a Life of Lettuce,* contains annotated cartoons. Three more are memoirs: *The Schooldays of Tom Popjoy, Popjoy: The Paris Years,* and *Wrong Turn: The Regrets of a Schoolmaster,* with an epigraph from screenwriter Ben Hecht's autobiography, *A Child of the Century:* "I once looked forward and now look back, and between those two looks is most of my life."

In *The Paris Years* Popjoy describes his time in the fifties at the École des Beaux-Arts, where he knew various writers, artists, and musicians—listing his evenings with "Bill Styron, Jean Seberg, Romain Gary, Thérèse and Niki de Saint Phalle, and Jimmy Baldwin, along with Langston, Juliette, Miles and Chet"—none of whose names mean anything to the boy. The memoir is filled with melancholy quotations from nineteenth-century French poets, particularly Baudelaire. "Now we will plunge into the frigid dark," Popjoy quotes, for instance. "The living light of summer gone too soon!" The boy copies this down, along with a sentence from a poem called "The Seven Old Men." "My soul danced in circles like a hull / Dismasted on a monstrous, shoreless sea."

"Did you leave Paris for the sea?" the boy asks Popjoy one day.

Popjoy puffs his pipe. "Actually, it was after the massacre of Algerians during the Algerian War. Corpses were floating in the Seine and hanging in the Bois de Boulogne. Enough seen, enough had, enough known, to borrow Verlaine's words. Politically and personally, I needed new scenery. By Christmas 1961 I'd left and may never return. As for the sea, I knew Charles Trenet, whose song, 'La Mer', you should listen to. Long, long, long after the poets have gone, he sings in 'The Soul of Poets', their songs are still walking the streets. And it's true. We create toward disappearance, in the hope that something might live on. They called him Le Fou Chantant, the Singing Fool, more fool them."

"I wonder what happens when you die."

"Your body matures, as does your consciousness," says Popjoy. "But as your body ages, so does your mind. What if, like my father, you become senile? If his consciousness survived death, what sort of consciousness would it be? If a baby dies, can it only ever have a baby's consciousness in the afterlife? And what about brain injury? Such questions quickly reveal the nonsense of the afterlife-thesis."

"Maybe senility is a mask," the boy suggests, "and infantile consciousness contains the essence of maturity? I imagine the core me will always be eleven, the age when I felt at one with myself. Since then we've rather drifted apart."

Popjoy looks at him curiously. "Maybe you have several selves and have found an important one in the Senior Art School. But as for the notion of an afterlife, the body and brain are part of the same fleshy mechanism. No brain, no consciousness."

"So there can be no life after death?"

"It seems incredible that we'll die. But the proof is everywhere. Tennyson said death seemed an almost laughable impossibility. He's now dead."

Bleakness covers the boy like a shroud. There seems little ahead to look forward to that won't merely repeat lives others have led. Maybe he'll get a job, marry, have children, and age, but he'll definitely die. What's the point? Part of him wants to amount to something. Another part feels like giving up before he's begun. Sometimes he wishes he were a cat, or bird. Surely only humans ask what the point is.

"Do you think it hurts to die, Mr. Popjoy?"

"Yes, I think it probably does."

Luckily, like Tennyson, the boy finds it almost impossible to imagine dying but he does ponder entrapment. On a typically rainswept afternoon, browsing Popjoy's books he reads Solzhenitsyn's *One Day in the Life of Ivan Denisovich*, identifying with the lack of privacy and the stultifying routine. "There were three thousand six hundred and fifty-three days like that in his stretch," the book ends. "From the first clang of the rail to the last clang of the rail. The three extra days were for leap years." Next to it is Dostoevsky's *Notes from the House of the Dead*. "Beyond this," he reads, "there are light and liberty, the life of free people! Beyond the palisade, one thought of the marvelous world, fantastic as a fairy tale. It was not the same on our side. Here, there was no resemblance to anything. Habits, customs, laws, were all precisely fixed. It was the house of living death." Turning to the end of the book, he finds the convicts saying goodbye to one another, freed at last. "Yes, farewell! Liberty! New life! Resurrection from the dead! Unspeakable moment!"

But a book by Arthur Balfour, *The Foundations of Belief*, provides perspective. "The energies of our system will decay," he reads, "the glory of the sun will be dimmed, and the earth, tideless and inert, will no longer tolerate the race which has for a moment disturbed its solitude." Initially, Balfour's observation threatens to wreck his already dismal mood. It reminds him of that moment in *Rebel Without a Cause* when the teacher at the Planetarium explains that humanity will disappear and not be missed. But then, painting with the rain battering the windows, he becomes exhilarated. What does life at Grimpton matter, anyway? It will dissolve, as will he. In the long run, nothing matters. For the first time in his life, like a hiker seeing empty sky, he recognizes our insignificance. In his head, he's the man in the fifties print in the Thornditch dining hall, looking over the vista, beyond the frame.

He's assumed he'll be painting alone all day but Popjoy walks in wearing a soaked raincoat, his silver helmet glistening. He pulls off the helmet and his white hair stands up like Einstein's. He shrugs off his coat to reveal a bright-red suit, shirt, and tie.

"Painting well?"

"After a while nothing matters, does it?"

"Been thinking again? Painting will do that. The mind won't keep still."

"Am I right? In the long run nothing matters?"

"But in the meantime?"

Popjoy enters his office. It's rained for days. Maybe it will rain forever.

"Mr. Popjoy?"

Popjoy grunts from his office. This means he hasn't time to say yes. The boy has never known anyone so busy as Popjoy, though what he achieves—beyond keeping up supplies and framing paintings—is a mystery.

"How important is it what others think of us?"

"Others?" Popjoy strolls from his office and stacks frames against a wall. He hammers a nail into a frame with such force he breaks the wood. "Damn!" He throws down the hammer and comes over to see the boy's painting—another seascape but influenced by the dark melancholy of de Chirico. "Decide for yourself," he says. "Personally, I'd rather be known as a good person but a bad artist than a good artist but a bad person."

"I don't care."

"Then you might succeed, but at what cost to you and your art? Art advertises your strengths and weaknesses. It's the opposite of escape. Whatever your apparent subject, writes Delacroix, it's always yourself that you paint. His *Journal* is on the shelves somewhere. Your painting will reflect your state of mind."

"Sometimes I feel anger at something someone has said. Resentment builds in me."

"Of course," says Popjoy. "The memory of an insult may make us angrier than the insult at the time. When you paint, your mind wanders so cultivate healthy-mindedness, even though, as William James reminds us, the skull will grin at the banquet."

The boy mixes French ultramarine with yellow ochre. Skull at a Banquet will be his next painting.

"Are you happy at Grimpton, sir—I mean Mr. Popjoy?"

"In my mind I often travel back to Paris, to École des Beaux-Arts, to my youth! Like Verlaine, je me souviens des heures et des entretiens et c'est le meilleur de mes biens—I remember those times and those conversations and they are my greatest consolations. Soon I'll leave this school and never return!"

"Me too," says the boy. "But why teach here if you can leave?"

"Retirement is dull. Besides, I'm needed. Why do you attend this place? You're not eight any more. You can just go."

"Where to?"

"New York. Paris. Tokyo. Tahiti—wherever you wish."

"Shouldn't I get educated?"

"Education saves us from discontent, but, in the widest sense, it comes from places other than classrooms. On the one hand, as Balzac notes, the history taught in schools is a collection of dates and facts of no significance. What use is it, he asks, to have heard of Joan of Arc? On the other hand, the Spanish poet Federico Garcia Lorca said that if he were hungry and helpless in the street, he'd ask for half a loaf and a book. Hunger for knowledge is as great as hunger for food. One cannot be content in ignorance. Well, I can't be. I work because it stimulates my emotions, and emotions are life's clothing."

Ah, thinks the boy. Popjoy wears clothes like emotions. Red is energy. Blue is melancholy. Brown is thoughtfulness. "Are colors emotions?"

"If you like," says Popjoy. "We define the world's coherence for ourselves."

Through such books and conversations, the boy experiences the Senior Art School as a store of possibilities in contrast to the windswept conformity of most of Grimpton. He finds Delacroix's *Journal* on the shelves. Enlisted as a long-term companion, the painter alerts the boy to "the traditional method of painting based on four tones mixed on the palette for shadow, halftone, light and reflected light." Popjoy then shows him what Delacroix means. Be bold, Delacroix urges, for "without daring, and even extreme daring, there is no beauty." "Is there anything more calamitous than being afraid?" he asks. Likewise, "cold accuracy is not art," he explains. "Skilful invention, when it is pleasing or expressive, is art itself." Emboldened by such encouragement, the boy follows paths of thought that expand as he paints. He also eventually becomes aware that many of Popjoy's observations, acknowledged or not, are taken verbatim from others, not least Delacroix and William James. Regardless, his words, or those he paraphrases or quotes, help shape a life.

Time passes and the boy continues periodically to request a canvas.

"Your strength," Popjoy finally sighs, "is that you badger until satisfied. Tuesday!"

That Tuesday afternoon is the wettest, windiest imaginable on the windswept, rain-drenched South Downs. December has arrived. Life in the Outer World goes on much as before. Trudging the leaf-strewn gravel outside the chapel, he passes Simon Fairfash, lead singer of school band, Rigid Plastic, along with the drummer, Hooleran. Their middle-parted hair flows back in the wind. Fairfash is seen as cool. He wears a silk scarf over his huge tie-knot, and never does homework. Rigid Plastic played in Great Hall last night. The boy smiles shyly at them, but even as he's about to say how much he enjoyed the show, Fairfash says to Hooleran, "More shit for my shoes," and Hooleran bares his mossy teeth in appreciation of the singer's wit.

Once in the Senior Art School, the boy leafs through a *History of Western Art* in the carpeted corner down one step, awaiting his canvas. Popjoy strolls from his office, tapping his pipe on a radiator. Offsetting his green face today is a white suit, the only bright thing on the worst of days. He hands the boy his canvas.

"Waste it and you'll never get another. What'll you paint?"

"Something always comes."

"You're lucky. I rarely paint now. Besides, whatever you do will be black in twenty years. Tout entiers perdu! as Lamartine warns us. Completely lost!" Popjoy's face darkens to a double gloom. "It's a world of diminishing returns." Passing the easels toward his office, he clicks his long, soft-looking fingers. "Twenty years, thirty. I'll retire in fifteen and be dead in twenty-five. Don't waste one day, young man. Remember the Grim Grinner of Grimpton."

"But what's a waste and what isn't?"

"Develop new grooves. I write or translate French every evening to keep my hand in. I also play jazz trumpet. Badly, but it brings back good memories. Arnold Bennett describes the hours of a day as a bag of gold. Rich or poor, important or unimportant, everyone gets to spend it. Each morning the gold is restored but," Popjoy holds his palms out, pipe between thumb and forefinger, "not forever."

His hands slap his white suit. "Hmm. Now where did I put the last twenty-five years?" He opens his office door. "One day you'll write about me but I'll be dead."

"I might be dead before I get to do that," says the boy.

"Not going to drop out, are you?"

"If they'll let me."

"Don't fall into the trap of thinking 'they' rule you. No one can do so unless you allow it. Note Marcus Aurelius. You can leave life right now. Let that determine your disposition. The choice is yours. But remember: freedom can be terrifying. All my friends who dropped out are dead. Still, they tried. Better than being a schoolmaster."

Popjoy turns away. His white suit stretches across bony shoulders, as if his generally upright frame is preparing to bend toward decrepitude. Whether to do with personal neglect, immersion in the Old Masters, or a problematic washing machine, Popjoy also today has a mustiness about him that betrays the brightness of the suit.

He pulls out his pipe. Spittle sparkles on his mauve lips. "Don't you know I'm telepathic? There's nothing strange. It's an ability most people neglect to develop. You think I'm old, that I smell musty. Well, my decay is an occupational hazard. I refer you again to Aurelius. Imagine you've lived your life. Now start living it properly."

Thrilled to have his first canvas, the boy paints long after Popjoy has left and the rectangles in the window are as solid black as his paintings will be. It's as if he's still listening to Popjoy's words after the art master has gone. He paints a seascape with a gigantic grape hovering above it, wearing spectacles with a shattered left lens, smoking a pipe, a screw thrust through bleeding eyes. Floating on the water are the numbers of his date of birth. The sky is stormy, the sea rough. He remains aware of the smell of pipe smoke, and smatterings of rain against the high crypt windows, if little else.

But what, he wonders, is "properly"?

16 MURAL

May arrives with a summons to the headmaster's office. Unlike at Thornditch, where the boy spent so much time in Glinty's and then Pug's study, he's only seen Dr. Magnus "Humpty" Lager sweep black-gowned across the quads, most recently to greet Prince Charles's red helicopter to show off to a king-in-waiting Lager's personal kingdom by the sea. He assumes it must be about his latest report, especially the English literature master's. *"And melancholy mark'd him for her own," wrote Thomas Gray about himself. He might well have had this young man in mind. He does what he's told but evinces no joy. He's been here years and we're still seeking him. Alas, he's tighter into his shell. His eyes have a blank look.* Maybe so, thinks the boy, but he'd rather that than the appearance—featureless but for a rosebud mouth and tiny eyes framed by goggle spectacles—of egg-headed Lager.

Humpty Lager's study appropriately resembles the Oval Office, except that the floor-to-ceiling windows overlooking the driveway are interspersed with pillars set with mirrors. These flood the room with brilliant light as well as dozens of Lagers, receding forever into glass tunnels. He crosses to the desk in front of the windows and mirrors. Lager and the infinite reflections that face the boy (an equal number face away but just look like eggs) all have eggheads with rosebud mouths and tiny eyes that peer through those spectacles as if the world were bright as the sun. The number of years Lager has spent in this office might account for this. Just entering risks cataracts. Lager and his forward-facing reflections often lick their little lips.

At Lager's shoulder stands Gurney, who, along with the boy, has multiple reflections receding, but Lager's egghead dominates. Gurney's forté, Popjoy has said, involves ladder-and-lightbulb installations. He works in the Institute for Conceptual Art that's part of the newly built Girls' House. Today, as ever, he's wearing his tweeds and his beard is trim. Popjoy seems excluded from this meeting. The boy suspects he alerted the headmaster to the boy's interests, but Gurney clearly wants the credit.

Beyond the real Humpty Lager the sun bursts from the clouds, causing tiny rainbows to sparkle in the mirrors. The sea now glints on the horizon like a slither of glass.

"The thing is, young man," says Lager, as if remnants of his last meal cling to the inside of his mouth, "Grimpton has to move with the times." He squeezes his eyes and licks his lips, as do his reflections.

"You'll be aware of the new Girls' House," says Gurney, "part of the new technology block to be attached to the Gurney Institute for Conceptual Art."

"We're naming it Lager House," says Lager, evidently unable to shift his oral residue.

"As part of the Gurney Institute for Conceptual Art," intervenes Gurney.

"Lager House, GICA," counters Lager. "After a history of being a school almost exclusively for boys, co-ed we will be."

"And," says Gurney, "the Gurney Institute for Conceptual Art needs a mural."

"Mr. Gurney has put your name forward as the school's premier painter—indeed only painter, now that Conceptual Art is so popular. He says you're the only boy who still uses the old Senior Art School, and that the oil painting part of the art show on Open Day will consist entirely of your work. How would you like to take on the Lager House commission?"

"I don't mind," says the boy. "If Mr. Popjoy agrees."

Lager licks his little lips, runs a hand over his egghead. "When the pope asked Michelangelo to paint the Sistine Chapel, do you suppose Michelangelo said, I don't mind?"

Lager pronounces Michelangelo *Mikkelangelo* and Sistine *Sistin*.

"Headmaster has addressed you," says Gurney.

"But you're not asking me to paint the chapel ceiling, sir."

Someone enters. Gurney's jaw muscles ripple. The boy can't see the entrant in the mirrors. He turns to see Popjoy, wearing a mauve suit, shirt, and tie but his usual white shoes. His pipe peeps from his top pocket. He seems to have been standing outside listening. He's sallower than ever in this bright room. Neither Humpty Lager nor Gurney, jaw muscles aside, pay any attention to his entrance.

"If I might intervene, headmaster?" says Popjoy. "When he says he doesn't mind, he means he'd love to. Wouldn't you, young man?"

"Would you *mind* doing it," says Lager, squinting at the boy, "or *love* to?"

"I'd love to, sir."

"Sorry to intrude, Headmaster," says Popjoy. "I must be going. Good luck, young man." The boy hears the door open and click softly shut. Gurney's jaw muscles ripple.

"Good, good. What'll you paint, eh? Come back with a design pronto."

Back in the crypt, Popjoy is puffing his pipe. "Any ideas?"

"Perhaps the World but with all the sea as land and all the land as sea."

"Admirably ambitious. But you'd be biting off more than you can chew. Here." The boy follows Popjoy into his office. "See that?" He points to a map on the wall. "Paris, as Gertrude Stein put it, is my hometown. To be Parisian is not to be born in Paris, said Sacha Guitry, it's to be born again there. But I've lived for so many years with the Paris of my youth, that if I returned I'd feel like a ghost. No one I knew is still there, the cafés will feel different. I'm giving you this map. Make of it what you will. Perhaps you'll go there but meanwhile the map may inspire your mural."

Popjoy shows him the Latin Quarter on the map, explaining that it's called that because a medieval scholar named Abélard took up residence there with his Latin-speaking students. "Here's Boulevard Saint-Michel, Cluny Museum, Les Deux Magots, Shakespeare and Company bookshop. My girl lived on Rue Galande so we'd meet in Square René-Viviani by the oldest tree in Paris. There's a little church here, Église Saint-Julien-le-Pauvre." He taps his pipe at each place. "Pilgrims returning along Rue Saint-Jacques from the latter's shrine in the Spanish coastal town of Compostela brought scallop shells to prove they'd been, which is why the French still call scallops Coquilles Saint-Jacques. And over here is École des Beaux-Arts. My own apartment was on Rue de Seine a short stroll from La Palette." As he talks, Popjoy's office fills with pipe smoke. The boy pictures himself in Paris. "The City of Light, they call it," puffs Popjoy, "although a philosopher named Walter Benjamin called it the City of Mirrors. Not unlike Lager's study, eh?"

So it is that the boy comes up with the design for his mural, a 360-degree, semi-abstract, dreamlike painting that he calls "My Imaginary Paris." Two days later he returns to Lager's study of extraordinary mirrors and windows. Again, he's confronted by infinite bespectacled eggheads licking their little lips, and Gurney standing in the corner, his tweed suit the only object in the room that doesn't reflect any light.

"Here's my design, Dr. Lager." The boy holds out the design. "My Imaginary Paris."

"Preposterous," says Gurney. "You haven't even been there. I know all about the Frogs. You know nothing. Moreover, I can't think this design will interest girls. Try again."

"It'll do," says Lager, licking his little lips and nodding along with his infinite reflections. "After all, isn't Paris a city of romance?"

"Best get on with it then," shrugs Gurney. "Be sure to use up all the oil paint."

17 KOLKATA

It's 2021 and again we slide into autumn. That March 2020 day—the last Tour Eiffel was open before the first lockdown—seems a lifetime ago. Soon masks replaced tourists and much has continued to change. Dislocation between Britain and the European Union proceeds apace. This past January, the EU halted the AstraZeneca vaccine rollout due to the risk of blood clots. British foreign policy is shifting cooperation from the EU to elsewhere. The government has curtailed the right to protest. Politicians now routinely appear with the Union Jack. Anyone trying to leave Britain without good reason risks a five-thousand-pound fine. To enter requires the completion of a Locator Form. A Day 2 and Day 8 swab has replaced a single test. With cases there reaching forty thousand a day, Johnson responded, "Let the bodies pile high," and declared 19 June UK Freedom Day. Other countries started a traffic light system, red-listing countries worst affected. People have been locked in hotel rooms for the duration of quarantine. But now, in September, the Louvre is near its busy norm and the Christo-designed wrapping of the Arc de Triomphe, unveiled days after Jean-Paul Belmondo finally expired decades after chain-smoking through *Breathless*, has drawn crowds.

Tour Eiffel had beckoned for months. Nicki and I have enjoyed cocktails at the top of the Hyatt Regency Paris Étoile and Tour Montparnasse, and the Pompidou escalator offers an unparalleled left-to-right city-rise from Sacré-Coeur, to Église Saint-Eustache, La Défense, Tour Eiffel, and Notre-Dame. But Tour Eiffel didn't appeal to her given the externality of the ascent. Awaiting the right moment I was barely in time. I clambered up the stairs alone, joined only by a German couple for the final elevator. At the top, I surveyed the city for the last time in a while, thinking of how Zola worried that the tower would affect the weather, and how Maupassant would eat in its restaurant as "the only spot in Paris in which one doesn't see *it*." To the west, the Seine flowed between an eerily quiet Pont d'Iéna and Trocadéro. Beyond lay the Bois de Boulogne bordering Neuilly. To the east a silhouetted Pont de Bir-Hakeim stretched across a silvery Seine split by the Île de Cygnes as far as Pont de Grenelle and the Statue of Liberty. To the north the inescapable Sacré-Coeur, that contentious Catholic monument, dominated the massacred Communards' one-time power base of Montmartre. A Gulliver surveying a Lilliputian Paris, I scanned the landmarks and whispered the statement on the roof of Parc des Princes, ICI C'EST PARIS, as it continues to be, however different life currently is for Parisians, as for us all.

Sometimes, with famous monuments, a scale model must suffice. While the Statue of Liberty in New York has smaller counterparts in the Orsay, on Pont de Grenelle, and elsewhere, so Tour Eiffel has a replica in Eco Park, Kolkata, which also has models of the Colosseum, Taj Mahal, *Cristo Redentor,* Great Pyramid of Giza, Great Wall of China, Maoi statues of Easter Island, and the Al Khazneh Temple of Petra. There's a Big Ben in Kolkata, too, but it's stuck on the busy junction of the Lake Town and VIP Roads. You chug through fume-filled traffic, rickshaws and all, and it pops up ahead. At school, racism against Indians was rife. They and all South Asians were labeled under "the P word." I was taught that the British dismantled their empire because colonized people had learned to self-govern. But it was still fine to mock "foreigners," especially Pakistanis and Indians, as inferiors with silly accents. Many years out of childhood and away from that so-called education, I was invited to Kolkata, and experienced an impromptu trip to the Bay of Bengal.

 I flew there with a colleague I'll call Agatha as part of our university's strategy for strengthening global links. Arriving via Dubai we were greeted with roses by Bangladeshi host Prithwish Debnath and his Greek wife, Kyriaki. The minibus driver took us to the Hyatt. Entering through high security and left to catch up on lost sleep by the palm-lined pool, this allowed us a brief respite from hospitality as overwhelming as the heat. In the late afternoon Prithwish and Kyriaki took us to Eco Park where, accompanied by requests for selfies, we strolled by the lake. Dusk descended and the scale models became floodlit.

 Eventually, Prithwish decided it was time to eat. Instead of relaxing in the balmy evening air, we climbed winding stairs for a meal in an air-conditioned grotto dark enough to leave Agatha and I in danger of falling asleep at the table. Agatha's solution was spicy food. Mine would have been beer, which Prithwish mentioned but which never arrived. Longing for bed, I tried to chat. The evening ended and the minibus took us back to the hotel. But in no time we were down in Reception for the first full-on day.

We reached our host university in a thunderstorm to attend management meetings and exchange gifts. The stormy weather continued the next day when—not yet knowing of Bengali Flexible Time (BFT)—we agreed to leave in midafternoon for the Bay of Bengal, four hours' drive southeast of Kolkata. In a manner of speaking that's what we did, except we left closer to six, the thunder and lightning cackling at our beach clothes, and the drive took six hours, during which Prithwish announced his Creationism.

"Do you think," he asked, "that homosexual priests should be allowed? If you accept the teachings of Christ, then you must accept that homosexuality is a sin, so a priest cannot be both a believer in Christ and a homosexual."

His subsequent arguments took up two hours. In particular he insisted that the whole of the Bible had been proved to be socially, historically, and scientifically true.

"And evolution?"

"Evolution is a theory," he replied. "But God is the truth. The Bible is the truth. It has been scientifically proven, whereas evolution has not."

Fortunately, Kyriaki spoke little English, which meant she couldn't join his argument, though she intervened in Greek punctuated with the word "metafrázo!"—"translate!"

"By the way," said Prithwish as we stopped at the Bengali version of Kentucky Fried Chicken, "the Digha hotels may not reach the standard of cleanliness you're used to."

Finally in Digha, close to midnight, while the driver argued with some men in the puddled street, Prithwish hurried into a dilapidated hotel. Rain clattered the minibus. Agatha tried to swat a mosquito. Kyriaki sang in Greek, perhaps of her homeland. When Prithwish finally reappeared he looked like he'd been in a fight.

"The hotel I booked is too dirty. We must find another."

Given how the night turned out, it's hard to imagine what he meant.

Around midnight, I got out of the van to spray Deet. Agatha was fearful she'd never see her children again. I said that one day we'd be in a meeting and catch one another's eye and think that at least we're not hotel-less at midnight in a rainstorm on the Bay of Bengal.

Just before 1:00 a.m. Prithwish found a hotel. We stepped over what appeared to be a spongy carcass functioning as a doormat and, watched from the porch by shoeless men in stained vests, entered a dingy hallway. Although the building was on a busy street, the interior felt institutional, like a prison or boarding school. The only downstairs lighting came from a fish tank. The concrete stairs and second-floor corridor were washed by the dim light of insect-spattered bulbs. The owner showed us three rooms. The men in vests followed and peered with us. Each room resembled a cell with a dusty cupboard, mirror, table and chair, a shower and nonflush toilet with a bucket and jug, and a single bulb dangling from the wall above a large bed with a patterned blanket.

"Indian families would share one of these rooms," Prithwish explained.

"You'll need to choose, Agatha," I said as we surveyed the third.

"This one," she said.

As if to greet her, from beneath the bed crawled a cockroach, which Prithwish crushed underfoot. Agatha chose another room but, when the others left, asked me to wait.

"Why are there bolts on the outside of the door?"

"I don't know, but there are two inside." I clicked both shut. "You try."

She did so. "I can't reach the top one."

"The bottom one is enough."

"Wait," she said. "What if the bolts on the outside are to padlock you in?"

We sat and talked and the conversation continued in the same fashion for perhaps an hour. I'd better go. I don't want to be alone. I'll stay. You can't. I'll stand outside your room. No. Then I'll go. But why are there bolts on the outside?

"Listen," I said eventually, "It's two in the morning and we'll be up at five to swim. That's three hours. All that really frightens you is the poverty."

"Yes," she replied. "I'm catastrophizing."

"I understand the fear."

"I don't want to get bitten either. Can I wear your socks?"

"I suppose so." I made to take them off.

"No. You keep them. I'll cover my feet in clothes."

"You'll be fine."

I waited to hear the bolt click after I closed the door then edged down the dark corridor to my room and cocooned myself in one of the sheets Kyriaki had brought. Only then, wrapped in the Indian night, listening to murmurs and bangs from the street and the whine of mosquitoes, did I realize why there were bolts on the outside of the doors. It was so you could padlock your room when you went out. But it remained true that someone could lock you in. I slept fitfully, unable to banish thoughts of that long-ago first night at boarding school, in a strange bed in a strange place, until Prithwish knocked and we set off to swim.

The morning was overcast but warm. Near the beach, a woodland pond resounded with bullfrogs—*Hoplobatrachus tigerinusis,* the largest species of frog in India—croaking beneath leaden skies. It being mating season the olive-green males had turned bright yellow with blue vocal sacs. Agatha and I plunged into the crashing surf and fought the undertow. Out of the sea we walked the beach collecting shells. Families swam or strolled, the women in dark-red saris. A man posed for photos on a white stallion, its forehead decorated with flowers. Preoccupied by the strange sights, we walked too far. The tide was encroaching. In our haste, Agatha dropped her phone in the water. We wrapped it in a shawl and splashed back to find Prithwish and Kyriaki huddled on rocks. After a café breakfast on Digha's dusty high street we explored a market and swam again before the long drive back past grassland and rice paddies to reach the hotel by nightfall.

Days three and four meant further talks to secure the links the university hoped for, but soon enough it was time to leave. My memories of the color, noise, and vibrancy are too jumbled to be separated into words. Kolkata was sweltering. The pollution induced a permanent raspiness to the throat. Our hotel was an oasis of quiet and order, with a yoga class on the lawn, and fine food and spacious rooms. But what stays with me, in terms purely of the cultural and geographic experience, is the Bay of Bengal, and that hotel in Digha, and those unexpected thoughts of boarding school. Above all, I'm a little haunted by the sense of transcending an imagined fate when dawn cracked and, watched by bemused Indians and a man on a white stallion decorated with flowers, we celebrated surviving the night by heading across the beach to the sea, and plunging into the waves.

18 EXHIBITION

The boy sets to work. At last he can produce a painting large enough to step into. He begins with the sky, dark blue at the top, becoming lighter toward the horizon. Below that he works on the imaginary city, increasing the contrast as it draws nearer.

"Delacroix's advice," says Popjoy behind him, "is that to give objects distance you should mute and flatten the colors."

The weeks pass. This, he thinks, is my mural to dreaming, to freedom. Open Day arrives. Popjoy wears a black suit, white shirt, black tie, and his white shoes. He looks like he's attending a funeral, even dressed for burial, his face is greener, more bloodless than ever.

"The suit," he says, "is to avoid distracting from your paintings. But in fact I'll be absent. Mrs. Popjoy has a hospital appointment, I'm afraid. I'm sure you can hold the fort."

On every available wall Popjoy has displayed the boy's depictions of severed heads, caged figures with screaming mouths (he's found Francis Bacon), weird juxtapositions, distortions: whatever he thinks might be uncomfortable to view. In one corner, ready for Lager-Gurney House, stands the perfectly pleasant mural.

The parents are in Spain. The latest postcard is of a cruise ship with a hand-drawn arrow and note indicating "our cabin." In contrast to last year's trip to Hong Kong, this year has seen a tightening of belts. But they're relieved that, once the boy goes to art college, the burden of fees will be over. They'll be back in time to collect him at the end of term. Other parents, though, do drop in. He feels as if the walls hold his mental entrails. Each painting seemed okay when he painted here alone, or with just Popjoy around, but now his secret world is open to anyone. Popjoy, though, has said he should answer questions. In the event, an elderly couple approach him.

"All yours?" asks the large lady, her dress pattern resembling an overripe banana.

"Yes, and for sale."

"We don't buy pictures."

"Which painting would you buy if you did?"

The woman's nostrils twitch. She looks at the paintings and over at the mural, then back at him rather as a doctor might before delivering a diagnosis of doom. She opens her mouth but hesitates before saying, "Lovely pictures, dear. You must continue."

"Aren't they!" exclaims her thin husband, hands behind his back. He has a bow tie, pebble spectacles over a blade-like nose, and very polished shoes.

"Want to buy a painting?"

"He doesn't," says the woman, tugging her husband's thin arm.

"Oh, I don't know." The man peers at one after another. "How much is that?" It's the Cézanne-inspired painting that Popjoy called a stage awaiting actors.

"Come on, Dirk," says the woman. "Don't tease."

"No, really, Melda. He has talent." Dirk holds out his thin hand and says, "Dirk Hallington. What do you want from life, lad?"

"To travel, sir," the boy says, "but creatively."

"Our son wanted that," says Dirk, "but it wasn't to be. You'll be a painter. Your subject matter is already in you." He pulls five pounds out a wallet. "I'll take it."

"You'll do no such thing," says Melda. "Put that money away!"

The boy fetches a stepladder and unhooks the painting. Looking down at Dirk and Melda Hallington, he thinks of the time years ago when he climbed on the bench and dented E. N. Gladmere's portrait, and of when the Colonel ordered him to stand on the lockers in front of the school to receive his Stripe.

"Wow," he says, "I've just sold a painting!"

"And I've just bought one," says Dirk.

"No, you haven't," says Melda. "Put it back."

Dirk winks at the boy. The boy climbs down and gives him the painting.

"Did you know our son?" says Dirk. "Stephen?"

"Of course," he says. "Hallington."

"Visiting helps us remember him. He loved Grimpton. Have you loved it?"

"Once I leave," says the boy, "I'll never return."

They look puzzled. "Why's that?" asks Melda.

"I'm off."

"Where?"

"Anywhere."

"Head for the horizon," says Dirk.

"Come on, Dirk," says Melda. "And don't you dare buy another!"

Popjoy returns near the end of Open Day. The Senior Art School has emptied.

"I've sold a painting to the Hallingtons," says the boy. "What happened to their son?"

"Stephen crashed a car into a wall only weeks ago," said Popjoy. "He seemed to have recovered from his injuries. Three days later Mr. and Mrs. Hallington were driving him back to Grimpton to restart his studies. They heard a groan. Stephen had slumped over in the backseat. He died of an internal hemorrhage. I can't believe they came today. His obituary will be in the magazine."

19　FREEDOM

Even though his report warns that *you will always have Grimpton,* the end to a decade of boarding arrives. For the final chapel service, the boy has to sit with Milford next to him, now a prefect so on guard at the end of the pew. The sacristans and choir file in behind Honey and Styke. The pillars soar through the haze of incense, but not only incense. The boy's vision has deteriorated since Milford hit him. He can't read with his left eye, which is permanently blurred, but he quite likes living in an impressionistic world where the sharpness of close contact with objects to his right eye mixes with the mistiness of the left. It lends his sight a painterly air reminiscent of Leonardo's technique of sfumato.

The school rises as Lager climbs to the pulpit.

"I'll begin," he begins in his food-clogged voice, "with a phrase from Isaiah, which you can take as my title. Winds of Adversity!"

As is the custom, the congregation sit down after his first few words. Lager surveys the ocean of bobbing heads, his own appearing as no more than an egg. The boy can't see the spectacles or little mouth, let alone the licking lips.

"Winds—of—Adversity! *Winds* of Adversity! Winds *of* Adversity! Winds of *Adversity!* Many of you boys have faced these. Many of you have not."

From a pocket, the boy retrieves a folded sheet of paper and a pen. On it he draws a grid with numbers in each square, ranging from one to seven. He puts various countries, including some he just enjoys the sound of, like Bolivia, Cambodia, and Fiji, into groups of four. Starting with England, Germany, Uruguay, and Brazil, he swivels the pen and stabs the chart. England two Brazil seven. He's thinking about how, when first sent away, he was among the smallest at Thornditch, the younger brother, inferior in every way. Now he's no longer known as Two or Minor, and is a gangly six feet. The dot World Cup advances. Until Uruguay and Brazil meet in the final, he can ignore Lager's voice, but then it intensifies.

"Remember this!" intones Lager from his pulpit. "As products of the private school system you number among the top percentile of the country. You aren't as likely to face quite the Winds of Adversity as the rest of the country. They may face gales while you face a breeze. But whether your Winds of Adversity turn out to have the full-blown sneeze of a hurricane or the sniff of a squall, remember the following facts. Firstly, there is one Truth, the Truth of the Lord our God. Secondly, all Truth is fixed and eternal. Thirdly, the world revolves around leadership and obedience. Fourthly, conformity and conventionality lead to strength. Fifthly, rebellion brings disorder and chaos. Sixthly, honor your father and mother. Seventhly, defend your queen and country, for it is an exceptional country in a world beset with untrustworthy foreigners. Eighthly, honor your class and race, for you are of the ruling class and, most of you, the finest race in the world. Ninthly, honor your school. Tenthly and finally, make money! Your wealth will trickle down like golden drizzle to nourish society as a whole. Let us sing the hymn of the Stonebrain Foundation, 'All Things Bright and Beautiful,' as indeed they are."

The boy raises his pen, stirs it in the air, and plunges it down. Brazil Nil. He does the same again. Uruguay One.

"Yes!" he hisses.

"Gammy git," mutters Milford. "Why don't you grow up?"

"When I do," says the boy, "I'll go to Uruguay."

"You'll never go anywhere or amount to anything."

"Crawl back under your stone, you stinking lizard."

Milford can't hit him in chapel, and isn't likely to get another chance. More hymns are sung, more prayers chanted. The service ends. Not for the first time, the boy watches the occupants file out like ghosts, as if he were dwelling in a memory. Our present will disappear, he thinks, even while this building, these chairs, and these hymnals remain. This congregation will crumble, as will I, after I've done more paintings, married, become a parent, and been to Uruguay.

After chapel, he descends the steps one last time to the crypt and Senior Art School. The door is unlocked. He tries the lights. They don't work. In the dimness from the small windows at the far end he sees Popjoy's office door open to a trace of lamplight.

"Mr. Popjoy?"

He edges through the dimness to the office door. Popjoy is at his desk, wearing the same dazzling blue suit as when the boy glimpsed him from the doorway that first time. Pipe smoke curls as if sucked into the lamplight.

"Mr. Popjoy?" Popjoy glances up, evidently preoccupied by whatever he's writing. "I came to say goodbye."

Popjoy puffs on his pipe. "Naturally," he says through the corner of his mouth. The way the lamplight glows on one side of his face reminds the boy of the skull in his first drawing session. *Skill is one letter from skull.* "Where will you go now, and to do what?"

"Go abroad and become an artist?"

"Everyone is an artist."

"What are you writing?"

"Application letters," says Popjoy. "Someone must need me."

He sucks on his pipe and continues to write. The boy feels, suddenly, that he's alone and that Popjoy, too, sees himself as alone, and that no further connection exists between them. How strange it is that none of the Senior Art School lights work except this lamp, its beam fixed so sharply on Popjoy and his pipe. Then he notices on the wall a poster of René Magritte's painting of a pipe—albeit an ordinary brown pipe, unlike Popjoy's—with the inscription that forms part of the painting: *Ceci n'est pas une pipe.*

That's when the hairs fizz on the back of the boy's neck. He stumbles from Popjoy's office out through the semidarkness thinking, *of course, of course,* as if the years to come have already tumbled away and the boy is no more there in the Senior Art School than is Popjoy. He sees what he should have seen all along. The days that seem to exist so solidly are no more substantial than his imagination—the Head Cinema of his childhood.

Is it an illusion, he wonders, that we were ever alive? Where did I read that? Wallace Stevens—a poem Popjoy showed me? That's it—"The Rock"!

"Imagine your present life from the distance of decades. Approach your life that way and you'll have a sense of perspective," said Popjoy. "Listen to Stevens: Regard the freedom of seventy years ago. It is no longer air. The houses still stand, though they are rigid in rigid emptiness. Even our shadows, their shadows, no longer remain. The lives these lived in the mind are at an end. They never were . . . The sounds of the guitar were not and are not."

So what, he asks himself, is the rock? What can you cling to? What makes sense? What's worth living for? It's true, he thinks, as he runs now up the stone steps, that however real the present moment feels, later it will feel like an invention, and in recalling it, will be one. His time at Thornditch, his love for Kalina Radeva, Karine, Anooshka, and Melanie, his trials and tribulations, even the beatings, are these all forms of invention? Stranger still, has he invented the mother and father, made them into caricatures of whoever they thought they were, or tried to present themselves as being? Has he invented the brother and sister? Has he, in perhaps doing so, betrayed them all? Can he retrieve them?

He could ask each of them in turn, Who are you? But he's not sure they'd understand the question. Perhaps they would. Perhaps each would in turn emerge from the shadows and say, Is it time we knew each other? But in truth, he thinks, they live in their worlds and he in his. Even though they exist now but won't in the future, he still creates his own version of each of them, just as they invent him.

He runs along the chapel corridor and out into the sea-salty air. Once in daylight, in the Outer World, his feet pound the gravel. He slows his run to a walk and crosses the top of the drive. His heartbeat slows and he feels calmer, more ordinary, as though the tangible world is something more than an ephemeral illusion.

He returns to his pit, puts the last of his belongings in his tuck box, turns the new padlock away from his date of birth, and closes the door. Carrying his tuck box, just as he did on arriving at Thornditch a decade ago, he climbs the stairs and, across Lower Quad, hears the large white clock strike the hour. How many circuits has that imperceptibly slow hour hand made since he first saw and heard it four years ago? How many other boys will witness it and think, before the clock is dismantled, or the buildings fall to ruin years hence, of the terror of time passing? He'll always recall it when he sees a clock face, and not least the two window clocks in Musée d'Orsay, especially when the Grande Roue is up and viewable across the Seine, circuits within circuits. He crunches to the wide steps that lead to the driveway. He has no idea what life holds, no idea where he'll go or what he'll do. But he'll go far away and keep moving. He'll wander like a ghost through foreign lands where he no more belongs than he does here. This is nothing like leaving Thornditch, where he'd actually been sad at the thought of his days there ending. His heart, he tells himself, has become as stony-sharp as the flint on the buildings' outer walls.

The mother and father, a decade older than when he first boarded, wave to him from a new car, this time sporting green. He'll never tell them, of course, for what can they hear? They've done their best for him, as for the brother and sister. He'll know this in later years just as he knows it now. They've done what they think is right, and for some boys, maybe even for the brother, perhaps it has been.

He isn't going to make definitive judgements. He isn't going to think any more about it yet, perhaps for years. He'll keep it locked up in the tuck box of his adult mind. Meanwhile he'll take up Dirk Hallington's suggestion and head for the ever-receding horizon. Perhaps he'll go to the Americas. He's always liked the idea of roaming that continent. Maybe he'll end up in Newfoundland or the steamy heat of the Amazon, or live in a hut in Labrador and wear finger mittens and paint the Northern Lights. Or become a Patagonian Goucho, fall from his horse and nearly die of exposure, or be shot by Colombian guerrillas, but not fatally. Or maybe he'll walk barefoot through Outer Mongolia or drink himself to oblivion in New Guinea, or take the Trans-Siberian Express to China and live off rice. Or maybe he'll just go to the States and find Kalina Radeva at Harvard, or search for her in Bulgaria.

Then one morning, when he's become whoever he's meant to be, and done what he's meant to do, he'll unlock the box. Time being subjective, it will feel like the evening he watched the sun burst and sink over the horizon on that journey to boarding school. It will feel immediate, even though decades will have passed. He'll probably be living in a foreign city where he feels finally at home—maybe Paris. Yes, Paris would be good. Then and there, he'll open the box and look at what once was but almost might not have been.

Taking the steps one at a time, slowly, deliberately, his feet echo to the chant forming in his mind. Remember this. Remember your young self. Don't dwell on it but keep it safe, filed, a static picture, a series of scenes, and meanwhile amount to something. He reaches the bottom of the steps knowing that the trials of his childhood and adolescence are over, and believing that, for the rest of his life, he'll be free.

20 RIO

A lot of time has passed. COVID is still with us, as is Brexit. With all Westminster political parties exercising what former politician Neil Kinnock called Brexomertà—a code of silence about Brexit's dire effects on the British economy—both now seem permanent. But Russia's massive expansion of its invasion of Ukraine has pushed COVID and Brexit down the headlines. 2021 saw further lockdowns and early 2022 periods of quarantine along with the mandatory testing. But these eventually ended, as did the Trump incumbency. Tour Eiffel being lit up blue with yellow stars through January lifted our spirits and we looked forward to spring until, on 24 February, Putin sent his troops into areas well beyond Crimea and Donbas. As I write Kyiv is under siege. A forty-mile column of Russian forces is heading for the Ukrainian capital. Olena Petrenka has WhatsApped that she and her mother have escaped to Poland but Bohdan is in the army. She hasn't heard from him in weeks.

Paris is again "Paris." Everything is open. Travel is unrestricted. But the pandemic, Russian aggression, and climate breakdown all contribute to a sense of unnerving uncertainty and perhaps an increase in hedonism. Celebrating a freedom we never expected to lose and that now feels temporary, I hurtle my Vélib' down the Champs-Élysées, round Concorde, and along Rivoli to take my seat in that far corner of the Louvre.

Taking advantage of the end of restrictions, I left the apartment one November morning and caught the 7:15 Ouigo from Gare de Lyon to the Côte d'Azur, a miraculous ride on Le Train Bleu from overcast Paris to Mediterranean sunshine. After a tunnel south of Lyon, even as my headphones thrummed Johnny Hallyday singing "Allumer le feu," the monochrome morning exploded into color. We passed a lake in mountainous landscape, yellow poplars, wide rivers, and splashes of red foliage. By midmorning we'd skirted Marseilles. Train, sea, and sky merged in shades of blue. We slid past white houses on hillsides dotted with umbrella pines and fields of crisply golden vines. After Toulon the train headed inland before rejoining the coast through Antibes. Soon enough I'd lunched on oysters and Chablis at Café de Turin, swum in the Mediterranean, and was strolling at sunset along Promenade des Anglais, thinking, not so surprisingly, of Rio de Janeiro.

Aside from its pebbly beach, Promenade des Anglais has much in common with Rio's famous coastline. Both are places to stroll and observe. Since art is one of my continuities, when I flew to Rio on a research trip shortly before the EU referendum, I planned to visit the Museu Nacional de Belas Artes. But procrastination took hold. Paintings could hardly compete with the brilliance of the beaches that stretch from Leblon to Leme, or the buzz of Estádio do Maracanã. Why visit a gloomy gallery rather than attend a game, or stroll with the cariocas, sip from a coco, and laze by the sea? The MNBA therefore became a duty to fulfil rather than a joy to anticipate.

Not that the weather was uniformly glorious. My cab splashed from the airport into the city through hammering rain, veering round overpasses, overtaking anything available, until the driver dropped me on Ataulfo de Paiva at the Leblon apartment of Toti and Marina, the latter a friend from student days in upstate New York. Drizzle rather than dazzle roused me on the Sunday morning. I ran the seven-kilometer rim of Lagoa Rodrigo de Freitas with other early risers. Across the lagoon *Cristo Redentor* loomed on Corcovado high above the Tijuca Forest. On the way back I headed down Garcia D'Ávila to swim in the sea. Marina and Toti joined me to walk to the peninsula of Pedro do Arpoador with its views back to the Two Brothers Mountains, Dois Irmãos, and forward across Devil's Beach to Copacabana, Leme, and the faint line of the cable car between Morro da Urca and Sugarloaf Mountain. Heading back and inland to the Hippie Market, we drank caipirinhas at their club then ate at Bar Lagoa overlooking the lagoon.

The next day a tropical storm suited my visit to the rainforest campus of Pontifícia Universidade Católica, PUC—pronounced "Pookie." I sat in Luis Delgado's class on "Young Goodman Brown" (Hawthorne is evidently taught from Istanbul to Rio). I was there with the half-dozen students at 7:00 a.m. Luis sauntered in, bespectacled in baggy trousers, shirt out, straggly beard, carrying a dripping umbrella which kept opening when he tried to prop it against the wall. He had no notes. I'm not even sure he had a book. He did, however, have a plastic bag, which I imagine held his lunch. But once he began to talk, he grew to a stature belied by his whippet frame.

Most of the students seemed to respect him but one girl, tetchy in class, accosted him in the corridor and complained about the lack of structure and the fact that he left no time for her presentation. "There are too many of you," he said. (The class had swelled to twelve). Eventually they conversed in Portuguese, perhaps to save him embarrassment. "Stressed students," he said afterward. I later learned he was on a zero hours contract. PUC released him within a year. He's now a performance poet in the bars of Lapa.

Trudging up through rain to the American School where Marina worked, I stopped in a shop to ask the way. No one spoke English. A customer gestured for me to get in his car and drove me up past a favela to the school. Through the library window on the rainforest campus, the gusts of rain curtained the world's largest favela across the valley. Rocinha had spread across the hillside during her lifetime, Marina told me. But she was sympathetic about its inhabitants, caught between the police and the drug barons. That past Friday the police had gone in. Gunshots echoed across the valley. The staff shut the children indoors away from windows. Due at a midafternoon meeting with a Professor Ricardo, in charge of PUC's international matters, I headed back through EARJ's sloping paths to catch the bus downhill.

Out came the sun, and the rest of my trip revealed the balmy Rio one expects. For a while I remained in my usual state of manic activity. I bought books and music in Leblon Shopping—Misha Glenny's *Nemesis,* Machado de Assis's *Dom Casmurro,* Clarice Lispector's *Água Viva,* and some Bossa Nova; dropped them at the apartment to stroll past futevólei players on Leblon Beach; jumped in a taxi to head inland for the train up to *Cristo Redentor;* took the bus back to Leblon past Sugarloaf and along Copacabana and Ipanema. Yet slowly I adjusted to the rhythm, hung out more on the beach, observed the cariocas as they trod the Avenue Delfim Moreira, and occasionally drank a caipirinha at Bar Veloso, where Tom Jobin, inspired by a carioca who walked daily to the beach in the sixties, wrote "The Girl from Ipanema." Most afternoons I'd swim until evening, pondering Marina and Toti's life. Brought up in Rio, they belong to a place in a way that I've always envied. In the city they have their gated entrances and private club, but on weekends they drive north beyond Petrópolis to their hillside house in Secretário with a view of Pedra da Maria Comprida.

Near the end of my stay I took the bus out to teach at the Federal University, UFRJ. On a bus back into the city, a student spoke to me.

"How are you, sir?" she said. "Enjoying Rio?"

"Sun, sea, sustenance, what more could one want? It's beautiful."

"Is it really?" she said. "I'm proud to be a carioca but not of the Brazilian economy, the corruption, the exorbitant cost of the Olympics, the extremes of wealth and poverty, particularly in Rio, the gated middle-class versus the poor folk of the favelas."

"The landscape is breathtaking."

"As is the pollution." I snapped photos as we passed shanties. "Such an outsider," she laughed. "Recording *everything* like it's all a mystery you're set apart from. You think you're safe but I never cross this flyover without imagining us plunging over the guard rail to the most ignominious of deaths. If it happens today you'll become part of Rio for eternity."

An outsider. Of course. Yet how seductive were those days of blue skies and white beaches, Sugar Loaf glowing orange in the sunset! Marina, Toti, and I climbed the hills south of Zona Sul, beyond Dois Irmãos, to look across at Pedra da Gávea and down on the shoreline. Many days I simply walked from Leblon to the low wall at Ponta do Leme where Lispector's statue sits with her dog at her feet. It reminded me of another girl-and-dog statue, that of Liliana Crociati de Szaszak and Sabú in Buenos Aires, forever (in Borges's macabre phrase) "tucked away in Recoleta." The newlywed died when an avalanche hit her honeymoon hotel. Dying at a later date, Sabú became the only nonhuman animal buried in the cemetery. Contemplating all this, I'd have a coco in the café by the sea wall with its walkway round the cliff sealed off with a sign warning, "Beyond This Point DEATH."

But with time running out, I could put off my visit to the MNBA no longer, so headed to a deserted downtown on the last Sunday. Drawn as ever to portraits I was moved by Cândido Portinari's 1932 depiction of his wife, Maria, another soul surely trapped in a place she'd rather not be. But other paintings led me to contemplate Brazilian history, not least Jean-Baptiste Debret's portrayal of the everyday lives of slaves, Victor Mereilles's romantic rendering of the first mass in Brazil, and Rodolfo Amoeda's *The Last Tamoio*. It's easy to imagine how beautiful Zona Sul must have been in the time of the Tupinambá, before the Portuguese arrived to enslave indigenous people, then brought in thousands of captured Africans. Freed in 1888, these slaves with nowhere to go made the hillsides home in what became known as favelas.

I fled the darkness for the sunlight, beaches, caipirinhas, and swimming until, on the final day, I took the 511 bus and walked to the secluded beach of Vermelha, climbed to Morro da Urca for the cable car to Sugarloaf, and chatted with an English couple about the referendum to be held in June. When they left, I lingered to survey the panorama of Rio, knowing it was again time to return to a land I've spent much of my life seeking to escape. But I saw, of course, that Rio has a side as dark as anywhere, and is no less a land of ghosts. You just can't see them in the sunshine.

A short time after I landed back in Britain, my father was found unconscious on the floor of his cottage in Dorset. My brother, sister, and I visited him in hospital but he seemed to exist in a fantasyland. From his hospital bed he invited us to take a tour of the palace he believed he was living in. He died a few days later.

PAST IN PRESENT

REUNION

Things are transformed into one another according to necessity, and render justice to one another according to the order of time.

—ANAXIMANDER IN CARLO ROVELLI, *THE ORDER OF TIME*

Two things of historical note happened in September 2022. In Britain the queen died, and in Paris, outside Église Saint-Germain-l'Auxerrois, Mayor Hidalgo inaugurated a memorial garden to the Saint Bartholomew's Day Massacre. The events are unrelated except that, while many educated people in both countries long ago rejected hierarchy and chose secularity, Britain is historically a Protestant nation and remains a constitutional monarchy, whereas France is Catholic yet long since a republic. In 2006 the authorities nailed a plaque to a wall in Square du Vert-Galant. But this new, higher-profile acknowledgment of the slaughter of my ancestors shows that events and beliefs of the past echo as powerfully as ever.

Now that even 2023 has "unspooled with negligent haste" (to use a Styron phrase) and 2024 is unraveling toward 2025, Nicki and I are wrapping up our time in France. This final year we're renting at a farm in Maisons-Laffitte. The main traffic on our woodland road, grandly named Avenue Champaubert, consists of mounted jockeys clipclopping to exercise their horses along the forest paths. Yet despite our rural surroundings evidence of history abounds. At nearby Place Napoléon a statue of the national hero commands a grassy roundabout, his eyes locked on Avenue de la Moskowa. Former residents with plaques to their name include two writers. One is Arthur Koestler, cited by Styron as belonging with Orwell and Camus in his triumvirate of engagé influences. The other is the uncompromisingly antihierarchical (and statue-hating)

Communard Jules Vallès. The center of Paris, too, remains close by. RER A flies high over the Seine before plunging down and through to Auber. Within minutes I emerge from beneath Opéra Garnier to stroll down Avenue de l'Opéra to the Louvre.

Beyond our own circumstances, much has happened. On a microscale, my Carte Louvre Professionnel has been renewed as a Carte CLEF. The COVID tides recede but debris lies in their wake, not least the closure of Alioto's and Castagnola's, two restaurants I passed on my way to the Golden Gate Bridge. Meanwhile on the night of 25 April, even while in the Louvre a renovated *Liberty Leading the People* wowed the ever-changing art-lovers' moshpit, the sails fell from the Moulin Rouge. Decay and restoration interweave. On a larger scale, a newly spired Notre-Dame is back to her prefire self. They removed the scaffolding in time for the Olympics, on the opening night of which an illness-stricken Céline Dion rendered Édith Piaf's words from "Hymne à l'amour" so beautifully from high on a storm-lashed Tour Eiffel that the rain seemed part of the show.

On the macroscale, Putin's invasion of Ukraine grinds on, Netanyahu's Israeli government has flattened Gaza in retaliation for Hamas' 2023 attacks, and from January 2025 Trump is back in the White House. AI is upon us and, for good or ill, the severing of eras continues apace. "They lived at the end of an epoch," writes Orwell in *Coming Up for Air* of parents shaken "when everything was dissolving into a sort of ghastly flux." In the same vein, Chateaubriand, in *Memoirs from Beyond the Tomb,* writes of the "transitory amalgam" of "a society which is dissolving and reforming" amid "the clash between past and future." Such are our times, if not all times.

This disorientation is not least evident in post-Brexit Blighty, with a succession of prime ministers and a need to process the loss of a monarch so long in situ. The royal demise coincided with the opening of my first London exhibition, at the Zari Gallery in Fitzrovia. Whatever one's attitude to notions of monarchy, Elizabeth Saxe-Coburg-Gotha, to use her family name before they changed it to the English-sounding Windsor, supported by her husband, Philippos (changed to Philip), was head of state for seventy years. Her death certainly affected the mood that rainy September night. My past and present were colliding at the very end of an era that began before I was born. But even that's behind us now, and the General Election of 4 July finally swept out a government who'd held power since 2010.

The past is a dream, writes Pessoa, over which we have some control. Perhaps the same is true of one's experience of a city. Always aware of Popjoy's map of Paris, I've developed an afternoon routine of cycling along the Left Bank to his one-time hangout, La Palette. Presumably he kept the map to help recall his youth. Maybe he gave it to me because he intuited I'd live here, or perhaps his gift gave me the idea. Now I'm the age of Popjoy when I knew him, and in much the same position as he'd have been in knowing this time in Paris is temporary.

But my childhood and adulthood have finally met. Since childhood I've rarely felt inside life and often outside. Living in Paris has mostly reinforced this. Like Maupassant's Georges Leroy, I pass cafés crowded with chatting strangers. Yet other times I'm one of those in the café. Were there a parallel universe that slotted onto this one, my insider self would catch the eye of my outsider self and we would nod to one another before the outsider passed on his way. But insider or outsider, in trying to tell my story and live a story I've told myself, I see that, despite my French ancestry and whatever my protestations, my base has always been the island I was born on. Therefore, I took the opportunity this past summer to take my family to visit my childhood home, and Thornditch on its Hundredth Anniversary. During the journey I was both middle-aged father and small boy.

We left Wiltshire at dawn and reached the house before nine. I had proof I'd lived there—the photograph taken on the driveway in April 1969—but the owners were out. Peeking through the windows was a shock. I'd lived for decades with an interior exactly as it had been, from the front porch through the peach-carpeted hall to the garden door, up the stairs to the landing, and up two more sets, each a little steeper, to the tower to look down at the garden and across to the hills beyond. Little of the ground floor remained the same. The hall had bare floorboards and an unfamiliar clock. The garden door opened onto a conservatory. The rockery and well had been dismantled and grassed over. The apple tree had gone.

Through the kitchen window the sight was starker still. All was now open-plan. It was the home of strangers. Nothing remained to suggest we'd lived there. Its outer shell hollowed from within, the personality I'd known had evaporated. The garden was overgrown. The hedge between house and road had dead patches. Everything seemed decayed. Although my parents moved away long before their seventies, the house resembled my memories of them in later years, when they'd grown too old to see the dust that was my mother's lifelong foe. Men don't see the dust, she'd explain. Well, in the end, nor did she, and not too long after, followed more recently by my father, she became the very dust she'd tried to hold at bay.

Back in the car toward Thornditch, I told Nicki and the girls one of many dreams of my childhood home. I open my bedroom door and walk barefoot in my pajamas down the landing. My parents stand at their open door. At first, the marks on their faces seem the effects of moonlight. Drawing nearer I notice the wallpaper disintegrating. My parents' faces are cracking. If I slow my pace, the decay slows too. The faster I advance the quicker the decay. When I reach them, their faces and bodies, and the doorway itself, crumble to ash.

"What I took to be a nightmare," I explained, "turns out to be the inescapable fact of existence. We must enjoy and celebrate life while we can."

"Hmm," said Tasha.

"Ha," said Ani.

"Maybe," said Nicki, "it's better not to look inside."

"Maybe so," I replied. "But it's tempting, given how long I've been away."

While some things disappear, other things remain. The route toward Thornditch barely resembled the one my father drove that Sunday evening long ago. Straighter roads had replaced the country lanes, but the driveway gate was unchanged. By the time we reached the Gothic turrets the shadows of the past were surely across my face.

The Thornditch event started with a service in the small chapel and an address from a headmaster much younger than me, an odd experience, given I'd regressed to eight. Drinks in Wellington—now emptied of beds and functioning as a reception room—preceded lunch in the dining hall, with its rubber table mats, Duralex glasses, and mounted House Shields for Armada, Poitiers, Trafalgar, and Waterloo, still red, blue, green, and brown. The afternoon cricket match was followed by tea. The print of the man looking out across the vista no longer presided over the dining hall, but Dalí's *Christ of Saint John of the Cross* still hung above the chapel door.

The event was sparsely attended. I didn't expect to see anyone of my year or even era. Certainly none of my peers were there. I felt like the lone survivor of a shipwreck in some B movie of the kind they showed on Film Night. Only halfway through the day did I catch the eye of a man in a blazer and old school tie. He seemed to recognize me.

"I doubt we were of the same era," I said, introducing myself.

"Danton-Hillier," he replied, surname only, as if in a time warp. "You were my dormitory captain. I remember you scoring for the First Eleven. I was quite in awe of you."

I was taken aback that a grown man might say such a thing. I was a boy of eight walking around, not a thirteen-year-old about whom a younger boy might have felt awe. It was not just that I was reliving my childish perception of adults, but that another adult was reliving his childish perception of me as his senior.

An Old Boy from the eighties explained his return. "This was my childhood," he said. Of course: we were returning to childhood, but not in any ordinary sense. To board in that era was to be there for two-thirds of each year. It dominated childhood and adolescence. When children lose parents, the psychological consequences are profound. I didn't lose them literally but must have reconciled myself to the fact that I couldn't expect my home to remain. I was on my own.

Still, I went through the day knowing that this was no longer my world. I was a husband and father. I showed my family the School Woods, which I'd assumed to be vast. I located the site of the trenches but they'd long since dissolved into the general woodland. Of the Headmasters, Splinter and Glinty were surely dead—well, Splinter's Latin lessons may continue yet—but Pug appeared as we were leaving. A car pulled up. The passenger window slid down to reveal a yellow-eyed old man with a dented-forehead.

"Is it?" he said from the passenger seat. I couldn't see the driver. "Gracious. There's a turnout for the books! Brigadier Danton-Hillier said you were around. Marvelous to see you!"

Even as he said this, however, his window slid back up and the car drove off. It seemed the car's driver deemed that Pug wasn't in a fit state to continue the exchange.

"Who's Brigadier Danton-Hillier?" asked Tasha.

"I don't know about the Brigadier bit but he was once a little boy in a dormitory."

"And who was that?" asked Ani.

"A long story."

"Best to record it," said Nicki, "before you get as old as him."

I thought of lines from Patrick McGuinness's novel *Throw Me to the Wolves*. "Does he recognise me? I'm not that different, and it wasn't so long ago," says a character. "Actually, it was, if you're measuring it in clocks-and-calendars time. But if you're measuring it in . . . what? Inside-time? Heart-and-blood time? Lining of our lives time? . . . in that case it's yesterday. It's always yesterday there, in the lining of our lives."

Springsteen writes of the pride we may feel in survival, but also of the role our multiple selves play in transcendence. "There's a car, it's filled with people. The 12-year-old kid's in the back. So's the 22-year-old. So is the 40-year-old." "The doors are shut, locked and sealed, until you go into your box." What matters is "who's driving." Our time in Paris is ending, but his music has energized me since leaving school. If the Thornditch event was a circling back to schooldays, his songs are always a circling back to when my journeys of escape began. It was therefore fitting that, shortly before the publication of my small tribute to his impact, I was able to fly with Tasha to see *Springsteen on Broadway*. With a copy of his autobiography from the Strand Bookstore, we stood for hours outside the Walter Kerr Theatre—spelled the English way—on the chance of meeting him.

Time passed. To protect Springsteen and guard us against latecomers, security men put barriers round the dozen or so of us waiting either side of the door.

"Since we're standing here," said Tasha, "tell me your Springsteen song of choice."

"The one that lit my youth was 'Badlands', no question," I said. "The fire of youth. 'Talk about a dream / Try to make it real.' And you?"

"None of your business."

People gathered across the street. Suppose the Boss was stuck in traffic? Did they shut the road for him? Halt the traffic? Part the waves?

Then, at 6:50, up pulled a limousine and out rolled Springsteen. Boots first, faded jeans, then the familiar visage behind shades, he looked like he'd slept fully clothed on a couch. A whoop from onlookers: Bruce! He glanced our way but walked to the other side.

"Well worth the wait, then," said Tasha.

But Patti Scialfa stood in front of us. She'd come to our little line at the barrier. In contrast to her husband, she looked ready for a night on the town: beige hat and suit, brown boots. The only obvious connections were their shades.

"Hello, Patti," I said. "Here's a flier for my book."

She took the flier to Bruce. He came over to where I held *Born to Run* open. I thought maybe I'd tell him that his music changed my life on leaving school.

What I in fact say was: "I've written a book about you."

He may have looked straight at me but all I saw was my reflection in his shades.

"That's so kind of you," he said, and moved on.

Just as quickly, it seemed, the show was over. Such are life's moments. Even the second run of *Springsteen on Broadway* has long gone and, with COVID no longer a source of restriction, he's been back touring the world.

The next morning the Empire State outside our Hotel 31 window was hidden in storm clouds. The streets streamed. Water cascaded into the subway. A woman opened an umbrella as a yellow cab sprayed by. Taillights pierced the avenue in glimmering daggers. We sheltered in the Metropolitan. I took Tasha to meet Rembrandt, or at least his self-portrait of 1660. "Hey, old friend," I said to another of my mentors. "There's magic in the night."

Some months later my family and I flew to Lisbon. Van Morrison, a key Springsteen influence, performed in Cascais. When he played "Precious Time" I thought of that time with a daughter in New York. Precious time slipping away. But now and then we touch base, through art, memory, travel, everyday life, with something all the more real for being fleeting. I thought of long-dead Emily Dickinson, her words so alive: "Since then—'tis Centuries—and yet / Feels shorter than the Day / I first surmised the Horses' Heads / Were toward Eternity—." Imagine *Dickinson on Broadway!* What price tickets? *Rembrandt on Broadway,* offering a nightly personal monologue and portraiture master class. Gone is gone. What will be your residue? Soon our daughters will join us in Paris again. We'll visit the Louvre, where I'll point out, among other portraits,

Duval's one-eyed flautist, recently elevated to sit behind glass alongside the museum's most significant patron, Francis I. In the Musée d'Orsay I'll introduce them to Madame de Loynes, happily back on display (along with Vicomtesse de Calonne) even if her Montmartre tomb has so crumbled that, while the sapling grows and the black cat resides, the headstone bearing her name recently fell, and has now vanished.

As for my portraits in words, many of these people are lost to me but not all. Luerty works in animal welfare. Dollaton lives in Dubai, Bunting in Nova Scotia. Dunn-Larkin is a prep school Latin teacher. Muscle Milford is a security guard at a multinational in Houston. I've discovered through Facebook that Karine, the Belgian girl from the Dordogne campsite in 1976, still lives in Brussels and is now a grandmother. But Kalina Radeva seems to exist only in my reveries of the past. Darius has retired from college football and moved to Prague. Carlotta still lives in Omaha. Tasha's first trip to America, aged nine in 2001, involved staying with her, her grain exporter husband, and their daughters, while I gave a talk on—and disconcertingly attended by—Joyce Carol Oates at the *Prairie Schooner* 75th Anniversary Conference in Lincoln. Zeki Kinali has an Instagram account and offers advice on how to carve spinning tops. Danny Kyalo tells me the environmental degradation of Kenyan lakes has worsened, with Soi Lodge itself now subject to flooding. TripAdvisor states that Vasca, the bar I was welcomed into as a stranger in Montevideo, is "permanently closed." Prithwish and Kyriaki have moved to Australia. Olena and her mother flew from Warsaw to Italy, where they're guests of a university. What awaits them, what awaits us all, remains uncertain.

But my task is almost done. "Humans generally have too complex a brain for the life they live," Michel Houellebecq said in a Louisiana Channel Interview. "A large part of their brain capacity isn't used and one life isn't enough." Certainly one book isn't enough. There's so much I haven't found room for, whether in terms of schooldays, travel memories, or the city I've called home these past five years. Narratives twist things out of shape. You always fail to do justice. If the family I grew up in were to read this they'd note the many things I've failed to mention, including their more redeeming characteristics and my own more damning ones. With travel, you can only include moments that yield a tale. With Paris, if I don't mention Philippe II Auguste's wall, or the Arènes de Lutèce, or Sainte-Chapelle, or the Conciergerie, or Blaise Pascal's sister waiting in vain in 1662 outside Église Saint-Merri for his latest innovation, the first omnibus, or the guillotined feminist Olympe de Gouges, or Dickens writing in *A Tale of Two Cities* of the death-carts carrying "the day's wine" to that horrifying contraption, or such Parisian ghosts as the Red Man of the Tuileries, or the Bouquinistes, or the builder of the Paris métro Fulgence Bienvenüe, or the tragic story of Modigliani's pregnant widow, Jeanne Hébuterne, or the art work in the Tuileries Tunnel, or a host of other things, then they'd find no place in the narrative.

Likewise, the multitude of people I've known here, from the Monoprix checkout girl who turned out not to be French at all, let alone Zola's Gervaise, but a Ukrainian named Oksana, to our Guyanan concierges in Neuilly, to the Indian guard at Montmartre Cemetery who shook his head at Madame de Loynes's disintegrated tomb before scrolling his phone to show me his remarkable seascapes, to the Air France pilot who crushed me at tennis, to the numerous bartenders whose stories I got to know. The details of all that and more must remain internal. Selected, stripped, sundered, sorted, shaped memories are all we ever offer.

Memories are akin to dreams. We dream when asleep and when awake. I've been reading a theory of consciousness. Russell Foster, Professor of Circadian Neuroscience at Oxford, explains that "sleeping on a problem really can help the brain find new solutions," but distinguishes between the fact that it's good for you and the question of why we sleep. "We have the idea that sleep evolved," he says, but maybe "wakefulness is low-level brain damage. Maybe we started out in a state of sleep then evolved to have wakefulness, but had to return to a proto-state."

A final dream, then: a boy aged eight falls asleep in a dormitory. He dreams he's an adult recalling his schooldays. When he wakes he's unclear whether he's still aged eight in a dormitory or an adult imagining this. He reflects that perhaps he's both, and has been many more people in the years between. He no longer dreams of candle boats but he does dream of the house where he grew up outside of term time, and he knows that, while we should honor and respect the viewpoint of our younger selves, and, for our own sanity, forgive perceived wrongs, our only actual life is the here and now. Realizing he is in fact not the child but the adult, he falls asleep....

Boy and man, he'll recognize this as a series of dreams, a collection of distorted portraits, a form of fiction rather than life itself. Clicking "save" on his laptop, he'll wander back through the Grand Gallery, past the Goyas, Leonardos, and Caravaggios, down Escalier Daru and out beneath Pei's glass pyramid. Climbing the steps by the Arc de Triomphe du Carrousel, he'll join Popjoy's ghost for a stroll in the Tuileries. It's good you finally came to Paris, Popjoy will say. It's all too easy to be one of those who, in Proust's words, "remain moored like house-boats to a particular point on the shore of life." For that, Popjoy will continue, is what became of me in middle age, whereas you found Paris, and Paris reminded you of discovering painting, and memories surfaced of how you found a treasured self. And now, as your Uncle Gaspard once wrote to his children, you just need to "persevere courageously."

Contemplating this exchange, the man will decide to live each day in fullness, keeping dreams in their place, on pages or canvases. We're all of us, he'll think, here to contribute and be contributed to. We're viewers and viewed, visitors to the Gallery of Life, and ourselves both the artists and the portraits. Were the boy with him they'd likely agree that a different childhood would have produced a different man, and life, and neither boy nor man would want his adulthood to have taken any shape other than the one it has.

I learned early from Delacroix that, since colors interact, we can enhance one by placing it beside another. The juxtaposition of violet and mauve brighten the cloaks in *The Execution of the Doge Marino Faliero.* Perhaps, then, contemplation of childhood bruises renders all the brighter the golden moments of adulthood; memories of discomfort enhance present comfort; imperfect physical vision sharpens mental vision; unfortunate experience begets fortunate wisdom. It would seem that happiness, inexpressible or otherwise, is simply to have family and friends, places to visit, people to help. But we also need our self-made homes. These may take many forms but for me they include a page awaiting words and, thanks originally to Popjoy, a canvas awaiting paint.

www.ingramcontent.com/pod-product-compliance
Lightning Source LLC
Chambersburg PA
CBHW031517060525
26260CB00002B/23